PRZEWALSKI'S HORSE

SUNY Series in Endangered Species
Edward F. Gibbons, Jr. and Jack Demarest, Editors

PRZEWALSKI'S HORSE

THE HISTORY AND BIOLOGY
OF AN
ENDANGERED
SPECIES

EDITED BY

Lee Boyd
and
Katherine A. Houpt

STATE UNIVERSITY OF NEW YORK PRESS

Published by
State University of New York Press, Albany

For information, address State University of New York
Press, State University Plaza, Albany, N.Y., 12246

Production by Diane Ganeles
Marketing by Fran Keneston

Library of Congress Cataloging-in-Publication Data

Przewalski's horse : the history and biology of an endangered species
    / edited by Lee Boyd and Katherine A. Houpt.
        p.   cm. — (SUNY series in endangered species)
    Includes bibliographical references and index.
    ISBN 0-7914-1889-8 (cl. : acid-free). — ISBN 0-7914-1890-1 (pbk.
    : acid-free)
    1. Przewalski's horse. I. Boyd, Lee, 1955–   . II. Houpt,
Katherine A.   III. Series.
SF363.P78   1994
599.72'5—dc20   93-2363
                                                     CIP

10 9 8 7 6 5 4 3 2 1

In memory of Erna Mohr
and in honor of Heinz Heck

Contents

Contents

Figures

Tables

Acknowledgments

―――――――

―――――

This book would not have been possible without the help of many people. First and foremost, our thanks go to our contributing authors. Not only did they consent to generously share their knowledge, but they good-naturedly put up with much badgering from us about getting things in on time and in the proper format.

To assure the integrity of the book, each contributed chapter was reviewed by an expert in that field. The comments provided by these reviewers aided us immeasurably in editing the volume. For their insightful reviews we would like to thank Jan and Inge Bouman, Sharon Crowell-Davis, Heinz Heck, Robert Hillman, Lon Lewis, Tracy McNamara, Richard Massena, Bruce McFadden, Elizabeth Thompson, George Waring and Peregrine Wolff.

The series editors, Ed Gibbons and Jack Demarest, gave us much advice and moral support, as did everyone at SUNY Press.

Many thanks go to Linda Phelps for providing us with her word-processing expertise. Without her, the book would have taken at least twice as long to complete.

We would like to thank our families and friends, and colleagues at Washburn University and Cornell University, for their interest in the book, and for providing us with moral and financial support as well as the release time necessary to get the volume done.

Lastly, none of the research included in this volume would have been possible without the interest and cooperation of zoos around the world. Zoo directors, curators, veterinarians, and keepers have our deepest thanks, and we hope this volume will be of help to you as you continue your task of preserving this magnificent endangered species.

A Note to the Reader

Chinese, Mongolian, and Russian words may be translated into a variety of English spellings. We have attempted to standardize these spellings in this volume, but other equally correct variations do exist.

1

Introduction

Lee Boyd and Katherine A. Houpt

The Przewalski's horse is an endangered species and is extinct in the wild. Only captive propagation in zoos has rescued the species from total extinction. At the end of World War II, there were thirty-one horses in captivity of which only nine reproduced. As a testimonial to the efforts of zoos to save this species, there are over a thousand Przewalski's horses at the time of publication of this book.

The size of the captive population has grown to the point where sufficient animals are available for reintroduction to the wild. The political climate is also favorable for cooperative efforts to return this species to the wild. If reintroduction attempts succeed, as seems probable, we will be able to add another species to the small number of successes aimed at slowing the accelerating rate of extinctions on this planet. While it is too late for other prehistoric mammals such as mammoths, we still have the opportunity of returning to the wild one of our other prehistoric co-habitants (see pages 5, 56). Indeed Przewalski's horses are already in semi-reserves in the Xinjiang Province of China where the species was last seen in the wild as well as in Takhi-Tal and Hustain Nuru in Mongolia, in preparation for their release into the wild.

There are two practical reasons for compilation of existing information on Przewalski's horses. Heretofore, comparatively little has been published about the Przewalski's horse. The few published references are difficult to obtain, and there is much informa-

1

tion that has never been published. The pre-eminent compendium on the species was written by Erna Mohr in 1959 and translated into English in 1971. Although Mohr's book can never be surpassed for its firsthand accounts of the early history of the species and its extensive illustrations, much has happened since this book was written. At the time of its writing the technology that we take for granted in studying the horses today was not yet available. At least twenty different research projects on various aspects of Przewalski's horse biology have been conducted in the past two decades and several international conferences concerning this species have been held. Secondly, when the horses were fewer in number and in fewer zoos, sharing information was much easier. Within the past decade the number of zoos holding Przewalski's horses has increased by 50% and now that there are over one-thousand animals in more than one-hundred twenty institutions (Volf 1981, 1991), it has become much more difficult to keep abreast of current knowledge. We felt the time had come to gather all information on Przewalski's horses in one place, to update what was known, provide easy access to the knowledge, and point out areas needing further research. This is especially important in light of attempts to reintroduce Przewalski's horse into the wild.

In order to facilitate the task of the keeper, veterinarian, and curator, especially in institutions which have not had Przewalski's horses before, information is presented on nutrition, management, potential behavior problems, and veterinary care of the animals. The value of these animals, which to some are not as charismatic as other endangered species, will become clear to the caretakers when they read the history of the species, both recent and paleontologic, and recognize the behavior patterns of their charges.

This volume should also serve as a guide to those embarking on research on Przewalski's horses. The research director will have a single source to begin a potential investigator's training. There are several reasons why continued research on Przewalski's horse should yield important theoretical information.

Domestic horses (*Equus caballus*) are those which are currently associated with, and under the control of, humans. Feral *E. caballus* are those, or descendants of those, which were once domesticated but have escaped captivity and are now essentially self-sufficient. All free-roaming horses in western North America and on the barrier islands off its east coast fall into this latter category. The only truly wild horse, for comparison with domestics is the Przewalski's horse, also referred to as the Asiatic or Mongolian wild horse.

Humans have long been interested in horses. Many of mankind's earliest artworks depict prehistoric horses. Horses were a source of food, and hides for clothing and shelter. Hooves, bones, and other connective tissues were used to make implements and glues. Eventually the horse revolutionized transportation, affecting agricultural practices, warfare, sports, and the mobility of human societies. Carrying riders and their belongings, pulling plows, carts and chariots, the horse, along with the dog and the cat, became our closest animal companion. Only the horse and the dog have so consistently and universally been "trained," necessitating a thorough understanding of their behavior and involving interspecific communication (whether realized on the part of the human participant or not). Although the horse is no longer an important source of transportation in industrialized societies, millions of people still own horses for aesthetic, recreational, and utilitarian reasons, as well as enjoying their companionship. Interest in these fascinating animals remains high.

Unlike the dog, where wild species closely related to it are ubiquitous and readily observed, wild relatives of the horse are rare. Wild zebras, asses, and onagers are neither ubiquitous in many parts of the world, nor very closely related to domestic horses. Imagine, then, the excitement generated when the existence of Przewalski's horses on the border between China and Mongolia became known to the western world. Within a short time it was realized that *Equus przewalskii* Poliakov, 1881, was the closest living relative of the domestic horse (*Equus caballus*). As such, they were of extreme interest for comparison with familiar domestics. Just how much do they differ physically and behaviorally from domestic horses?

Przewalski's horses conform to other wild equids in body size, and like other wild equids have short erect manes and a standard coat color. They are of interest in clearly showing how humans have selected for different sizes, coat colors, and long flowing manes in domestic breeds.

Przewalski's horses are also of intense interest as an example of evolution at work. One species is thought to give rise to two, when different populations of the same species become reproductively isolated from one another. With no intermingling of genetic material, enough changes accumulate over time that eventually the populations can no longer interbreed. The equid species show this process in action. Although domestic horses and Przewalski's horses have different chromosome numbers, they have not yet diverged sufficiently to make hybridization impossible. The two interbreed freely and the offspring produced are fertile. Horses and asses show the next step in divergence; although the two species can hybridize, their offspring (a mule) is sterile, because the chromosomes from either parent are not sufficiently similar to pair properly at meiosis.

In addition to pointing out intriguing ideas for research, we hope that this volume will be a valuable reference to zoo curators and keepers, zoo veterinarians, and biologists charged with caring for Przewalski's horses in captivity and implementing their reintroduction. The book may also be helpful to those interested in the conservation and reintroduction of endangered species in general. The Przewalski's horse studbook is the model upon which other species' studbooks have been based, and it is hoped that their return to the wild will serve as a model for the reintroduction of other species. This volume may also be of interest to horse enthusiasts, and those biologists with an interest in particular topics such as nutrition, genetics, or behavior.

Assembling information for the book was an international effort. Such international collaboration is essential for the well-being of the horses in our care, and will be critical for reintroduction attempts to be successful. If this book fosters international cooperation, contributes to the dissemination of knowledge about Przewalski's horses, stimulates further discussion and research, helps to improve the care of Przewalski's horses in captivity, and improves their chances of a successful return to the wild, we will consider our job to be well done.

2

The History of Przewalski's Horse

Inge and Jan Bouman

REFERENCES PREDATING PRZEWALSKI

The First Visual Evidence

The very first visual account of the existence of Przewalski's-type wild horses dates from about 20,000 years ago. Rock engravings, paintings, and decorated tools dating from the late Gravettian to the late Magdalenian (20,000–9,000 B.C.), consisting of 2,188 animal pictures were discovered in caves in Italy, western France and northern Spain; 610 of these were horse figures (Leroi-Gourhan 1971). This gives some evidence of how abundant wild horses must have been in this area at that time. These prehistoric artists were gatherers and hunters. Although their culture was still at the stage of stone implements, they had become skilled hunters. Animal painting in caves probably played a role in the rituals accompanying their hunts. Many of the figures painted in the caves and on tools are drawn with remarkable skill showing details of conformation and coat. Of course, these drawings may not always have been true-to-life. The prehistoric horse figures were not uniform in appearance. Many of them, however, show clear characteristic signs of the Przewalski's horse type, such as upright manes, the shape of the lower jaw and compact profile and both summer and winter coat. Some very evident examples are the paintings in the caves of Labastide, Niaux, Le Portel, Limeuil, La Madeleine and Combarelles in France, and Altamira in Spain. A beautiful neighing wild horse carved in ivory was found in Mas d'Azil in France. Some tools were also found which were decorated with Przewalski's horse heads in Arudy (Leroi-Gourhan 1971).

The discovery of the paintings in the caves gives us the opportunity to form some idea of the physical appearance of the wild horses living at that time. Remains of fossil bones can give some broad idea of their conformation, but unfortunately complete skeletons or skulls were rarely found. About 20,000 years ago there was a sharp peak of cold temperatures: from that period on, the osteological evidence suggests that only medium- to small-sized horses were found in central Europe and central Asia, standing from 125 to 134 cm at the withers (Nobis 1955, Bökönyi 1974, Azzaroli 1985, Sher 1986). It is certain that the very large horses which lived until the initial phases of the last glacial died out (Nobis 1955, Herre 1961). After the last ice age around 10,000 B.C., the steppes in large parts of Europe and Asia were replaced by forests and wooded areas.

The horse, a truly steppe species, must have experienced difficult times. Some of the wild horses adapted themselves to these changes, while other horses retreated further into the Eurasian Steppe. In the Mesolithic (10,000–8,000 B.C.) and Neolithic (8,000–4,500 B.C.) horses became rare. They had been exterminated in most of southern Europe, but survived in small numbers in central Europe, possibly in Spain, and were somewhat more abundant on the Russian plains (Azzaroli 1985). Remains of skeletons, found in the whole of Eurasia, revealed horses, which according to Nobis, belonged to one species, varying in size from small to medium. He thought that the medium-sized ones were in the majority, while the small ones lived at the two ends of the distribution area from western Europe to central Asia (Nobis 1955). Maybe as a result of improved conditions of life in the steppes of Russia and the Ukraine, the size of horses here increased to between 144 and 153 cm at the withers (Bibikova 1967). Several of these wild horses were domesticated in the steppes east of the Dnepr during the Bronze Age (Azzaroli 1985).

The history of the Przewalski's horse is an extremely difficult one to trace, especially after the beginning of horse domestication. From then on it is very difficult to decide whether some osteological remains found at a particular site belonged to domestic or to wild animals. Early horse domestication took place around the middle and lower course of the Dnepr and extended eastwards to the Volga or perhaps as far as the Ural River, but not farther east (Azzaroli 1985, Barclay 1980). Recent radiocarbon datings show that horse domestication was accomplished in the first half of the fourth millennium (Azzaroli 1985).

From there the first domesticated horses plus the art of domesticating them were brought to Asia Minor, east Asia and Europe, mostly to regions where highly developed cultures were flourishing, based on sedentary farming, trade and urban life. In some of those regions the domestic horse was brought beyond its natural habitat. It cannot be ascertained if the wild horses, from which the early domestic horses were derived, resembled the present Przewalski's horse or perhaps the Tarpan, which lived in the Ukraine and in eastern Europe. It makes sense, however, to suppose that local wild horses may have been used to improve the early domestic ones. In some of the regions where the Przewalski's horses lived, they have certainly been used for this purpose (Bökönyi 1974). Pictures of Przewalski's horses on vases and images carved on ivory tools give evidence of the acquaintance of the people with wild horses resembling the present Przewalski's horse.

At Maikop at the northern part of the Caucasus, a silver vase was found from the early Bronze Age, dated between 2,200 and 1,800 B.C. It was decorated with animal figures and among these were a Przewalski's-type horse and a lion (Azzaroli 1985; Brentjes 1967, 1972). At Susa and in Tal-e-Malyan in Iran, decorated pieces of ivory were found with a picture of a neighing Przewalski's horse dating from 2,700–3,000 B.C.

With the spreading of the domestic horse, the art of taming it and above all of riding it, the pattern of human life changed radically. The horse enabled both the expansion of the specialized cultures of the riding nomads and their wars of conquest in Asia Minor, east Asia and parts of Europe. As a result of the rapidly growing population and the consequently increased cultivation of land for agriculture and cattle-breeding, the wild horse population drastically diminished. Some wild horses even had to withdraw to the remotest corners of middle Asia. The Tarpans became extinct in the wild around 1897 (Heptner 1955), more or less unnoticed, and once this was a fact it was thought that the last species of wild horse had become extinct. No one could expect that in Asia real wild horses, known today by the name Przewalski's horses still existed.

Written References of the Existence of Przewalski's Horses

The very first written accounts of Przewalski's horses originate from Tibet. The monk Bodowa, who lived around 900 A.D., made notes on them in his writings (Zevegmid and Dawaa 1973).

Another early written reference is in the "Secret History of the Mongolians." It tells how in 1226 Genghis Khan set out on his

campaign against Tangut and suddenly saw wild horses cross the
path in front of him. His horse reared and Genghis Khan fell to the
ground (Bökönyi 1974). For centuries nothing was heard of the species. Then around 1630, it was announced that Chechen-Khansóloj-
Chalkaskyden, an important Mongolian, had presented a Przewalski's horse as a gift to the emperor of Manchuria (Zevegmid and
Dawaa 1973). This gives an indication that the wild horse must
have been highly appreciated and difficult to catch (Bökönyi 1974).
Visitors to Manchuria seldom saw the Przewalski's horses as they
were very shy and could easily hide in the many mountains. The
few reports of Przewalski's horses mostly came from native hunters. Mention is made of a very large hunt with three thousand
beaters which was organized by the emperor of Manchuria in 1750.
In one day two hundred to three hundred Przewalski's horses were
shot (Mohr 1971). In a Manchurian dictionary, which was compiled
in 1771, the Przewalski's horse is mentioned as a "wild horse from
the steppe" (Dovchin 1961). The explanation given is: "Wild ancestor of the domestic horses" (Bannikov and Lobanov 1980).

The first reports from a westerner of sightings of Przewalski's
horses were from John Bell, a Scottish doctor in the service of Czar
Peter the Great, who went on a journey in 1719–1722 (Mohr 1971).
His book, "A Journey from St. Petersburg to Peking," was published in 1763. Then for another one and a half centuries nothing
was heard about Przewalski's horses. Linnaeus (1707–1778) does
not mention the Przewalski's horse in his famous, "Systema Natu-
rae." This shows clearly to what extent this wild horse was unknown in the West.

THE 'DISCOVERY' OF THE PRZEWALSKI'S HORSE

The Expeditions of Colonel Przewalski

It was Colonel Nikolai Michailovich Przewalski, who made
mention of the wild horses again. This eminent explorer, descended
from Polish ancestors, lived from 1839–1888. By the order of Czar
Alexander the Second he made one expedition of discovery to eastern Siberia and three to central Asia, aiming to reach Tibet
(Rayfield 1977).

In 1878, Przewalski returned prematurely from his second expedition in central Asia due to illness. At the Chinese-Russian
frontier post, Zaisan, he received a horse's skull and hide as a present from the commissioner, A.K. Tikhanov. The horse had been

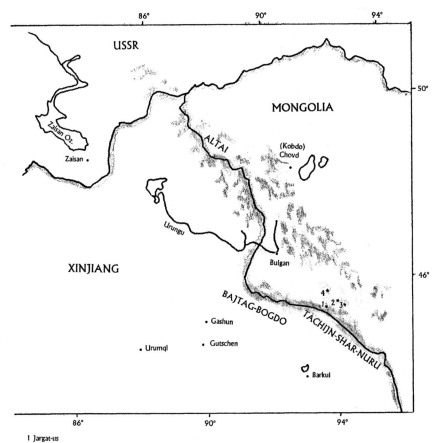

Figure 2.1. Map of the known geographical range of Przewalski's horses prior to extinction. Starred locales are natural wells or springs where wild horses were sighted.

shot by Kirghizian hunters some 80 km north of Gutschen (Figure 2.1). Colonel Przewalski initially doubted if the remains were from a wild horse. He took them to the Zoological Museum of the Academy of Science in St. Petersburg. The conservator, I.S. Poliakov, studied them and concluded they really belonged to a wild horse. It was given the official name, *"Equus przewalskii Poliakov, 1881."*

Nikolai Przewalski made an official announcement of his discovery of the Przewalski's horse in 1880 after returning from this third expedition to central Asia (1879–1880). During this journey

Przewalski discovered two groups of wild horses on his way from the Bulugun River to Barkul (Rayfield 1977). The specimen which he had received from Tikhanov came from the same area. In his statement, he not only described the build and the appearance of the wild horses, but gave some additional information about this species as well. For example, he said that the horses lived in groups of five to fifteen horses guided by an older stallion. They were very shy and possessed a keen sense of smell, hearing and sight. They seemed to keep to the saline steppes and were able to survive a long time without water. According to Przewalski, hunting them was extremely difficult. Winter was the best time for hunting since the snow provided the hunters' water supply. Przewalski tried to shoot the horses, but the stallion fled at full speed, its tail and head raised, the whole herd following him. He succeeded in approaching the herd from the side and sneaking near them. Suddenly, they noticed him, and like a windstorm they fled and disappeared. Przewalski found it rather peculiar that these wild horses had never been discovered outside the most remote areas of the central Asian deserts (Przewalski 1884). The question of whether what he saw was a real horse or an Asiatic wild ass was not resolved satisfactorily.

The Reports of the Brothers Grum-Grzhimailo

The first Europeans, who not only saw the Przewalski's horse but successfully hunted them, were the brothers Grigory and Michael Grum-Grzhimailo, who from 1889 until 1890 travelled through western China (Grum-Grzhimailo 1892). G. Grum-Grzhimailo was a Major General of the Russian General Staff, famous for his travels through China, Pamir and Tien Shan. By order of the Russian government, which expressed great interest in the study of central Asia, the Grum-Grzhimailos compiled maps, described the local populations and made detailed notes about the fauna and flora. According to the Grum-Grzhimailos, Colonel Przewalski never saw the wild horse which now bears his name with his own eyes, but saw the Asiatic wild ass (*Equus hemionus hemionus*).

In 1889, the expedition of the Grum-Grzhimailos was in the Gashun area where they discovered a harem of Przewalski's horses near a watering place. It took them several days before they were able to shoot four Przewalski's horses: three stallions and a mare.

During these days they were able to observe the horses from short distances.

> "Wild horses are very careful at night, during the day they skillfully use the features of the country to camouflage themselves. Chasing a herd three hundred to four hundred steps behind, we often completely lost sight of it and found it only by the tracks. Wild horses keep in bands of no more than ten, each herd having a dominant stallion. There are other males, too, but they are young, and judging by the hide of the two-year-old colt that we killed the dominant treats them very cruelly. In fact, the hide showed the traces of numerous bites." (Grum-Grzhimailo 1892)

In this diary the brothers Grum-Grzhimailo (1892) described the stallion as very vigilant, mostly hiding himself in the bushes and letting the herd walk two to three hundred steps forward. When danger was observed he signalled his band by snorting. The horses immediately formed a file with a young stallion at the head and the foals in the middle, among the mares. When chased, the stallion took a position at the back. When a foal could not catch up with the herd, the stallion urged it on. He even pushed the young with his muzzle and dragged it along by the withers. Occasionally, he kicked the air threateningly.

The four hides, and the skulls of the three stallions collected by the Grum-Grzhimailos together with an incomplete skeleton, were taken to the Zoological Museum of St. Petersburg and there added to the collection of this institution.

Following the reports of Colonel Przewalski and the Grum-Grzhimailo brothers, articles on the Przewalski's horse also appeared from the hands of W.J. Roborowski, P.K. Koslow, M.W. Pevzov and A.N. Kasnakow (Garutt et al. 1965). However, none of these explorers had ever seen a Przewalski's horse in the wild. Their knowledge was based on information obtained from local inhabitants. The question of whether the Przewalski's horse was a real wild horse kept many scientists busy for twenty years after the publication of these reports. Among them there were even some who thought the Przewalski's horse to be a hybrid of a domestic horse and a Dziggetai (*Equus hemionus hemionus*) (Garutt et al. 1965). The thorough investigations of A.A. Tikhomirov (1898–1902) and W.W. Salensky, who studied over ten skins, about ten skulls, and some skeletons of Przewalski's horses, proved that the

Przewalski's horse was a genuine wild horse and put a stop to this speculation (Salensky 1902).

LAST SIGHTINGS OF THE PRZEWALSKI'S HORSE IN THE WILD AND ITS EXTINCTION

Last Sightings

The original distribution of the Przewalski's horse is assumed to have covered the whole Eurasian steppe belt. By 1900, the sightings by Przewalski in 1883 and Grum-Grzhimailo in 1896 plus the reports of Pevzov in 1879, Noack in 1902 and Clemenz in 1903 described by Garutt et al. (1965), made clear that the population range had severely contracted. In 1958 Bannikov stated:

> "The wild horse was to be seen only in Dzungaria and its area of distribution was limited in the north by the Urungu and the northern slope of the High Altai. The most northerly point where the wild horses had been seen lay at the point of intersection 46°N and 90°E; the limit to the east was 95°E. The southern limits followed the slopes of the Tien Shan (44°N), as far as 86°E. The focal point of the area is a quadrant, limited by 89°–94°E and 44°30'–45°30'N and by the chain of mountains from Bajtag-Bogdo and Tachijn-Shar-Nuru." (cited in Mohr 1971, p. 31)

No reports were published after 1903 of sightings of Przewalski's horses until 1947, when one Przewalski's filly was captured on the northern slopes of the Tachijn-Shar-Nuru mountains (Figure 2.2), and was sent to Shargalantu, formerly Kobdo. When the captured filly was ten years old, she was moved from Shargalantu to Askania Nova, where she became known as Orlitza III. In the thirties and forties wild horses must have been relatively abundant in the Dzungarian Gobi (Barun-Hurai Hollow) in southwest Mongolia (Zevegmid and Dawaa 1973), but they diminished progressively thereafter. Several Arats (Mongolian herdsmen) related that at times as many as fifty to a hundred Przewalski's horses could be seen grazing in small groups between the hills (Paklina and Pozdnyakova 1989). In 1947 the Russian botanist Junatov discovered six to seven Przewalski's horses, and the Mongolian Zanciv eighteen horses (Zevegmid and Dawaa 1973). From then until 1960 there were sporadic records of hunters and Mongolian Arats sighting small groups of two to three horses in the limited area between the mountain ridges of the Tachijn-Shar-Nuru and Bajtag-Bogdo

Figure 2.2. The Tachijn-Shar-Nuru (Yellow Mountains of the Wild Horse) range; one of the last refuges of the Przewalski's horse, and possible site of future reintroductions.

(Zevegmid and Dawaa 1973, Mohr and Volf 1984). The horses were mostly seen during spring and summer near natural wells like the Cagan-Salyn-Choloj, Salyn-us, Nutz-us, Chonin-us, Todgijn-us, Tachijn-us, and Aratyn-us (Figure 2.1). The Przewalski's horses would travel south along the northern hills at the foot of the Ih-Havtag and the Baga-Havtag to the Bajtag-Bogdo range, which straddles the Mongolian-Chinese border. According to the Arats the horses avoided the higher mountains and crossed the border by way of the valleys (Paklina and Pozdnyakova 1989). Two Mongolian expeditions in 1955 and 1962 returned without sighting Przewalski's horses (Volf and Chagdarsouren 1975).

Further reports relating to sightings of Przewalski's horses came from the Mongolian Arats named Tuvden and Chisge (Zevegmid and Dawaa 1973) who respectively saw eleven and seven horses in 1966. Expeditions organized by the Academy of Sciences of the People's Republic of Mongolia sighted only one harem in 1967 and in total five animals in 1968. In 1969, the Mongolian scientist N. Dovchin was the last person to see a Przewalski's horse, a stallion, in the wild. It happened near a spring called Gun Tamga (Figure 2.3), north of the Tachijn-Shar-Nuru, meaning "Yellow Mountains of the Wild Horse" (Paklina and Pozdnyakova 1989). One of the latest expeditions in search of Przewalski's horses was organized in 1979 by Academician Sokolov, director of

Figure 2.3. The spring Gun Tamga, where one of the last sightings of a Przewalski's horse in the wild took place.

the Institute for Evolutionary Animal Morphology and Ecology in
Moscow, but no horses were seen, nor were tracks of them found.
Later expeditions in 1988 and 1989 by the same Institute in cooperation with Mongolian zoologists all were without success (Paklina and Pozdnyakova 1989). It can be assumed that Przewalski's
horses are now extinct in the wild in Mongolia. Unfortunately, not
much is known about the last Przewalski's horses in Xinjiang
(China) at the other side of the border. The director of the Peking
Zoo, Tsai Chan-ping, reported that his zoo sent out expeditions in
1955 and 1957 in order to capture Przewalski's horses. These expeditions had no success (Volf and Chagdarsouren 1975). Tan Bangjie
(1981) published a report in China which caused a great stir. It
was based on information from Pen Xi Ling, a geologist, who had
sighted seven to eight Przewalski's horses on the northern slopes of
the Ke-La-Mai-Li mountain, south of the Tachijn-Shar-Nuru, in
1958. He saw another wild horse in the same region in 1980. Dr.
Dolan from the Zoological Society of San Diego, visiting Urumqi in
1986, stated that the last authentic sightings in China were in the
late fifties. According to the Chinese authorities, the 1980 sighting
is incorrect (Dolan, personal communication 1986).

The Causes of Extinction

Why did the numbers of Przewalski's horses in the wild decrease so drastically after World War II?

It is clear, that the Dzungarian Gobi cannot be seen as an optimal habitat for the Przewalski's horse, but was in fact their last refuge, from predation by humans for meat and skins, and from competition with domestic livestock. Pushed away into the peripheral zones of their original range of distribution, their survival was subjected to great pressure. In the last decades Mongolia too has been swiftly settled. Historically, a large portion of the Mongolian people were nomads with large herds. By utilizing the best parts, the herdsmen (Arats) penetrated into the areas inhabited by the Przewalski's horses. The Dzungarian Gobi is an extensive desert basin, surrounded by mountains. The Mongolian Arats developed the tradition of leaving the northern Altai range in autumn and travelling south with their cattle. In winter they grazed their cattle on the dry steppes in the mountains and the foothills of the Bajtag-Bogdo range, the Baga-Havtag, the Ih-Havtag Nuru, Huh Undrijn Nuru, the Tachijn-Shar-Nuru and the Huvchijn Nuru mountains. These were feeding areas which the Przewalski's horses frequented because even in winter there were nutritious grasses to be found like the feathergrasses (*Stipa orientalis* and *Stipa glareosa*) (Sokolov et al. 1990). In spring the Arats would gradually move north again, reaching the foothills of the Mongolian Altai by summer. The arid territory of the Dzungarian Gobi offers few watering places, most of them situated in the central desert part and some 10–30 km away from their feeding areas. Many animals assemble in the areas around the wells, which are small oases, some of them with high grass that offers protection to a host of smaller species. The vegetation of oases is mostly scarce with specimens such as reed (*Phragmites communis*), a type of lyme grass (*Elymus secalinus*), tamarisks (*Callipogonum*), and halophyte plants like *Achnatherum splendens*, caragana bushes (*Caragana spinosa*), *Halimodendron halodendron*, the shrub-like saxaul (*Haloxylon ammodendron*), and *Reaumuria songarica* (Sokolov et al. 1990). Until 1950 the Arats were not allowed to graze their cattle south of the spring Honin-Us, where a border crossing point had been established some 40 km north from the border with China (Paklina and Pozdnyakova 1989). In 1950 the crossing point was moved up to the border, which enabled the Arats to herd their cattle to the wells and in the surrounding areas where the Przewalski's horses had been feeding up to then. The frontier guards have always kept their own livestock including domestic horses roaming around for their own food supply. Naturally, the Arats and frontier guards went hunting as well, but not being regular horse-meat eaters, this posed no great threat to the Przewalski's horses. However, the Chinese Kazakhs do consume horse meat, and between 1945 and 1947 they had been given permission from the authorities to settle in southwest Mongolia. The Kazakhs had no cattle of their own and relied heavily on hunting for their subsistence, thus forming a threat to the Przewalski's horses (Paklina and Pozdnyakova 1989). The winter of 1945 was extremely harsh, the snowcover was very high and the temperature very low, -50°C. Glazed frost or "dzud" as the Mongolians call it, is one of the greatest hazards of winter for many ungulates, covering every blade of grass in ice. In 1948 this glazed frost persisted for a long time. A large portion of the livestock died. Because of the severity of the winter, hunting was intensified and the wild hoofed stock were weakened by lack of food. This happened again in 1956 (Zevegmid and Dawaa 1973). Until 1940, the hunters had used primitive rifles which fired only one shot at a time. Consequently, losses among the swift Przewalski's horses had been minor. This changed radically when modern rifles were introduced, making it possible to annihilate whole groups of horses at once. Also, in the 1930s and 1940s the religious climate among the Arats had gradually changed. Before the Mongolians came under the influence of the USSR, they were Buddhists and their religion prohibited them from killing more animals than they needed. After 1950, Buddhism lost its hold to communism, resulting in greater hunting pressure by the Mongolians. Hunting the wild horses has been forbidden since 1926 (Zevegmid and Dawaa 1973). Unfortunately, the observance of this protective measure was never enforced. Real measures to protect the Przewalski's horses in their last remote refuge in southwest Mongolia and Xinjiang came too late to prevent total extinction.

THE CAPTURE OF PRZEWALSKI'S HORSES

Early Plans

Colonel Przewalski's rediscovery of the wild horses attracted the attention of many zoologists as well as animal lovers. Plans were made to catch Przewalski's horses alive. D.A. Clemenz and

C.E. Büchner were particularly interested in these plans. Clemenz was a well-known ethnographer, who had been in Mongolia for five years by order of the Russian Imperial Academy of Sciences towards the end of the nineteenth century. During that time he had been able to establish very good relations with many prominent Mongolians. In Bijsk he had made the acquaintance of Nicolai I. Assanov, who owned a trading business at Kobdo. This man hoped to catch a number of Przewalski's horses, provided that ample money was made available for a well-equipped expedition. Therefore, the three men approached Friederich E. von Falz-Fein, a rich estate-landowner, German by birth and living in the Crimea of Southern Russia. Von Falz-Fein possessed a herd of some 500,000 sheep at his estate, Askania Nova. He also bred cattle and horses for the Russian army. One part of his estate was reserved for keeping exotic and rare animals (Heiss 1970). When Clemenz and Büchner proposed to capture Przewalski's horses, von Falz-Fein was highly interested. After another meeting at St. Petersburg, von Falz-Fein commissioned Assanov to organize the expedition. The latter had two catchers, Wlasow and Sacharow in mind, who would start the capture of Przewalski's horses with the help of the native population. However, it proved to be impossible to catch adult horses, as they were too fast and too shy. Only the capture of foals would stand a chance of success. This plan had to take place in early spring, when the mares would just have foaled. The first effort was probably made in 1897. Not much is known of this first endeavour, except that some foals were caught, but they died soon thereafter. According to Clemenz, success was not achieved until 1898 (Mohr 1971).

The First Successful Capture

Two foals were caught by Sacharow and his helpers in the Dzungarian Gobi, and four by Wlasow near the well Emtsche (Garutt et al. 1965). Wlasow thought he could keep the foals alive with sheep's milk, however, the foals soon died. The filly caught by Sacharow also died quickly. The second foal, a colt, which was kept in Assanov's garden at Kobdo, died of poisoning when it was five months old. The skulls and hides of these animals were sent to the Zoological Museum of St. Petersburg, together with the hides of an adult Przewalski's mare and a yearling stallion shot by local people. By now it had become clear that the capture of living Przewalski's foals was possible. The problem was how to keep very young

foals alive. The solution found was to obtain domestic horse foster
mothers to nurse the Przewalski's foals.

The Second Successful Capture

Erna Mohr (1971) quotes Waldemar von Falz-Fein (1930) who
described how in 1899 a new attempt was made to capture foals,
this time with more success. Seven foals were caught, six fillies
and one colt. One colt and one filly proved to be so weak, however,
that they could not cover the distance from Kobdo to Bijsk, 500
kilometers, and so they were left at Kobdo. The remaining five
were taken on foot with their foster-mothers to Bijsk. From there
they were transported by train to Russia. They arrived at Alekse-
jewska, situated 70 kilometers from Askania Nova at the end of
February or early March of the following year. During the transport from the station to Askania Nova another young foal died, so
that at last only four fillies arrived at Askania Nova. What became
of the two foals left at Kobdo, is not quite clear. Most probably the
monarch, Uchtomski, who paid a visit to Assanov, had seen the
two foals and purchased them from him for the purpose of present-
ing them to Czar Nikolai II. The filly must have died before the
transport to the imperial stables at Tsarskoe-Selo could have taken
place. Assanov transported the colt to the imperial stables together
with a filly that was caught in 1900. Unfortunately, she died at
Tsarskoe-Selo in 1901. The colt was given by the Czar to von Falz-
Fein in 1904, and became the breeding stallion at Askania Nova.

The Third Successful Capture

The catch in 1900 was small, only three Przewalski's foals
were caught, i.e., the above mentioned mare and two colts given by
Assanov to the Moscow Zoo as a present.

Hunting Przewalski's horses was a very difficult job, as they
were very shy and had a very good sense of smell. One was rarely
able to get within shooting distance, let alone catch the horses
alive. The catchers needed a number of very fast horses to pursue
the fleeing Przewalski's horses. During the long chase they frequently had to change to fresh horses, which they had brought
with them. At that time there were already so few wild horses left
that often it would take weeks before a group of Przewalski's
horses was discovered. When a group of Przewalski's horses with
their foals had been sighted, the time-consuming hunt could start.
In the pursuit, the Arats tried to separate the foals from the mares.

If this succeeded, the confused and exhausted foals would stop running, and they could be caught by "uraks," long sticks with a loop of rope at the end.

The Fourth Successful Capture

The 1901 catch can easily be called a surprisingly large one. Fifty-two foals were caught. Probably at least 20–25 harems had to be traced and pursued to achieve this. Many adult Przewalski's horses must have been shot. The news of sighting wild horses in southwest Mongolia got around fast. The first Duke of Bedford, Herbrand, was, like von Falz-Fein, a great animal lover. He was president of the London Zoological Society and kept many rare mammal and bird species on his extensive estate at Woburn. Between 1888 and 1912 he succeeded in acquiring the last Pere David's Deer (*Elaphurus davidianus*) from China and successfully bred them. Thanks to him this rare deer species was saved from total extinction. After hearing the reports on the wild horses in southwest Mongolia, the Duke of Bedford was very much interested in obtaining this species as well.

Carl Hagenbeck, the famous animal catcher and dealer from Hamburg, who had already imported various species such as Asiatic deer, wild sheep, ibex and Siberian roe deer from central Asia, and who did a lot of business with the Duke of Bedford, was asked to obtain a number of Przewalski's horses. According to the reports of Waldemar von Falz-Fein (1930), Hagenbeck succeeded in buying from Assanov the fifty-two foals from under von Falz-Fein's nose. According to Hagenbeck (1926) the story was quite different. He ordered his Russian agent, a travelling trader named Grieger, to organize the capture of Przewalski's horse foals for him. N. Paklina (personal communication 1990) told the following story about the captures in 1901. It confirms Hagenbeck's report and gives some additional data on the method of transportation of the foals. In 1969 the Mongolian zoologist Dovchin interviewed several old Arats from Altan Sojombo, a hamlet on the northern edge of the Dzungarian Gobi and the southern slopes of the Altai mountains. One of them, a man called Bazar, gave this account:

> "Grieger asked us to catch Przewalski's foals. He traded flour, tea, and winter boots for furs of wolves, and foxes, and horns of saiga antelopes. Many local people were willing to help Grieger, as he paid them in Russian currency. The capture took place in April and May. Fifty-six foals were captured. Grieger had not counted

on such a large catch, and did not have enough condensed milk, which he had brought to feed the animals. Goat's milk was used as a substitute. Six foals died in the period between capture and the transport. The survivors were put into bags and loaded onto camels, one on either side. Ten camels were necessary to carry the milk, the remainder of the hundred camels in the caravan carried luggage. After crossing the Mongolian-Russian border the foals were transferred to another caravan. During the transport another four foals died."

Only twenty-eight of these foals reached Europe alive; many died during the exhausting journey. They first covered the long distance from the capture site to Kobdo and to the river Ob by foot, which took fifty days and was made under the most unfavorable weather conditions. Domestic mares were obtained as foster mothers to nurse the Przewalski's foals. The journey continued by ship along the Ob to Bijsk and by train from Bijsk to Hamburg where on 27 October 1901, only fifteen colts, thirteen fillies and their foster mothers arrived safely (Hagenbeck 1926).

Of these twenty-eight foals, five colts and seven fillies went to the Woburn estate; one colt plus one filly went to the London Zoo, while another colt and filly were temporarily housed in London and sold to Manchester in 1908. One colt and one filly went to the Tierzucht Institute of the Halle University and one pair went to the Berlin Zoo. Moreover, Hagenbeck sold a pair to the New York Zoo. This pair was not accepted by the Zoo, as they were considered to be in bad condition. Hagenbeck then transported them to the Cincinnati Zoo. Finally, one stallion went to the Paris Zoo and one pair to Mr. Blaauw, who owned the extensive estate, "Gooilust," near Hilversum in The Netherlands. Three colts remained in Hamburg (Mohr 1971).

The Fifth Successful Capture

In 1902 many foals were again caught, but the exact number is not known. Eleven arrived alive at Hamburg for Hagenbeck, and four went to Askania Nova: three mares and a young stallion. The catch must have been much larger, as a large number of skulls and stuffed foals date from this time. It is likely that the men in charge of this Hagenbeck transport sold or gave the foals that died along the way to traders of stuffed animals. The Przewalski's horses that arrived in Hamburg were in poor condition; five died during that year. Two were sold to the New York Zoo where they arrived in

1905; another pair was sold to Professor Ewart of Edinburgh, and the remaining two were kept in Hamburg. One of the latter, a mare, died in 1908 and the other, a stallion, was sold in 1920 to the Artis Zoo in Amsterdam. It lived there for another two years and then died. Of the three mares which reached Askania Nova, only one later produced foals.

The Last Captures

The last catch of Przewalski's horses around the turn of the century took place in 1903. Not many animals were caught. Two of them, both mares, arrived at Askania Nova early in 1904. During the 1930s and 1940s just a few Przewalski's horses were caught. Something is known about only two of these. One filly was caught in 1938 on the northern side of the Tachijn-Shar-Nuru mountains and was sent to Shargalantu about 75 kilometers northwest of Ulan Bator, the capital of Mongolia. In 1962, the mare came into the possession of the Mongolian War Ministry. From 1966 until 1967 she was kept on an estate near the town of Enderchaan, 300 kilometers east of the capital. This mare was cross-bred with Mongolian domestic horses. In 1947 another Przewalski's mare (Orlitza III) was caught as mentioned above. She was also sent to Shargalantu and then sold in 1957 to Askania Nova. She died in 1973, having given birth to four foals, which was of great importance to the breeding of Przewalski's horses.

The Founders of the Captive Population

The first adaptation to captivity was very difficult for the shy and easily stressed Przewalski's horses. Individuals which possessed few preadaptations for coping with the small and impoverished captive environments experienced rather intense negative selection.

Of the Przewalski's horses that survived after arrival at their destination, only a few produced foals. The mare of the pair that arrived at the Imperial Stables of Tsarskoe-Selo died in 1904. Of all the horses sent to Askania Nova, every stallion died during transport. The Czar therefore gave his remaining stallion to Baron von Falz-Fein in 1904 for breeding purposes. Of the three horses in the Moscow Zoo one mare died in 1902, and the remaining pair did not reproduce. Nor were any foals born in Berlin, Manchester or Edinburgh, while the breeding at Carl Hagenbeck's Zoo in Hamburg was not successful either. The Paris Zoo, Menagerie du Jardin des Plantes, bought a stallion from the first Hagenbeck transport and in 1906 the first filly was born at Woburn, which later was sold to Paris. This pair produced their first filly in 1909. Another three foals were born after this, a stallion and two mares. The colt soon died. The fillies and their parents all lived to a ripe old age. Yet no foals were born to the second generation so that this line died out in 1941. The same thing happened on the estate Gooilust, belonging to Frans Ernst Blaauw. The pair he bought in 1907 from Carl Hagenbeck's first expedition had three foals: two colts and a filly. One colt went to Woburn. In 1909 the mare born at Gooilust died and in 1914 the stallion bought from Hagenbeck died, too. Until 1922 Blaauw tried to breed using the stallion that was born at Gooilust in 1913, but without success. So he bought a stallion from Woburn in 1922 and a mare from Halle. Although this mare had produced five foals in Halle, no success was achieved at Gooilust. When Blaauw died in 1936 he left all his animals to the Duke of Bedford. One of the stallions died before the transport took place and the other went to the London Zoo. In spite of a good beginning, Gooilust and Paris played no part in the subsequent breeding of Przewalski's horses (Mohr 1971).

THE HISTORY OF CAPTIVE BREEDING OF THE PRZEWALSKI'S HORSE

To continue the history of the Przewalski's horse we will look at those zoos which succeeded in rearing them. The breeding of Przewalski's horses is not an easy matter. There are only five places—New York, Cincinnati, Woburn, Halle and Askania Nova —where several generations of horses were reared from horses caught in the wild. This led to the situation where only eleven of the Przewalski's horses caught around the turn of the century have influenced the present population (Bouman 1977).

Four periods can be distinguished in the history of captive breeding of the Przewalski's horse:

1899–1935

1935–1968

1968–1979

1979–until the present

Period I (from 1899–1935)

The initial breedings, mostly by pairs in isolated zoos and private parks, were not very successful. Throughout the first period the total number of Przewalski's horses in captivity remained around twenty to thirty distributed over twelve to fifteen zoos and private parks. Unilateral breeding within small groups in Askania Nova (Ukraine/USSR), Woburn (U.K.), Halle (Germany) and North America occurred until 1935–1940, with no exchanging of horses between the groups to broaden their founder-base. Only in the U.S.A. were Przewalski's horses exchanged between New York and Cincinnati. In Berlin, Edinburgh, Moscow and Hamburg the horses did not breed, while in Paris and Gooilust breeding was initially successful, but the descendants of the first generation did not reproduce. Consequently, the total number of founder animals decreased in this period from fourteen to eleven (Bouman-Heinsdijk 1982a). It was an unfortunate circumstance that one of the Mongolian domestic foster mares was used once for breeding at Halle in 1906; including her, the total number of founder animals before World War II is twelve.

Askania Nova. Of the nine Przewalski's horses caught wild which went to Askania Nova: eight mares and one stallion, only two mares foaled, when they were bred to the stallion presented by the Czar to von Falz-Fein. One mare gave birth to eight foals, and the other three, and the stallion subsequently covered some of these offspring of his. In the following generations mares continued to be covered by closely related stallions, causing high inbreeding. Prior to World War II, thirty-two Przewalski's foals were born in Askania Nova. Baron Friedrich von Falz-Fein occasionally crossed Przewalski's horses with domestic horses and zebras. In 1918 he fled to Berlin where he died in 1920. His entire property, a 100,000 hectare steppe and 2,600 hectare reserve and zoo were taken over by the state.

The animal dealer Ruhe bought two stallions from Askania Nova in 1925, plus a mare in 1927; one stallion and the mare were sold to the Berlin Zoo, where they produced three colts and three fillies. In 1937, a couple of Przewalski's horses from Askania Nova were sold to Warsaw, where they had no offspring. Single stallions were sold to Moscow and Leningrad. During the Second World War a couple of Przewalski's horses were sent to Germany, but these never arrived, probably having died by bombing during the transport. In the course of the Second World War all the remaining

Przewalski's horses in Askania Nova died. The offspring of the couple which arrived in Berlin in 1927 did not fare well either. Hermann Göring, Hitler's Reichsmarschall, was an avid hunter, and he conceived the idea of instituting a huge reserve on the Schorfheide (moor) to be populated by all of the kinds of animals which used to live in the Great German Reich. Consequently, several Przewalski's horses arrived in this "reserve." The area was attacked with fire bombs in 1943 and all the Przewalski's horses lost their lives. Only one mare, Ella (#140 Hellabrunn 13), descending via Berlin from Askania Nova, survived the Second World War, and she became one of the breeding mares in Munich in the second period. Through her, the original "Askania Nova blood" was saved for the future.

The United States. On December 30, 1902, a couple of Przewalski's horses arrived at the Bronx Zoo in New York; Carl Hagenbeck had exchanged them for two pairs of bison. The stallion was in good condition, but the mare was not; she had difficulty standing. As no one had a notion of what to do with Przewalski's horses, people tried to handle them as domestic horses, making efforts to harness them and put them to a cart to drive around the zoo. The more it was tried, the wilder the horses became, so ultimately the effort was abandoned (Bridges 1974). Although the mare had improved by the spring of 1903, the management of the Bronx Zoo wanted to have another pair. Therefore, this couple was sent in 1905 to the Cincinnati Zoo, Hagenbeck's American depository, where the director was his agent (Bridges 1974). In 1912 they produced their only foal, a colt. The replacement pair did not arrive in New York until late in 1905. From this pair six foals were born, and through breeding among them another seven, causing New York to possess a good breeding group for years.

The foundation studbook published by Mohr (1959) lists four animals as arriving in the U.S.A. up until 1905, but in fact there were six (Dolan 1982). The last two horses were shipped directly to Mr. Davenport, one of the early Arabian Horse breeders in the U.S.A. It is not known when they arrived in the United States, nor is it possible to tell from which of the Hagenbeck importations they are derived (Dolan 1982). Nothing is known about descendants, if any.

Descendants of horses in New York and Cincinnati bred successfully with each other at Philadelphia from 1914 onwards. Progeny from the lines established at Philadelphia, New York (Bronx) and Washington, D.C. (from Philadelphia breeding) were sent to Australia and Europe.

In 1916–17, New York sold a stallion plus two mares to the Sidney Zoo in Australia. One of these mares foaled twice, while the stallion sired three foals by his daughters, and that was the end of breeding in Sidney. However, one colt (#225 Sidney 4) was sold to Carl Hagenbeck of Hamburg in 1932, who resold him to the Paris Zoo in 1942. Another horse, a mare, was sold in 1935 to Hellabrunn, the zoo in Munich. The story of these two Sidney horses will be continued in the next period.

Around 1924, the director of the Bronx Zoo considered the inbreeding of his herd too high, so he obtained from the Philadelphia Zoo a descendant of the stallion born in Cincinnati by a mare that New York had previously sold to Philadelphia. Upon arrival in New York the director did not regard this stallion as suitable for breeding because he had a white forefoot and a blaze; and no further breeding took place at New York. Unfortunately, in the United States only a few Przewalski's horses from the earlier period of successful breeding remained. So it happened that the death of the mare #119 Philadelphia 6 in 1959 meant the end of the Przewalski's horses in the United States. Yet the influence of their offspring was continued in Europe.

In total the U.S.A. line produced twenty-nine foals. The last foal was born in 1937. This breeding line ended in the 1950s leaving one stallion from Washington siring descendants in Prague, and a mare from Washington and a mare from Sidney became the breeding mares in Munich. A stallion from Sidney sired one foal in Paris.

Unfortunately, the inbreeding of the progeny of this line had increased considerably by the end of this period.

Halle. Out of the first Hagenbeck transport one pair went to Halle, which was not a zoo but the Zoological Department of the Agricultural Institute of the University of Halle in Germany. Counselor J. Kühn wanted to investigate whether the Przewalski's horses were real wild horses—a fact questioned by many at that time—as well as study their relationship with domestic horses (Spöttel 1926). The Przewalski's pair at Halle produced three fillies. Kühn experimented by crossing a Przewalski's horse with a domestic one and produced various hybrids. Furthermore, he crossed a Przewalski's horse with a Mongolian domestic horse, this being one of the foster mothers which had joined the transport.

This combination produced only one colt. After the Przewalski's stallion died in 1908, the four remaining Przewalski's mares were covered by the stallion which was half Przewalski's horse and half Mongolian domestic. Nine foals were sired by him, six of them by pure Przewalski's mares, and the other three by his "mixed-blood" daughters. Only two of these nine foals produced descendants, the stallion Ali (#62 Halle 5) and the mare Minka (#65 Halle 8), out of pure Przewalski's mares, therefore carrying 25% Mongolian domestic horse blood. In 1932, they were transferred, via the Research Station of the Agricultural High School in Prague, to the newly founded Praha Zoo, which continued the Halle breeding line (Mohr 1971). There they had five foals, of which two died young. Two went to Munich where they were not used for breeding because they were not pure, and the last one, Helus, remained in Prague and had foals sired by a Przewalski's stallion from the U.S.A., who also covered her mother. The last Przewalski's horse in Halle died in 1928. As one will understand, the inbreeding in this line had increased considerably. Eighteen foals were born in this line. The introduction of the Mongolian domestic horse into the Przewalski's breeding group has from that day onwards been the cause of much discord.

Woburn (U.K.). Herbrand, Duke of Bedford, purchased five colts and seven fillies from Carl Hagenbeck. They arrived in 1901 at his estate, Woburn Abbey, along with one stallion and a mare for the London Zoological Society of which he was president. Because of this close bond between London and Woburn, occasional exchange of horses occurred. Not much is known about the first period at Woburn, because a great part of Woburn's archives was lost in a fire. As far as is known, twenty-four foals were born in this line. After 1920 most of the horses were moved to the London Zoo, and later to its country branch, Whipsnade Park, when it was completed. Reproduction was not successful in this line. The stallion Neville (#182 London 6) is the only Przewalski's horse from the English line whose blood is continued in the present Przewalski's stock. In 1938 he was sold to Hellabrunn-Munich. Neville was the successor of the stallion Pascha (#187 Askania A) who was moved in the same year to Berlin. This story belongs to the history of the second period.

There were only a very few horses from the first period available for breeding in the second period. No more than three stallions and five mares produced offspring thereafter. The original breeding areas: Askania Nova (Ukraine/USSR), Halle (Germany), England and the U.S.A. had ceased to function as such.

Period II (from 1935–1968)

Fortunately, the second period brought some new developments. Some exchanges of Przewalski's horses took place. The Munich Zoo received one mare from Washington and a stallion from London out of the Woburn group. Together with mares which carried blood from the original founder group at Askania Nova, a herd with members from three different breeding centers was formed. The Prague Zoo obtained an unrelated stallion from the U.S.A. for their breeding mares from Halle. The stallion, #225 Sidney 4, who originated from the early American line, at a great age sired in Paris a colt by a mare from Prague. These exchanges gave a new impulse to breeding. The number of Przewalski's horses increased. The Second World War, however, caused an enormous reduction in number by acts of war. Only thirty-one Przewalski's horses survived the war. The significance of the year 1945 becomes clear when it is realized that at that time only nine Przewalski's horses (three males and six females) produced offspring for future captive propagation (Bouman 1977, 1982). It took at least another ten years after World War II to recover from this loss. Thanks to breeding in Munich and Prague the Przewalski's horses passed the narrow bottleneck situation after 1945. In 1955 the prewar number was again reached. The unrelated Przewalski's horses imported to Munich and Prague in 1934, 1937 and 1938 produced descendants with low inbreeding coefficients.

One of these descendants, the stallion Uran (#76 Praha 9), became the breeding stallion at the Prague Zoo. He was very prolific and sired thirty-five foals, producing descendants from his half-sisters, his sisters and a few times from his own daughters.

In Munich Neville (#182 London 6), was the breeding stallion at first, producing nineteen foals. His son Severin (#150 Hellabrunn 23), was then used in Munich, and after 1956 at the Catskill Game Farm in the United States. He was extremely virile. He produced thirty-seven foals altogether in Munich and in the U.S.A.

In 1965 the number of Przewalski's horses had increased to 134, an increase of 84% in five years. They were kept in thirty-two zoos and private parks, mostly in pairs or small groups.

Some developments in the fifties had long lasting effects on the captive breeding of the Przewalski's horses. One such development was the controversy of the Prague versus the Munich blood-lines.

As was mentioned before, two mares descending from the Halle/Prague line were kept at the Munich Zoo after 1932. Their offspring were covered by the stallion Neville and his sons Severin (#150 Hellabrunn 23) and Sidor (#154 Hellabrunn 27). The descendants all carried some "blood" of the domestic Mongolian pony once used for breeding at Halle. As Heinz Heck, the director of the Munich Zoo at that time, did not want any Przewalski's horses with domestic blood, several Przewalski's horses were euthanized between 1951 and 1955. Two horses were euthanized in 1951, when the total population contained no more than thirty-five horses in captivity, two were destroyed in 1953 from a total number of thirty-seven, and four in 1955 from a total of forty-one horses (Heck, personal communication 1976). Because of this "selection" the influence of three founders diminished considerably.

The destruction of these horses at a time when the captive breeding stock was extremely vulnerable and when the number of Przewalski's horses in the wild was at the verge of extinction, caused considerable controversy among the breeders of Przewalski's horses. Heck also advocated selection on the basis of configuration to an ideal type, which led to much discussion about the differences in breeding wild animal species and domestic breeds (Herre 1967). His action and thoughts caused a strong controversy between the Prague and Munich line breeders, resulting in long-lasting unilateral breeding at Munich, and most breeding groups in the U.S.A. which were based on offspring from Munich. An isolated sub-population was created with breeding stock carrying only the influence of nine original founders, because two wild-caught founders are strongly associated with the domestic mare's bloodline. Some re-evaluation of Heck's opinion that only Przewalski's horses bred at Tierpark Hellabrunn, Munich, should be considered "pure" occurred after the publication of Dolan's (1982) article. As a result of new information and of some interesting photographs of the founders of the Munich line, showing markings and feature clearly deviant from Heck's ideal type, it was impossible to maintain the distinction between "pure" and "impure" Przewalski's horses based solely on external features.

Another important development in the 1950s was the creation of a studbook. With the help of Dr. Heck and many others, Dr. Erna Mohr collected data on the Przewalski's horses since the first consignments, modelling the studbook of the Przewalski's horse after the one kept for wisents. The first publication appeared as a supplement to the monograph "Das Urwildpferd" (Mohr 1959) and contained entries for the 228 animals in captivity between 1899 and 1958. The European union of Zoological Gardens of which she was a member, asked Dr. Jiri Volf to be the studbook keeper. Updated studbooks were published annually thereafter by the Prague Zoo (Volf 1960 et seq.). These were recommended by the First International Symposium on the Preservation of the Przewalski's horse organized by the Prague Zoo in 1959. Four more symposia were held in 1965, 1976, 1980 and 1990. The proceedings of each symposium were published as a volume of "Equus" by Professor Dathe, Tierpark Berlin (then GDR), giving information on many aspects of the Przewalski's horse morphology, ecology, behavior and captive breeding.

Period III (from 1968–1979)

Thanks to several exchanges of Przewalski's horses and the establishment of two prolific unrelated breeding groups at Prague and Munich, the total captive population had increased considerably in the second period. But a reversal occurred, when after 1965 unilateral breeding started again in these main breeding centers without exchanging horses. Due to the fact that the Munich line had a maximum number of nine founders, and the old Prague line only five, Munich had the most genetically diverse breeding group, so inbreeding could be kept at a lower level.

In Prague the situation became worse when a son of the stallion Oscar (#78 Praha 11) took over the harem group. He sired thirty-five descendants, covering his sisters as well as his daughters. The inbreeding coefficient of some of his offspring became as high as 0.504. With the increased number of horses, the Prague and Munich zoos started to sell their offspring. Prague sold fifty-six related Przewalski's horses as breeding pairs to many zoos in Europe: Antwerp, Askania Nova, Leipzig, Whipsnade, East Berlin, Riga, Warsaw, Cologne, Port Lympne (U.K.), Nuremberg, Arnhem, Rotterdam, and also to Havana in Cuba. Consanguineous matings in those zoos produced generations of horses that were more and more inbred, driving the inbreeding coefficient of some horses up to a peak of 0.597. In most cases this consanguineous breeding was successful only for one or two generations, after which no more foals were produced.

Of all the zoos, Paris initially stood in the best position, having bought the stallion #225 Sidney 4, then ten years old, of American descent, from Hagenbeck in 1942. At the age of twenty-nine, he sired a colt out of a mare from Prague but died before its birth. However, this meant that Paris had at its disposal an outbred stallion, Pacifique (#281 Paris 5). Pacifique, who covered the mares from Prague, reduced the inbreeding coefficient of their progeny.

Over-employment of certain stallions for breeding also occurred in Munich; Neville's son Severin produced a total of thirty-seven foals, some of them in Munich and most of them in the U.S.A. after he was imported there. He was succeeded by his half-brother Sidor, who was bred to his sisters and half-sisters to produce twenty-nine foals, thereby re-introducing heavy inbreeding in Munich. Munich sold most of its offspring to the U.S.A. Chicago obtained a pair in 1955, which did not breed. Between 1956 and 1963 five stallions and eight mares were bought by the Catskill Game Farm (U.S.A.). Because of successful breeding there, thirty-seven Przewalski's horses were sold to other American zoos in this period, but these horses were closely related. The average inbreeding coefficient of the imported horses was 0.138, but by 1979 it had increased to an average of 0.365 for the offspring of the fourth generation from the mare's side.

Around 1970, the influence of the new genetic input of the last wild-caught horse, the mare Orlitza III (#231 Mongol), became perceptible. She was caught as a foal near the Bajtag-Bogdo Mountains in southwest Mongolia in 1947 and transferred to Askania Nova in 1957. From the Munich stallion Orlik (#146 Hellabrunn 19), Orlitza produced four foals and became the twelfth wild founder of the present captive Przewalski's horse population. One daughter died early without offspring. The other, Volga (#244 Askania 1), gave birth to four foals sired by her father, brother, son and cousin. Orlitza's son, Pegas (#259 Askania 2) became the breeding stallion of the new Askania Nova stud with mares imported from Prague in 1965 and 1971. Her son Bars (#285 Askania 3) became the breeding stallion at Prague. Fortunately, both were very prolific breeders. The Prague mares were very inbred themselves but the offspring of these matings had greatly reduced inbreeding coefficients and the genetic variability increased. This had an associated effect on the rate of population increase, although this was not immediately obvious from the figure of 253 horses at the end of 1975, an increase of 38% compared with 1970. However, a closer scrutiny showed that in 1974, descendants of the last wild-caught Przewalski's mare with their low inbreeding coefficients, produced ten more foals than did the inbred mares. Without their influence the increase in 1974 would have been 9% instead of 12% and in 1975 2% instead of 4% (Bouman 1977).

After 1970 other new developments took place. Przewalski's horses from Munich and Prague were bred with horses possessing or lacking the influence of the mare Orlitza III, mostly by bringing a stallion from Munich or the U.S.A., to cover mares originating from Prague. This first happened in Nuremberg, East Berlin, and Leipzig, and later in Cologne. New breeding groups were established like the ones in Marwell Zoological Park (U.K.), Oberwil (Switzerland), Port Lympne (U.K.) and the Minnesota Zoological Garden (U.S.A.).

These sites offered the horses larger paddocks with grass to improve the living conditions. Three of these groups had a broad founder representation and the inbreeding coefficients of their offspring were low. The population increased considerably, reaching 384 horses by January 1980. Unfortunately, except for Minnesota, these groups did not exchange stallions and kept breeding within the same family during the third period, so the inbreeding of their offspring increased once again.

Some developments during the third period of the history of captive breeding of the Przewalski's horses should receive special mention. No confirmed sightings of Przewalski's horses in the wild have been made since 1968 (Bannikov and Lobanov 1980). It became evident that the Przewalski's horse was nearly or completely extinct in the wild, so no new genetic input could be expected from the wild in the future.

The Third Symposium on the Preservation of the Przewalski's Horse was held at Munich in 1976. It was stated there, that although the last years had seen an improvement in the numerical status of the species in captivity, there was cause for concern about the long-term survival of the captive population of Przewalski's horses. The demographic and genetic analyses of Bouman (1977, 1980) and of Bouman and Bos (1979) demonstrated that consanguineous matings produced generations of horses increasingly inbred. Increased juvenile mortality and decreased life-span indicated a reduction in fitness through succeeding generations. The natural reservoir of genetic variability within the gene pool of the species had been diminished by management procedures such as small population sizes, artificial selection, and over-employment of certain stallions for breeding (Ryder and Wedemeyer 1982). Bouman emphasized that with the help of the Prague studbook, and his partly computerized pedigree card system, which he offered at the Symposium to the breeders, guidelines could be formulated for a comprehensive international breeding program (Bouman 1977). Inbreeding had to be minimized and the influence of the founders should be represented equally in the population to maintain its genetic diversity. The Symposium recommended consulting the Bouman card system, when disposing of or acquiring stock, in the hope of changing sales practices. Przewalski's horses were mostly sold as closely related pairs. Such sales caused inbreeding with its deleterious effects for the preservation of the species.

Unfortunately, the time was not yet ripe for organizing Prze-walski's horse breeding programs. An optimal and well-balanced genetic management should, of course, include participation of all breeders of Przewalski's horses throughout the world. However, communication and cooperation between them was influenced or even prevented by differences in organization, knowledge, and also by geographical and political problems of competition. The difficult financial position of most owners and the lucrative animal trade in Przewalski's horses restricted the chances of cooperation. A pair of Przewalski's horses could be sold for $10,000 to $18,000 at that time.

In 1978, the Arnhem Study-Conference was organized by the newly established Foundation for the Preservation and Protection of the Przewalski Horse (FPPH). An international group of scientists was brought together to present results of their investigations on genetics and hereditary diseases of the Przewalski's horse in comparison with the extensive knowledge available from domestic horses (de Boer et al. 1979). Results of comparative genetic blood research for Przewalski's horses and Mongolian ponies was presented, important because of the genetic influence of the Mongolian pony once used for breeding at Halle in 1906. The aims and functions of genetic research for future breeding programs were discussed in detail. For the first time a detailed pedigree analysis of the occurrence of certain diseases like ataxia or infertility had been undertaken (Ashton and Jones 1979).

An international working party to study these diseases of the Przewalski's horse was established during the Arnhem Conference and reports published thereafter (Ashton and Jones 1979, Ashton 1984, Ryder and Wedemeyer 1982). Unfortunately, the working party had to stop work through opposition by some zoos.

The Fourth Period (from 1979 until the present)

In 1979, seventy-five institutions maintained Przewalski's horses. The 385 individuals were divided over sixteen European countries, North America and Cuba (Volf 1960–1988).

The stringent laws concerning the importation of exotic animals forced the zoos more than ever before to draw on their own supply or to exchange animals with colleague zoos. Two developments are characteristic of this period: recognition of the need for mutual breeding programs for endangered species in captivity, and a growing interest in reintroduction.

Breeding programs for the Przewalski's horse. The American zoos were the first to become increasingly aware of the problems of long-term captive breeding of small populations of wild animal species. It was a milestone in zoo history that in November 1979, breeders of Przewalski's horses in the U.S.A. met to establish a North American breeder's group for Przewalski's horses with the aim to manage their stock as one population rather than isolated groups. Genetic considerations would be taken into account in order to maximize the preservation of genetic diversity (Ryder and Wedemeyer 1982). The breeding program was called the Species Survival Plan (SSP) for the Przewalski's horse. Apart from the herd in the Minnesota Zoo, the sixty-three Przewalski's horses at that time (1/1/1980) were closely related, originating from thirteen horses imported from Munich to the Catskill Game Farm between 1956 and 1963. It was anticipated that the breeding group at the Minnesota Zoo (ten horses), genetically the most diverse group but containing domestic horse blood, should be kept segregated from the others. Munich line stallions were used for breeding the mares in that zoo. As we have seen before, the inbreeding coefficients in the U.S.A. had increased considerably up to an average of 0.339. The reproductive rate of the Munich line sub-population compared with the population of those Przewalski's horses descended from the domestic mare was much lower (Keverling Buisman and van Weeren 1982). New genetic input was very important.

Outcrossing to non-U.S.A. Przewalski's horses could reduce inbreeding and increase the genetic variability. The American breeders group succeeded in 1982 in exchanging Przewalski's horses with Askania Nova (Ukraine/USSR), which had until then not exchanged Przewalski's horses either, since 1957. Through the genetic input from the "pure-blooded" offspring of Orlitza III, the average inbreeding coefficient of the Munich line American Przewalski's horses could decrease. The breeders' group further agreed to pool information on necropsy examinations, non-breeding animals, and research on genetics, reproductive physiology and behavior.

In 1984 an exchange of stallions took place between the Munich and Prague Zoos. In Prague the breeding had stopped. The valuable stallion Bars (#285 Askania 3), the son of Orlitza III (#231), showed pathological behavior; he attacked his mares fiercely and killed some of their foals. In Munich the inbreeding had increased dramatically through unilateral breeding within the family since 1951. Several mares and stallions showed reduced fertility or infertility (von Hegel et al. 1990). Like the Americans, Munich looked for new genetic input and exchanged their breeding stallion, Simon, with the twenty-one-year-old stallion Bars. Bars produced four foals in Munich.

In the meantime the zoos of the British Isles had established the Joint Management of Species Group (JMSG), based on the model of the American Species Survival Plan (SSP). Unfortunately, Port Lympne with the biggest collection of Przewalski's horses did not participate in this national breeding program.

In 1986, a Continental European cooperation between zoos started officially. The European Breeding Programs (EEP; Europäisches Erhaltungszucht-Programm in German) were accepted for several endangered species (Schmidt 1987). Dr. W. Zimmermann (Cologne Zoo) became the first coordinator of the Przewalski's Horse Breeders Group. A growing number of zoos from different countries participate in this group. The species coordinator presents updated genetic and demographic information on the status of the Przewalski's horse, coordinates research and bi-annually discusses possible movements of horses and tactics to be employed with other members. Like the American model, the group was founded on the supposition that management should be based on the loan or exchange of animals, rather than selling them. Besides research on diseases like ataxia and infertility problems, much more attention is paid in the European group to the phenotypic selection of Przewalski's horses for breeding purposes. In Europe an increasing number of Przewalski's horses show a lack of black pigmentation in their coats, which is probably caused by recessive genes. This phenomenon is also occurring in fallow deer, steppe zebras and other species. Because of consanguineous breeding in captivity these recessive genes are more commonly expressed. The EEP decided that due to the increased population in Europe, it should be possible to exclude proven fox gene carriers from the breeding program without losing wild genes.

In the near future cooperative breeding ventures should certainly be undertaken between the species coordinators of the SSP (U.S.A.), the EEP (Continental Europe) and England, although it will be far from easy to extend this worldwide. As of January 1,

1990, the captive population numbered 961 Przewalski's horses divided over 129 institutions in thirty-three countries and on four continents, among them far-flung countries like Sri Lanka, Korea, Japan, Uruguay, Australia, China and Cuba (Volf 1960–1990). Fortunately, at present there is a mutual concern for long-term conservation. After 10–14 generations in captivity, a reduction of genetic variation took place through inbreeding depression, unequal founder representation, genetic drift and selection (Ryder and Wedemeyer 1982, Keverling Buisman and van Weeren 1982, Bouman and Bouman 1989). The negative effects of adaptation to inappropriate social and/or environmental conditions while in captivity must also not be underestimated (Volf 1967, 1989, Bouman and Bouman 1989). As few wild species have been kept in captivity without new genetic input, it can be expected that the Przewalski's horses, if released into a presumed natural habitat, will be far less successful in surviving than were their wild ancestors.

Growing interest in reintroduction. Although the importance of future reintroduction into the wild was mentioned on several occasions prior to 1980, no real steps had been undertaken (Dathe and Wünschmann 1980, Dathe 1984). The growing captive population, which increased from 338 Przewalski's horses in 1978 to 961 in 1989 caused several zoos to have the problem of surplus animals within the restricted space typical of zoos.

Organizations like the International Union for the Conservation of Nature and Natural Resources (IUCN), and the World Wildlife Fund (WWF) had until 1980 shown no interest in captive breeding of wild animal species, concentrating their efforts mainly on conservation projects for threatened environments and the species they contained. No funds could be expected from them for restoration of the Przewalski's horse to Mongolia, a country largely dependent on foreign help for such an expensive conservation project. With support from Sir Peter Scott, chairman of the Survival Service Commission (SSC) of the IUCN, a first step was taken to study future reintroduction of the Przewalski's horse by setting up the Przewalski's Horse Captive Breeding Group of the SSC. A variety of experts in wildlife management, behavior research and captive breeding were invited to participate in a meeting during the Fourth Symposium for the Preservation of the Przewalski's Horse in Winchester, England in 1980. The Foundation for the Preservation and Protection of the Przewalski Horse (FPPH) proposed a plan for reintroduction into a wild reserve based on the principle that Przewalski's horses cannot be released directly from zoos into the wild. An intermediary stay in semi-reserves is essential. The necessity of establishing semi-reserves for the Przewalski's horse was discussed, accepted and later endorsed by the Symposium (Dathe 1984).

In the same year the Foundation Reserves for the Przewalski Horse was established in The Netherlands, a joint enterprise was undertaken between the FPPH and WWF-Netherlands, aiming at establishing semi-reserves (IUCN/WWF project 3077) (Bouman-Heinsdijk 1982b). With the financial support of the WWF-Netherlands, Przewalski's horses from a variety of bloodlines could be bought from zoos in the U.S.A., the U.S.S.R. and the rest of Europe. Breeding groups with unrelated stallions, and bachelor groups were released in five large nature reserves in The Netherlands and Germany varying in size from 30 to 265 hectares (ha). There, the animals exist without supplemental feeding and with a minimum of human intervention, thus enabling them to develop a more natural behavioral repertoire, and become accustomed to running wild. This intermediate stage between captivity and their ultimate reintroduction may have to extend for more than one generation to build up a population of healthy, outbred, behaviorally competent Przewalski's horses, suitable for successful release into the wild (Bouman and Bouman 1990).

Although not based on the principles of the IUCN semi-reserve project, the North American zoos succeeded in finding larger pastures for new breeding groups in Front Royal, Virginia (10 ha); Topeka, Kansas (24 ha); Calgary, Canada (65 ha); and Wagon Mound, New Mexico (243 ha).

A conference sponsored by the Food and Agriculture Organization (FAO) and the United Nations Environmental Program (UNEP) was held in Moscow in May 1985 to discuss the possibility of reintroducing the horses into parts of their former range in the steppes of eastern Asia and western Mongolia. It was decided that under the leadership of the Russian academician Sokolov, expeditions would be organized in search of suitable areas for release. Long-term sources of funding, and a program for gradual reintroduction would be explored carefully. In close cooperation with the Mongolian Academy of Sciences and the Joint Biological Mongolian and Soviet Union Expeditions, a suitable reintroduction area was found in Hustain Nuru in Mongolia some years later (1989).

The Chinese government also showed interest in the reintroduction. In 1985 the Zoological Society of San Diego was approached by the Ministry of Forestry in Beijing to assist them in obtaining wild horses for a captive breeding program in Urumqi, which would ultimately lead to reintroductions into the wild in Xinjiang north of Jimsar. In 1986 Przewalski's horses were bought from several zoos; they are kept in large walled enclosures without grass. In 1989 two groups of Przewalski's horses (twenty-five animals) were released into a large enclosure of 200 ha. Within the next two years, horses will be released in southeast Xinjiang (Oswald, personal communication 1992).

The Mongolian Government had expressed interest in the reintroduction of the Przewalski's horses long before the Chinese, but realization of the plans was a long time coming. On June 5, 1992 the first sixteen Przewalski's horses from semi-reserves at Askania Nova (Ukraine) and The Netherlands, transported by the Foundation Reserves for the Przewalski Horses (FRPH), returned to Mongolia. After an acclimatization period of a year they will be released in Hustain Nuru, a mountainous steppe reserve of 50,000 ha situated some 115 km from Ulan Bator. A total of eighty horses will be transported to Hustain Nuru through the year 2000 to be able to build up a free-roaming, self-sustaining population in the wild. The Mongolian Association for Conservation of Nature and Environment (MACNE) is responsible for the execution of the project in Mongolia. Along with the FRPH, MACNE prepared a long-term reintroduction program for the Przewalski's horses and a special program for management of the undamaged steppe biotope at Hustain Nuru and the conservation of its biodiversity. The government of The Netherlands fortunately decided to help the Mongolians financially with this prestigious project for a period of five years, beginning in 1993.

A second group of five horses obtained by Oswald from Askania Nova (Ukraine) arrived in Mongolia on June 6, 1992, and was released in a large enclosure of 160 ha at Takhi-Tal, on the northern border of the Dzungarian Gobi. As in the Urumqi model, the Przewalski horses will be kept some years in the enclosure for breeding. When sufficient offspring are available, they will be released in the surrounding Dzungarian Gobi.

It can be concluded that the fourth period of captive breeding was characterized by a strongly expanding population. Thanks to the breeding efforts in zoos and private institutions in Europe and North America, the species has been saved from extinction. Recently population biology became an integral part of what is now called conservation biology (Soule and Wilcox 1980). It was postulated that genetic diversity is the most important condition for the long-term survival of a species. But if captive groups are not subject to management based upon rigorous long-term strategies taking into account genetic, demographic, behavioral and ecological models, all advantages of longevity are likely to be lost. Conway (1980) mentioned the crisis facing the Przewalski's horse as an example of a lack of such management. Fortunately cooperative breeding groups were formed in North America, England and continental Europe in the last ten years to maintain the present gene pool. The growing number of horses in captivity justifies their reintroduction.

3

Morphology, Habitat, and Taxonomy

Colin P. Groves

MORPHOLOGY

External Characters

Because of the problem of the Mongol pony ancestry, and possible changes over generations of captive breeding, Mazak and Dobroruka (1967) found it necessary to reconstruct the characters of Przewalski's horse as a basis for future selection in the Prague line. Their sources included descriptions, photographs and measurements, from ten authors, of horses shot or captured in the wild, beginning with the type description by Poliakov in 1881. Where no other data were available, they used the first-generation captive-born offspring of the Hagenbeck imports, and their own observations on preserved material and the appearance of the last Przewalski's horse to be captured in the wild, Orlitza III, caught in 1947. Contrary to fears expressed by cynics from Lydekker (1912) onward, the result was the discovery of a consistent type, homogeneous to the extent that all wild taxa are homogeneous. The validity of the standards laid down by these authors was corroborated by observations and measurements on the subadult stallion Bars (#285 Askania 3), offspring of Orlitza by a stallion of the Munich line (Mazak 1966).

Heck (1970) illustrated his own criteria for recognition of purebred Przewalski's horses from those with some domestic ancestry. The basis of his argument is not stated, but presumably relates to the characteristics seen in the reputedly purebred Munich line as

contrasted with those which recur in the Prague line, which is
known to contain some Mongol pony ancestry. It is interesting that
his results generally agree with those of Mazak and Dobroruka.

Still further detailed information was given by Mohr (1959,
and the 1971 English edition), who paid special attention to age
changes; and by Heptner (1961) who was anxious to establish criteria for detection of domestic admixture as an approach to the problem of "purity" in European wild horses. The conclusions of these
authors are the basis for the description which follows.

Stature. The stature is recorded for ten first- or second-generation
horses, more than three years old, born in Askania Nova before the
Second World War. Six males were 138–146 cm high at the
withers; the four females were 134–140 cm high at the withers.
There was no difference between first- and second-generation specimens. Only one record from the wild exists: a male shot by Grum-
Grzhimailo was claimed to be 146.8 cm, though the method of measurement was not stated. These figures, collected by Mazak and
Dobroruka (1967), must be regarded as more reliable than those
given by Bannikov (1958), Sokolov (1959), Mohr (1959) and Heptner et al. (1961), all of whom give values going down to 124 or even
120 cm (sources not given, but certainly including some immature
specimens, under three years old), and none of whom take possible
sexual dimorphism into account.

Weight. Three first- and second-generation males in Askania Nova,
all five years old or more, weighed 278–297.2 kg; a three-year-old
male weighed 260 kg. Two females, five and eight years old,
weighed 244 and 280 kg (Mazak and Dobroruka 1967).

Body conformation. Typically, Przewalski's horse has a low-slung
robust build with a remarkably thick, rather short neck; the
withers are not prominent; the limbs are comparatively short but
slender (Mazak and Dobroruka 1967).

Heck (1970) considers that the croup in the purebred Przewalski's horse should be narrow, and the thick neck is not held upright
like a deer ("Nicht hirschartig aufrecht getragen"). The legs he describes as short, very sturdy, and strong-boned, and that long fine-
boned legs are a sign of domestic ancestry; this may be true, but
Mazak and Dobroruka's discussion shows that the "stockiness" can
be overstated.

Head form. The muzzle is short and high and the lower margin of
the jaw is straight, so that the profile line of the jaw meets the

dorsal profile line of the head at an angle of some 16°–18°30' (21° in a subadult), compared to about 25–32° in a domestic horse (see Mohr 1971:43); the upper lip protrudes somewhat beyond the lower lip (Mazak and Dobroruka 1967). As described below, Volf (1970) has documented some differences in the ventral profile of the mandible between wild-caught and captive-born specimens; for the moment it need only be noted that any changes that have occurred do not close the gap between Przewalski's horse and domestic horses.

According to Heck (1970), the interorbital distance should be relatively narrow, and the eyes project laterally. Too broad a forehead, and eyes that are too forward-looking, indicate domestic blood. Frechkop (1965) described the craniological basis for this feature, but found that some domestic ponies do not differ much, if at all, from Przewalski's horses.

Body color. The foals caught by Hagenbeck were of two color types: one pale grey-yellow, the other a bright yellowish red-brown. There has been considerable discussion over this: were there two subspecies, even two species, involved? Matschie (1903) thought so and distinguished a new species, *Equus hagenbecki,* from *E. przewalskii* (see below). Mohr (1959) argued against this; there is no evidence that the two morphs were from different geographic areas, indeed she quotes a record from Pallas that two color types occurred within the same herd, and draws attention to a photograph of the two morphs in the same herd published by Bannikov (1958).

The head and neck are darker than the body, as Poliakov (1881) himself noted; this contrast is less marked in the dark morph than in the light one. The underparts are lighter than the flanks; Heck (1970) emphasizes the manner in which this light tone extends upward behind the forelegs and in front of the hindlegs, creating with the brownish flanks a saddle effect. The distal segments of the limbs are also dark, even black, from the tarsus and carpus (or even higher) to the hooves; this tone is more expressed on the anterior than the posterior surfaces, at least on the forelimbs. Three to ten thin dark stripes are present on the carpus, and there are generally a few on the tarsus, too (Figure 3.1).

A dark dorsal stripe, or "eel-mark," runs from the mane down the back and dorsal side of the tail to the tail-tuft (Figure 3.2). It is much clearer and darker in adults than in the young, and in summer than in winter. The type specimen, a juvenile in winter coat, had no noticeable dorsal stripe at all, a circumstance which was

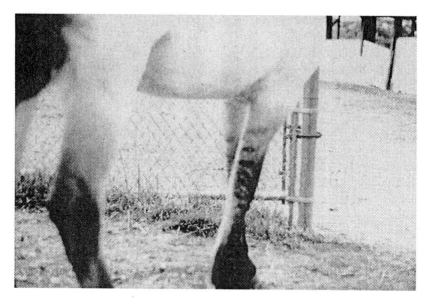

Figure 3.1.   Leg stripes on the mare Misha (#952). Photograph by Lee Boyd.

Figure 3.2.   Dorsal stripe in the summer coats of the mare Bogatka (#504) and her two-year-old daughter Bobelia (#1071) who is suckling. Photograph by Lee Boyd.

unfortunately used as a diagnostic character in the type description (Poliakov 1881).

Across the shoulders, just in front of the end of the mane, there is at least a trace of a thick dark cross-stripe. It may be present on one side only.

The muzzle tends to be light colored, often actually white, but the lips and the margins of the nostrils are dark. The region round the eyes is also somewhat lighter than the general tone of the head.

Hilzheimer (1909) went even further than Matschie, and recognized three different subspecies: *Equus equiferus equiferus* from Bajtag-Bogdo, with light muzzle and black limbs; *Equus equiferus typicus* from Zagan Nor, with dark muzzle and black mane; and *Equus equiferus hagenbecki* from the Urungu River, with light limbs and muzzle and red-brown mane. Volf (1974) found no evidence that these differences were geographic; he suggested, however, that captive breeding in some stocks has tended to make the type more homogeneous.

White or dark marks on the face and elsewhere are expected to be more frequent in crossbred horses, but are not necessarily indicative of domestic ancestry, according to Mohr (1959), who described and pictured an apparently purebred Munich line stallion with a white star between the eyes.

While the iris of the eye is generally brown, a few blue-eyed individuals are known (Lee Boyd, personal communication 1991, and see Mohr 1971:63).

Mane and tail. The mane, dark brown to black, begins between the ears and reaches the withers; there is no forelock. The mane is upright, or falls slightly to one side, especially in older animals; it never, however, hangs like the mane of a domestic horse. In winter, whitish hairs some two-thirds the length of the dark mane-hairs border the mane on either side. The hairs forming the mane are 16–20 cm long (Mazak and Dobroruka 1967).

Perhaps the most striking difference from domestic horses is that in Przewalski's horse the dock is short-haired: that is to say, the proximal region of the tail is free of the long "horse-hairs" which form the tuft; it is nearly always a lighter shade of the dorsal color of the body (Figure 3.3). On the sides, the hairs get longer and darker distally, grading into the long dark tuft hairs. The long tail hairs reach to the level of the fetlocks.

Body hair. The natal coat is yellowish and curly; it is shed within the first few weeks of life. The mane of the newborn foal is short

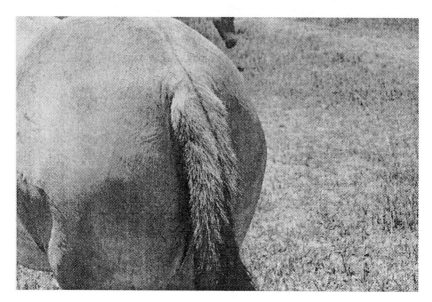

Figure 3.3. The dock of the tail is short-haired, as seen in the mare Selenga (#635). Photograph by Lee Boyd.

and curly, and does not begin to grow in adult fashion until some six months of age.

The hair in winter is markedly longer than in summer. On the cheeks and posterior half of the lower jaw it forms a "beard" 5–8 cm long in winter (Mazak and Dobroruka 1967), which almost disappears in summer. The mane may hang to the side more in winter than in summer, but a hanging mane may indicate poor health, or a delay in molting.

The timing of the spring shedding seems to depend on ambient temperature. In 1958 at the Prague Zoo horses began to molt between April 2nd–22nd in different individuals, in 1959 a month earlier (March 10th–28th), and in 1960 in between (March 21st–April 5th); in all cases the mean daily temperature was on the order of 5 to 7°C at the beginning of the molt (Mazak 1962). Shedding takes 48–69 days in adults, with a slight tendency for it to last longer in older animals; and even up to 87 days for foals in their first molt. The sides of the face, a spot behind the ear, and a spot on the upper haunch are the first areas to molt; further flank spots are then shed, followed by the forehead and midface, the upper third of the neck, and the remainder of the neck and the flanks, in that order. The belly, lower limb segments, angle of the jaw, and throat retain their winter hair longest (Mazak 1962). Domestic horses shed in more diffuse and irregular fashion.

Skeletal Morphology

Cranial characters. Frechkop (1965) was the first author to point out differences between the skulls of Przewalski's horse and domestic horses. The orbit is oval, dorso-ventrally compressed in the Przewalski's horse skull, but it is rounded in the domestic horse; the orbital rim is more prominent anteriorly, less so posteriorly, than in most (not all) domestic horses (Figure 3.4). The Przewalski's horse skull has a higher nasal cavity than most domestic horses (a few pony breeds excepted), so that the facial angle is smaller, a difference which is appreciable in the living animal (see previous section). In the mandible, the corpus is deeper and the ascending rami are shorter and more vertical (less convergent towards the jaw angles).

Azzaroli (1966) compared in detail the skulls of Przewalski's horses with those of domestic horses. The Przewalski's horse skull

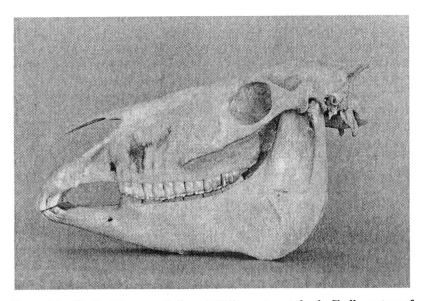

Figure 3.4. Skull of the mare Colleen (#549), age ten at death. Skull courtesy of the Topeka Zoo and the Dyche Museum of Natural History at the University of Kansas. Photograph by Lee Boyd and Barb Clauson.

differs in the following three features: 1) the convexity of the braincase roof is less pronounced; 2) the narial opening is longer, its posterior end being above the distal margin of premolar 2 (P2), whereas in the domestic horse it is above its mesial lobe; 3) the palate is longer, reaching the level of the distal lobes of the third molar (M3), while in domestic horses it reaches only the M2/3 boundary. An interesting finding was that the skulls of Upper Pleistocene horses from Europe (Italy, Germany and Russia) resemble the domestic horse, not Przewalski's horse, as apparently does the skull of the tarpan (see below).

According to Eisenmann (1982), craniometrically Przewalski's horse belongs to a long-snouted group along with certain North American species and the heavy horses among domestic breeds; European and Alaskan fossil horses, and pony breeds are short-snouted.

Forsten (1988) compared Przewalski's horse skulls with those of tarpans and late Pleistocene wild horses from Europe and Siberia, using log ratio diagrams. In comparison, the Przewalski's horse skull has a narrow snout and short, broad braincase.

Volf (1970) has, however, put some of these differences into perspective. Studying the mandibles of six Przewalski's horses caught in the wild, six that were first- to third-generation captive-born, and ten domestic horses (five Mongol ponies, five Kladrub horses), he found that the captive-born Przewalski's horses approach domestic horses somewhat compared to the wild-born ones. The height of the mandibular corpus decreases, leaving the mandibular angle much more prominent, and the toothrow shortens. Volf comments that this could be simple genetic plasticity, brought out by inappropriate feeding with its consequences for jaw mechanics, or it could reflect the need for stronger selection-to-type in the captive stock. A possible criticism of this study is that the ancestry of four of Volf's captive-born specimens is not absolutely clear according to the studbook, but his point about the need for selection is well taken, and further studies need to be made.

Postcranial skeleton. Stecher (1961) found that fifteen out of twenty-one Przewalski's horse skeletons had eighteen thoracic vertebrae, the rest nineteen; eleven had five lumbars, the remainder six; seventeen had five sacrals, three had four. These figures differ somewhat from those of domestic horses, which generally have eighteen thoracics like the Przewalski's horse, but six lumbars (89/94 skeletons).

Forsten's (1988) comparison of postcranial measurements with those of upper Pleistocene horses refutes the idea of any consistent differences apart from size (the Przewalski's horse is smaller). The skeleton of a tarpan had shorter, broader phalanges than the Przewalski's horse series.

DISTRIBUTION AND HABITAT

Bannikov (1958) has recorded all that is known of the distribution and habitat of Przewalski's horse in recent times. Przewalski himself met with wild horses only in Dzungaria; he had earlier reported them from Tsaidam and Lop Nor, but subsequently admitted that this was in error. Pevzoff described its range as from the Manas River in the west to the latitude of the eastern border of the Tien Shan range (so about 95°E), in saxaul (*Haloxylon*) steppe. Grum-Grzhimailo found them in the Gashun district, north of the Gutchan Mountains. Clemenz met with them south and southeast of the Bajtag-Bogdo Mountains; Bannikov himself saw one in Ulan Bator which had been captured on the northern slope of the Bajtag-Bogdo. Bannikov summarizes the turn-of-the-century distribution as limited in the north by the Urungu and the High Altai, extending to 46°N, 90°E; in the southwest by the Tien Shan, down to 44°N; and extending east to 95°E. Most of this range is in the northern part of Xinjiang (i.e., Dzungaria); only its eastern edge extends into Mongolia itself.

By the early 1950s, they appear to have been restricted to the Bajtag-Bogdo, and as far east as the Tachijn-Shar-Nuru ridge. Photographs of what were identified as wild horses, in the distance, taken by Kaszab in 1966, were considered to be *Equus hemionus* by Volf (1967), but Kaszab himself (1968) strenuously defended his original identification and was supported by Bökönyi (1974). Even if these animals were wild horses, none—not even tracks—have been seen since. It seems, therefore, that Przewalski's horse is extinct in the wild: hunted for meat, and excluded from their pastures and watering points by domestic stock.

The region they were known to inhabit is not a sandy or rocky desert, but better described as semi-desert, at some 1000 to 1400 meters altitude. Vegetation in some regions is surprisingly dense, consisting of saxaul (*Haloxylon ammodendron*), wormwood (*Artemisia incana*), tamarisk (*Salicornia herbacea*) and various grasses; elsewhere it is very sparse, with only isolated tufts of the salt-grass

Salsola breaking the flat desertscape. It is this latter habitat which is shared with kulan (*Equus hemionus*). Przewalski's horses, however, were not as nearly independent of water as kulan, although they were said to be capable of digging into the sand for water with their hooves.

In this area mean January temperature is −15° to −18°C, plunging to a minimum of −35°C, and mean July temperature +20° to +25°C, reaching a maximum of +40°C; annual rainfall is not above 400 mm (Bannikov 1958). The same habitat supports, even today, other large ungulates, notably kulan (*Equus hemionus hemionus*), Saiga antelope (*Saiga tatarica mongolica*), Goitred gazelle (*Gazella subgutturosa hillieriana*), Mongolian gazelle (*Procapra gutturosa*), wild camels (*Camelus ferus*) and, in the desert ranges, Argali sheep (*Ovis ammon darwini*). The main predator is the wolf (*Canis lupus*), but small cats such as the wild cat (*Felis silvestris chutuchta*), and Pallas's cat (*Otocolobus manul*) are also present. Desert hares (*Lepus* spp.) and rodents constitute the remaining terrestrial mammalian fauna.

TAXONOMY

Przewalski's Horse

Mohr (1959) gives the following local names for Przewalski's horse, as collected by various authors: Take, Tachi, Takke, Tekke, Statur or Dzurlikadu (Mongol), Surtake, Surtaken, Syrtach or Kertag, Kurtach (Kirghiz), Jauwat or Takky (Turfan). There seems to be some dispute about these names. Falz-Fein, according to Mohr, gives the Mongol (sic) word for horse as Tach, while Syr means desert and Kur means mountain: hence Syrtach and Kurtach, which would be the light and dark color morphs, respectively.

Przewalski's wild horse was mentioned in literature and even known to the scientific world long before it was described taxonomically. Bökönyi (1974) cites a description of a wild horse hunt, in what would now be Gansu, by Genghis Khan in 1226, and of a wild horse captured at Tachijn-us (central Mongolia) by order of Chechen Khansóloj and presented to the Emperor of Manchuria in 1637. Mohr (1959) draws attention to the observation of wild horses in the region east of the Ob, about 45°N, 85–90°E, by John Bell in 1719–1722. Przewalski's horse was certainly among the *Equiferi* mentioned by Pallas (1811, see below).

An intriguing interlude between these old mentions and the

scientific description of *Equus przewalskii* is the Yo-to-tse. Smith (1841), after recording information received from various sources about wild horses in Central Asia (among which certainly is Przewalski's horse), described (pp. 304–307) and figured (Pl. 17) an equine called *Asinus equuleus*, the Yo-to-tse, which had been drawn by the editor, Lizars, at the request of Sir Joseph Banks, who had obtained from Earl Rivers information that there was "an undescribed species of diminutive horse brought from the Chinese frontier northeast of Calcutta, and was then to be seen in a livery stable near Park Lane." It was a male, slightly under three feet high although nearly four years old (by its teeth), rather slenderly built, with a "coarse abundant mane, larger than the ass, but still standing upright"; the tail was long-haired nearly to the root (and, indeed, the plate does show a horsehair-free basal portion to the tail); there were chestnuts on the forelegs only; it was a "yellowish-red clay color," with black mane and tail hair and dorsal stripe, a vague shoulder-cross, knee- and hock-stripes, and black fetlocks, the rest of the lower limbs being brown. Smith states that he had "hesitated long" over whether it was not really a horse rather than an ass. The plate, by error labelled *Asinus hippagrus*, corresponds more or less to the description except that the mane is unexpectedly short. Lydekker (1912) was the first to draw attention to the reputed locality, Chinese Tatary (= Mongolia), and to the close fit of this description to Przewalski's horse; only because the muzzle was not described (nor figured) as white he considers it "impure." He is surely right that this was the first Przewalski's horse to be described in a scientific work; only the residual uncertainty that must always remain where there is no type specimen prevents the name *equuleus* from becoming the senior synonym for *przewalskii*.

Poliakov (1881) described *Equus przewalskii* from a subadult (fifteen-month-old) specimen forwarded to him by N. M. Przewalski, who in turn had obtained it from A.K. Tikhanov in 1878. It had been killed by Kirghiz hunters, not, as at first thought, in the Lop Nor district but in eastern Dzungaria (see Mohr 1959, 4:71–72). Matschie (1903) proposed to restrict the type locality to Zagan Nor and Bajtag-Bogdo, but there is no evidence to support this action; Harper's (1940) proposal of Gashun Oasis (44°30′N, 90°E) seems more acceptable, based as it is on other known early collecting localities. Matschie's *Equus hagenbecki*, described on the supposition that the light and dark morphs are actually distinct species, was from Ebi Spring, Njursaul and the Urungu River district. Lydekker (1912) ascribes it to "an admixture of blood," but, as we have seen above, there is no evidence that it is other than a simple polymorphism.

The only other name given to a Mongolian wild horse is *Equus caballus gutsenensis* (Skorkowski 1946). This name was given to the supposed "pure component" of the Przewalski's horse, as part of an elaborate attempt to get back to the original pureblooded subspecies of *Equus caballus*, all domestic breeds and even wild stock being, it was supposed, crossbred (see below). The type of *E. c. gutsenensis* was a skull from Gutschen (=the Gashun Oasis or the Gutchan Mountains).

European And Western Asian Wild Horses

The mouse-grey tarpan of western Russia, Ukraine, Poland and northern Germany has been endlessly discussed in the literature, both from a taxonomic standpoint and with regard to its nomenclature. Herodotus (Book 4:51–52) mentioned wild white horses living around the great lake in Scythia which forms the source of the Hypanis (=the River Bug) (de Sélincourt 1954); the Bug does not today originate in a lake, but alterations of river courses are not unknown historically, and the upper course of the river is in the same general area as the Pripyat marshes, in the region of the Poland/Byelorussia/Ukraine border. Smith (1841) cited Schneebergius as saying that the wild horses of Prussia were "mouse-colored," with a dark dorsal stripe; he also, interestingly, gave two Roman sources for them in North Africa (one described them as "whitish ashy grey," the other as "rufous"—but were these really wild horses, as opposed to, say, wild asses?). Lydekker (1912) and Bökönyi (1974) have conveniently summarized some of the other historical sources, as early as Roman times (when wild horses occurred as far west as Spain). Von Heberstein, between 1517 and 1528, saw cream-colored wild horses in Lithuania. On the other hand, in the early thirteenth century Albertus Magnus described those in Prussia as being "cinereus" (ashy), with a dark dorsal stripe; despite the claim of Bökönyi (1974), this does not sound like the "creamy" of von Heberstein, but as we shall see, a seasonal color change seems likely.

The first detailed description of European wild horses was provided by Gmelin (1774), who met with them in 1769 in the region of Bobrovsk, near Voronesh. They were, he said, "hardly as large as the smallest Russian" [pony]; they had very thick heads, pointed ears, short frizzly mane, and "tail-hair shorter" than in domestic horses (perhaps referring to short hair on the dock?). They were mouse-colored, with white or ashy-grey belly, and the limbs black from the knees and hocks down. Their hair was very long and thick. Gmelin and the peasants assisting him killed a stallion and two mares, together with a Russian mare that had run wild with the herd, and captured the hybrid she had produced as well as a purebred foal.

Pallas (1811) described the Russian wild horse as a variety of *Equus caballus* under the name *Equiferus*; a name not intended in a scientific sense, but as a simple descriptive term in a book written in Latin, despite its adoption by later nineteenth century and early twentieth century authors as a scientific name (discussed in Mohr 1959). In fact, he mentioned wild horses between the Dnepr and the Altai, but did not distinguish clearly between the western and eastern ones, though he mentions their color as being reddish or pale grey—most subsequent commentators have felt at liberty to interpret this as meaning that the western ones were the grey ones, as the reddish ones would be satisfactorily accounted for by the Przewalski's horse.

Smith (1841) provided a wealth of interesting information on wild horses: admittedly second-hand from Tatars and Cossacks whom he had interviewed in 1814, but in the main quite consistent with other evidence. Referring to true wild horses as *tarpan* and *tarpani*, to distinguish them from feral horses (*Takja* or *muzin*), Smith's informants told him that the purest wild horses were found on the Karakorum, south of the Aral Sea, on the Syr Darya, near Kusneh (presumably the Kuznetsk-Alatau region of the Dzungarian border, not Kuznetsk on the western Kazakhstan border), and east into the Gobi; while in Russia there were mixed herds near settlements. Like Pallas, Smith referred to a variety of colors: tan, "isabella" (yellowish-grey), or mouse, with a whitish surcoat.

Then, curiously, Smith went on to describe as a genuine wild horse (whether on the same authority or no, it is difficult to say) "the white woolly animal of the Kara Koom and the high table land of Pamere," fourteen hands high, with large head, thick muzzle, short ragged mane, a "beard," "grisly white, somewhat darker in summer." On page 262 and the following page, what seems to be the same horse is mentioned again, and figured (Pl. 4), as "The White or Grey Stock" from the Pamir Plateau, the steppes north of the Black Sea, Armenia and Cilicia; but the horse under description this time would seem to be domestic.

On the question of "impurity" in wild horses, Pruski (1959)

and Heptner et al. (1961) have some remarks. Because of the intensity of competition which purebred wild horses would offer, domestic horses would have a rather low probability of survival and
breeding if they ran wild, and any crossbreds they produced would
again be subjected to strong competition. In fact, the influence of a
wild stock on local domestic breeds is likely to have been much
more significant than the reverse. Only in the last stages, when
the wild horses were disappearing, would domestic genes begin to
predominate.

And as agriculture and stock-breeding gradually took over the
steppes, the tarpans disappeared. But Heptner et al. (1961) argue
that even the last survivors remained fairly true to their basic
color and conformation. The last survivor died in 1918 in captivity
near Poltava. This last individual, known as the Dubrowka or Tau-
rian tarpan, was described (Heptner 1955) as being 140–145 cm
high, with a big head, small ears and short neck; "field-mouse-
grey" with a broad dorsal stripe and an ill-defined shoulder-cross;
the mane, tail and shanks black; and a thick mane, semi-erect but
falling somewhat to both sides of the neck; the forehead broad,
vaulted, the profile straight. The only other tarpan to be described
in the literature was the Shatilovski or Cherson tarpan, caught in
1866 on the Zagradoff steppes, north of Crimea (Figure 3.5a). The
Cherson tarpan, which was gelded and lived for twenty years in
the Moscow Zoo, was a dark mouse color with the shanks black; the
mane hung down on the left side and, unlike Przewalski's horse,
had a forelock. (The tendency of the mane to fall to the side, and
the development of a forelock, are discussed by Heptner 1961).

The skull of another tarpan, killed on Rachmanov steppe in
1854, was studied by Gorgas (1966) who measured its cranial capacity. The finding that its cranial capacity was small, like domestic horses, while that of Przewalski's horse is larger, was widely
interpreted to mean that the tarpan was not a genuinely wild
horse at all, but feral (because brain reduction is widely acknowledged as a consequence of domestication). Against this may be
weighed both the reputed homogeneity of tarpans, as already discussed, and the finding that some subspecies of a given species may
be naturally smaller-brained than others (and so, in a way, more
"domesticable"—see Hemmer 1983).

In general, Heptner et al. (1961) distinguish what they call
Equus przewalskii gmelini, the South Russian steppe tarpan, as
having been dark grey with a black mane and tail, black dorsal
stripe, and black lower limb segments; the young rusty-tinged; the
winter coat long, dense, slightly wavy, and "dirtier looking" than

the summer coat, evidently fading to ash-color during winter; the facial skeleton rather short, molar teeth small, and frontal profile slightly concave. It lived as far east as the Ural River, or more probably only to the Volga, and west perhaps to Rumania.

Antonius (1912) gave the name *Equus gmelini* to the tarpan, although he considered that it was not the only wild horse of Europe: "*Equus ferus* Pallas" on which name (see above) the Przewalski's horse had lived in Europe during the Upper Palaeolithic, as had "*Equus gracilis* Ewart", a supposed pony-like species for which there is in fact no hard evidence, and six other species for some of which there is fossil evidence (mainly, in fact, Middle Pleistocene), for others not. But there is no doubt that the name *gmelini* is antedated by more than a century: Boddaert (1785:159) founded a species *Equus ferus* largely on Gmelin's description, and it is this reference, rather than Pallas (see above), which is the original technical usage of the name. The earliest name for the tarpan is therefore *Equus ferus* Boddaert, and *Equus gmelini* Antonius is a junior objective synonym.

Nobis (1971), apparently not realizing that *gmelini* is an objective synonym of *ferus*, used both names, for different horses, associating them with different fossil samples: *Equus ferus ferus* from Mezin, and *Equus ferus gmelini* from Sungir.

A further name that seems likely to apply to the steppe tarpan is *Equus scythicus*. This was founded upon teeth of latest Pleistocene age from Dobrogaea, Rumania, but some domestic horses were also referred to the species (Radulesco and Samson 1962).

In addition to the steppe tarpan, Heptner et al. (1961) also distinguish a forest tarpan, *Equus przewalskii silvaticus* Vetulani. This would be smaller than the steppe form, and less robust, and the color fading was more intense in winter. It lived in western and southwestern Byelorussia, Lithuania, Poland, and Germany. The last representatives survived in the Bialowiecza forest until about 1814, when they were all caught and either tamed or killed (Pruski 1959). The name *silvaticus* Vetulani is actually long antedated by *Equus sylvestris* Brincken, 1826, a name applied to wild horses which had lived "forty year previously" in Bialowiecza forest, which were described simply as "graufarbig, mit einem Aalstrich über den Rücken" (gray colored, with an eel-stripe down the back).

Vetulani (1936) described how, from the 1920s on, he collected koniks from the vicinity of Bialowiecza, which were known to incorporate tarpan blood from as recently as about 1820, and after a period of selective breeding reintroduced them to the wild (Figure 3.5b). The males averaged 129.4 cm high, the females 128.0; they

Figure 3.5. a. One of the last tarpans prior to their extinction; the Cherson Tarpan in the Moscow Zoo in 1884. b. Polish koniks, bred to resemble their tarpan ancestors. (From Volf 1979b, reprinted with permission of Zeitschrift des Kölner Zoo).

varied in color from brown to black or isabella, and he selected them, in accordance with Brincken (1826), to be grey at least in summer—but it has been found that the coat grows white in winter (except for the distal limb segments, dorsal stripe, mane and tail), as does that of the primitive Hutsul breed of the Carpathians according to Bökönyi (1974). The white horses of Herodotus and von Heberstein can doubtless be understood in this light. The mane is erect in foals only, and falls to the side in adults. Volf (1979a and b) has most recently described their appearance and behavior.

Any Other Wild Horses?

Skorkowski (1946, 1961) was convinced that the wild horses known to us and to history are all mixtures between six originally pure types. Przewalski's horse, tarpan, and even ten out of fifteen fossil horse skulls which he examined, all are "mixed." Before dismissing these views peremptorily, we should remember that in the first half of the century this sort of analysis was widespread in a sister science; anthropologists, dismayed at the great variability within human races, and the wide overlap between them in measurable characters, hypothesized the former existence of "pure races" which had, during prehistory, inconsiderately intermingled. All that Skorkowski did was to apply the same principles to hippology (and refuse to modify them as time went on).

There are also those who believe that there were not merely different subspecies of *Equus ferus*, but different full species of wild horses, which all formed part of the ancestry of the domestic horse. This model has most recently been summarized by Kapitzke (1973), based on the work of Ebhardt, who never published his conclusions fully. There were four such species, according to this model: The Urpony (surviving in its purest form in the Exmoor Pony); the Tundrapony; the Ramshead Horse (best represented by the Sorraia Horse today); and the Ur-thoroughbred. Trumler (1961) allocates scientific names to the four types. The Przewalski's horse is (mainly) a Tundrapony; the tarpan was a mixture of types three and four. As with Skorkowski's model, so with Kapitzke's; even known wild horses are deemed not to be purebred representatives of one type or the other; again, fossil material that can be definitively allocated to one or the other is rather scarce, but the different types can, it is claimed, be recognized in European Upper Paleolithic cave paintings—leaving no room for stylistic variation

or artistic license, of course. Thus, the Urpony is represented at
Lascaux, Les Combarelles and Le Portel; the Tundrapony at
Niaux, La Madeleine and, again, Les Combarelles; the Ramshead
Horse at Spanish sites and Tassili; the Ur-thoroughbred at Fezzan.
(It should be noted that Groves [1986] questioned the existence of
wild horses in North Africa at all; but while his paper was in press,
evidence at last became available finally resolving this much discussed question [Bagtache et al. 1984]: a true wild horse really did
live in North Africa.)

On the question of the accuracy of Upper Paleolithic represen-
tations, Ucko and Rosenfeld (1967) urge caution. There are numerous hypotheses of the meaning of this prehistoric art—art for
art's sake, sympathetic magic, mythological illustration, sacred
decorations for religious sanctuaries—and it covers an immense
period of time, and extended over vast areas of Europe and Africa.
Surely not all, perhaps not even most, animal depictions are meant
to be photographic? Yet hippologists, in particular, have tended to
treat them as if they were: Blanchard (1964), for example, sees
nearly twenty different species in European cave art. Even Mohr
(1959), though realizing that there are drawbacks to treating the
paintings realistically, suggests on the basis of the Pech-Merle
spotted horses (illustrated by Ucko & Rosenfeld 1967:60, and
again, among twenty-two horse depictions on a double page spread,
1967:154–155) that dapple-grey morphs existed at that time.

There are perhaps just a few things that one can say about the
latest Pleistocene horses of Europe on the basis of Upper Paleolithic art: that most, at least, had upright manes and grew
"beards" on the jaw-line, and that there were some with light muzzles, light underparts, and dark legs. Some of the most realistically
depicted horses, such as the truly brilliant drawing from Niaux
(Mohr 1959:22), show all these features and are irresistibly remi-
niscent of Przewalski's horse, which means only that there was
(among others?) a kind of wild horse in western Europe at that
time which was of that general type.

That there were in fact other wild horses in latest Pleistocene
and early Holocene times was convincingly argued by Lundholm
(1947), who distinguished West European wild horses (France,
Switzerland) from both tarpan and Przewalski's horse by the complex enamel of the cheekteeth, and by the fact that M3 was not
longer than M2; and Swedish wild horses of early postglacial times
by a combination of skull characters, the enamel being simple. It is
studies like these that do most to establish that there really was

more than one taxon of wild horse in Eurasia in the last 20,000 years, although whether there was more than one distinct species, as opposed to just subspecies of *E. ferus*, is disputable: see Groves (1986) and Forsten (1988) for a summary of some evidence suggesting that there might have been two or more species in the late Pleistocene, but hardly three distinct genera, as proposed by Samson (1975).

Summary: Taxonomy of Recent Wild Horses

Present knowledge is reviewed most recently by Groves (1986). The three postglacial wild horses for which there is osteological evidence are *Equus ferus przewalskii*, the tarpan *E. f. ferus* (of which Polish and Ukrainian representatives cannot, on present evidence, be distinguished from one another), and the unnamed Swedish form.

On the steppes east of the Volga, as Heptner (1955) argued, was a zone of intergradation where both grey (tarpan-like) and reddish (Przewalski-like) wild horses occurred. This is evidence that the European tarpan and Przewalski's horse were actually conspecific. (East of the Ural, in Kazakhstan, wild horses were predominately of red type, so probably, according to Heptner, were the true Przewalski's horse).

Tarpan skulls average very slightly longer than Przewalski's horses in basal skull length, but slightly shorter in vertex length (upper length of skull), they have a less extended occipital crest, and the diastema is longer; the single complete Swedish skull is smaller than either, but again with a rather long diastema (Groves 1986, Table 1). The tarpan has on average smaller teeth than Przewalski's horse; in the Swedish horse the teeth are smaller still (Groves 1986, Table 2). Forsten (1988) found two tarpan skulls to have a longer, narrower braincase than those of Przewalski's horse; Eisenmann (1982), though she studied no tarpans, noted a relatively short muzzle in various European late Pleistocene horses, which would seem to confirm Forsten's finding from a different perspective.

In summary, then, I would recognize just two subspecies of wild horses in historic times, as follows:

1) *Equus ferus ferus* Boddaert, 1785. The tarpan. Synonyms: *sylvestris* Brincken, 1826; *gmelini* Antonius, 1912; *silvaticus* Vetulani, 1928.

2) *Equus ferus przewalskii* Poliakov, 1881. Przewalski's horse. Synonyms: *hagenbecki* Matschie, 1903; *typicus* Hilzheimer, 1909; probably also *equuleus* Smith, 1841.

Wild Horses in Perspective

The question of the relationship of horses to other equids has been reviewed by several authors (Azzaroli 1966, Bennett 1980, Groves and Willoughby 1981, Groves 1986). There are problems with all of these models: whether true asses and hemiones form a clade, whether all zebras form a clade, and whether horses are (1) the most divergent of surviving equids or (2) the sister-group to hemiones and/or asses or (3) part of a clade including some or all zebras—these are still topics for lively debate. A further question, more perhaps a matter of taste than those listed above, is whether all living equids should be placed in a single genus, *Equus*, or should be split into several genera. Fortunately any of the possible answers to this last question would be effectively the same as far as horses are concerned, since *Equus caballus* is the type species of *Equus*.

Is, then, *Equus ferus* to be maintained as a species separate from *Equus caballus*? Yes, for two reasons.

First, if domestic horses are not descended from the tarpan or any of its conspecifics, then the separation is warranted on taxonomic grounds. This is still an open question; a version of the multiple-origins theory may be correct, or domestic horses may be descended from some unknown ancestor, not the tarpan. Note that the chromosome difference (see Ryder, this volume) seems to exclude Przewalski's horse from the ancestry of domestic horses, unless the mutation occurred almost at the moment of domestication (but before breed diversification).

Even if domestic horses are descended from the tarpan, or from a wild ancestor conspecific with the latter, the question of whether or not wild horses are *Equus caballus* becomes a non-question, to be decided on convenience alone, and, as discussed by Corbet and Clutton-Brock (1984), who advocate keeping them separate. Note that the chromosome characters which apparently rule out Przewalski's horse as the ancestor of domestic horses do not exclude the tarpan, since karyotyping of koniks and "bred-back tarpans", which are descended in part from the Bialowiecza tarpans, has picked up no trace of heterogeneity. Note, incidentally, that the chromosome difference does not require that the Przewalski's horse and tarpan be separate species, as it is a simple Robertsonian one, which does not affect interfertility and indeed is well-known between conspecifics in other mammalian groups. As we have seen, Heptner's (1955, 1961) evidence suggests that there was in fact an intergrade zone between the Przewalski's horse and the tarpan.

4

The Studbook

Jiri Volf

In the 1950s the number of Przewalski's horses in the wild rapidly decreased. The horses became so rare that no accurate records about their occurrence were available (Mohr and Volf 1984).

Also, the problems of breeding of these animals in captivity raised serious fears. Their total number was 30–40 individuals and this was in fact balancing on the verge of extinction.

These facts led Dr. Erna Mohr of the Zoological Museum in Hamburg to write a comprehensive monograph about the endangered species. The largest Przewalski's horse herd was at the Prague Zoo at that time and I served as its curator. Therefore, in 1956 Dr. Mohr asked me for my cooperation in a questionnaire activity; this activity made it possible to prepare an inventory of all wild horses that had been kept in captivity and put their genealogy together. In this way the first studbook was founded and was published as an appendix of the above mentioned monograph, "Das Urwildpferd," in 1959 (Mohr 1959, 1971).

The activity also had another positive effect. Breeders became more interested in these animals, so that the number of wild horses in captivity increased by 50%, i.e., from 41 to 59 individuals, during four years (1956–1959).

Alarming reports about the decreasing number of Przewalski's horses in the wild, and their highly limited numbers in captivity, induced the Prague Zoo to organize the 1st International Symposium on the Przewalski Horse in Prague in 1959. The symposium showed that considerable attention should be devoted to encouraging reproduction by the wild horses in captivity and cataloging the world herds in detail. The symposium also put the Prague Zoo in charge of maintaining a worldwide record of horses kept in captivity and of publication of a studbook. The zoo continues to fulfill this task.

The studbook card is the basis of registration of Przewalski's horses. Each studbook card consists of two originals. The first, blue for stallions and pink for mares, remains in our worldwide card index, and the second, in opposite colors, i.e., pink for stallions and blue for mares, is sent to the owner of a given horse.

Data concerning a given horse are listed on the front of the studbook card; i.e., species, studbook number, sex, studbook name (name of breeding station and number in the succession of offspring born at that zoo), house name, date of birth, place of birth, owner, date of death, place of death, post-mortem findings, disposition of the corpse, characteristics and remarks. On the opposite side ancestors through the third generation (great grandparents) and all descendants are listed including their sex, date of birth, studbook number and name, and the other parent (Figure 4.1).

Studbook cards of Przewalski's horses were found quite satisfactory due to their accuracy and simplicity, so they have been recommended by the International Union of Directors of Zoological Gardens (IUDZG) and International Union for Conservation of Nature and Natural Resources (IUCN) as a model for registration of other endangered species.

Having completed the basic registration of all previous wild horses kept in captivity, we make only studbook cards for newborn foals at present. It is our aim that the owner has the studbook card as soon as possible after announcement of the birth so that the foal can be transferred to a new owner with the above birth certificate. As the release of the studbook card is fast, it is not possible to present the studbook number. This number has to be completed by the owner according to chronological numbering listed in the subsequent studbook. The owner is also obliged to complete data about descendants on cards of breeding animals.

When the horse comes to a new owner it is accompanied by its studbook card with the indicated change. When the horse dies, the last owner sends the properly completed studbook card back to us and we place it in the so-called "dead card index."

A photoarchive is an indispensable component of the worldwide card index of Przewalski's horses. The archives consists of as many photographs of individual animals as possible. The photo-

A

Zoological Garden Prague, Czechoslovakia

International Studbook for the Przewalski Horse

Species: **Equus przewalskii Poliakov, 1881**   Studbook No.: 84

Sex: F   Studbook Name: Praha 17

House Name: Arna

Date of Birth: 20.V.1953   Place of Birth: Praha

Owner: 1. Zoo Praha   since: 20.V.1953

2. Fa Behrend,Buenos Aires   19.VI.1954

3. Diergaarde Rotterdam   22.IX.1954

4. Zoo Amsterdam   8.XII.1960

Date of Death: 22.VII.1969   Place of Death: Amsterdam

Post-Mortem Findings: probably lead poisoning

What Happened with the Corpse: to Zool. Museum, Amsterdam

Characteristics: Colour reddish bay, light coloured around
the nostrils only; height 131 cm

Remarks:

TZ 42-5820-84

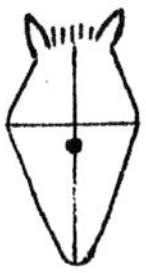

Figure 4.1.   Studbook card for the Przewalski's horse. a. Front Side. b. Reverse.

B

Father

Studbook No. and-Name		
76.Pha 9	120.Wash.1	118.Phil.5
		119.Phil.6
House name	65.Halle 8	56.Halle 1
Uran		58.Halle C

Mother

Studbook No. and-Name		
75.Pha 8	120.Wash.1	118.Phil.5
		119.Phil.6
House Name:	65.Halle 8	56.Halle 1
Vlasta		58.Halle C

Descendants

	Sex	Date of Birth	Father (Mother)	Studbook No. and-Name
1.	F	11.XII.56	85.Pha 18	219.Blijd.1
2.	M	23.I.58	85.Pha 18	220.Blijd.2
3.	M	27.I.59	85.Pha 18	232.Blijd.3
4.	M	4.III.60	85.Pha 18	239.Blijd.5
5.	F	14.VI.61	85.Pha 18	264.Amst.1
6.	F	24.VII.66	220.Blijd.2	360.Amst.3
7.				
8.				
9.				
10.				
11.				
12.				
13.				
14.				

Guaranteed By ....
Studbook Keeper

archives serve as the direct documentation of identity to help to prevent occasional mistaken identity during transport.

Deaths or transfers of Przewalski's horses to a new location are continuously reported by the breeders, most frequently on a special questionnaire card (information card) we send them every year for this purpose (Figure 4.2). We think that we save the breeders from administrative work in this way, and that the uniform record makes it possible to obtain accurate information. In January we also send a summary of the data to all breeders including data that were sent to us during the last calendar year. If the data are complete it is sufficient for the breeder to sign them prior to returning them to us. Otherwise he or she must complete them.

Thanks to the excellent cooperation of all Przewalski's horse breeders it is possible to supplement continuously the worldwide card index and make it up-to-date. On its basis we publish annually the International Pedigree Book of the Przewalski Horse (Volf 1960 et seq.).

The Pedigree Book is divided into several chapters. It contains the official register of Przewalski's horses born during the previous

PRZEWALSKI HORSE INFORMATION CARD

Owner: ...WHIPSNADE WILD ANIMAL PARK..

Address: DUNSTABLE, BEDFORDSHIRE, LU6 2LF., ENGLAND.

Studbook Number	♂ ♀	Studbook Name	House Name	Parents		
				Studbook No	Studbook Name	House Name
1759.	F	London 93	ZARA	♂ 824	Chester2	Boris
				♀ 705	London 38	Svetlana

INFORMATION	DATUM	Remarks: born dead, aborted, cause of death, etc.
BIRTH	30.6.1988	
DEATH		
ARRIVED		~~From~~/to: Oberwil Zoo, Oberwil,
TRANSFERRED	9.10.1989	Switzerland.
		(Owner's address)

Date......11th January 1990

Mrs. Christa Datlen

(Records Office)
Signature

Figure 4.2. The information cards used by breeders to inform the studbook keeper of changes in their herd.

calendar year, aborted and stillborn foals, and changes in Przewalski's horse herds (transfers and deaths). The largest part of the book is the Official Register of All Przewalski Horses alive on January 1 of a given year. Each animal's data from the studbook card are presented, namely studbook number, sex, studbook name, house name, date of birth, father, mother, and current location. Current data in the introductory chapters of the Pedigree Book are presented chronologically and in the Official Register of all living Przewalski's horses the data are listed alphabetically by breeder's site (Figure 4.3).

Particular attention is devoted to the rapid publication of the Pedigree Book. Only a pedigree book with up-to-date information can fulfill its task as a real guide for the breeders, e.g., for offering surplus horses for transfer or when looking for required animals.

In 1970, 1980, and 1991, we issued General Pedigree Books containing data about all Przewalski's horses kept in captivity beginning with the wild-caught imports in 1889 and ending with foals born before the end of 1969, 1979, and 1989, respectively (Volf 1980, Volf et al. 1991).

On the basis of the data presented in the General Pedigree Book it is possible to answer a number of breeder's questions, such as determining the population curve during a certain period of time, the age structure of the present population, distribution of parturitions during a given calendar year, age at onset and end of sexual activity for stallions and mares, and other statistics (Mohr and Volf 1984). On the basis of the General Pedigree Book it is also possible to create a complete genealogy of each registered individual and thus determine its inbreeding coefficient.

Individual volumes of the Pedigree Book and of the General Pedigree Book served as a basic source of information for many publications (Amos 1987, Bouman 1977, Boyd 1988a, Gruenerwald 1982, 1985, Ryder et al. 1989, etc.).

In 1976, the Przewalski's horse inventory "Bouman system" became established for elaborating the complete genealogy of each registered individual. On the basis of this material the representation of the original wild-caught founders for each Przewalski's horse and for the complete population in captivity could be calculated as well as the inbreeding coefficients. The data were used for new computer programs developed first in the U.S.A. and later in Europe, which could be used to manage the horses as biological populations by applying the fundamentals and methods of demography and genetics.

1589.	M	Springe 18	Spring ins Feld	29. V. 1987	1162. Bern 12 Alexander	1245. Springe 8 Spora	Springe
1683.	F	Springe 20	Spreta	29. IV. 1988	1007. Köln 11 Askan	398. Köln 1 Verena	Springe
1735.	M	Springe 21	Spriegel	8. VI. 1988	1007. Köln 11 Askan	856. Springe 1 Springia	Springe
1737.	F	Springe 22	Spinnerin	9. VI. 1988	1162. Bern 12 Alexander	1245. Springe 8 Spora	Springe
558.	M	Praha 113	David	5. VI. 1973	285. Askania 3 Bars	403. Praha 94 Helada	Stuttgart
588.	F	Praha 116	Elipsa	28. V. 1974	285. Askania 3 Bars	250. Praha 39 Háta	Stuttgart
859.	F	Stuttgart 2	Edose	15. VII. 1979	558. Praha 113 David	588. Praha 116 Elipsa	Stuttgart
1286.	F	Nürnberg 37	Maud	7. IX. 1984	397. Hell. 63 Rochus	741. Nürnberg 17 Mausi	Stuttgart
1767.	F	Stuttgart 4	Maura	13. VII. 1988	558. Praha 113 David	1286. Nürnberg 37 Maud	Stuttgart
1168.	M	Bern 13	Maxim	11. VII. 1983	632. Nürnberg 9 Peter	540. Praha 111 Donna	Taipei
1218.	F	Springe 7	Spritze	7. V. 1984	749. Marwell 31 Ilka	398. Köln 1 Verena	Taipei
1247.	F	Halle 12	Julia	3. VI. 1984	627. Marwell 22 Josef	625. Marwell 21 Joan	Taipei

B

Číslo karty Studbook number	Pohlaví Sex	Číslo evidenční Studbook name	Jméno House-name	Datum narození Date of birth	Otec Father	Matka Mother	Stanoviště Site
1252.	M	Bern 14	Jiří	13. VI. 1984	519. Praha 109 Cyklon	651. Nürnberg 11 Mimea	Taipei
571.	M	Marwell 13	Bedal	14. I. 1974	293. Catskill 17 Basil	95. Praha 28 Leda	Tallinn (Leningrad)
636.	M	Askania 25	Graver	4. VII. 1975	391. Askania 9 Gordyj	489. Askania 10 Grena	Tallinn
953.	F	Tallinn 2	Milly	19. IV. 1981	605. Askania 21 Vorat	355. Praha 78 Mirta	Tallinn
1112.	F	Nikolaev 1	Nika	24. IV. 1983	391. Askania 9 Gordyj	823. Askania 46 Granka	Tallinn
1194.	F	Askania 88	Pena	28. III. 1984	821. Askania 45 Parad	524. Askania 12 Viola	Tallinn
1235.	M	Askania 96	Purik	20. V. 1984	821. Askania 45 Parad	602. Askania 20 Geran	Tallinn
1258.	M	Moskva 13	Gnev	20. VI. 1984	636. Askania 25 Graver	901. Askania 58 Vestnica	Tallinn
1435.	M	Tallinn 3	Bele	12. V. 1986	571. Marwell 13 Bedal	1112. Nikolaev 1 Nika	Tallinn
1593.	M	Tallinn 4	Ben	31. V. 1987	571. Marwell 13 Bedal	1112. Nikolaev 1 Nika	Tallinn

C

	Sex			Date			
1765.	F	Tallinn 5	Nancy	9. VII. 1988	571. Marwell 13 Bedal	1112. Nikolaev 1 Nika	Tallinn
1044.	M	Askania 72	Listok	8. V. 1982	259. Askania 2 Pegas	528. Askania 14 Vjuga	Taškent
1184.	M	Rostov 3	Cukat	12. IX. 1983	652. Askania 27 Luč	709. Askania 35 Galka	Taškent
1259.	F	Askania 99	Pava	21. VI. 1984	821. Askania 45 Parad	600. Askania 18 Groza	Taškent
842.	M	Askania 52	Poker	7. VI. 1979	259. Askania 2 Pegas	396. Praha 91 Vada	Termez
1116.	M	Oberwil 19	Irkuts	5. V. 1983	478. Hell. 65 Silvester	577. Praha 114 Etna	Thot à Thonac (Oberwil)
1197.	F	Oberwil 21	Kurleja	4. IV. 1984	478. Hell. 65 Silvester	308. Blijdorp 10 Juliana	Thot à Thonac (Oberwil)
899.	F	London 58	Jovanka	16. V. 1980	517. Marwell 3 Haldo	581. London 26 Fay	Tokyo
913.	M	London 59	Nureyev	4. VI. 1980	517. Marwell 3 Haldo	389. London 14 Petruschka	Tokyo
1160.	M	Bern 11	Leo	1. VII. 1983	519. Praha 109 Cyklon	651. Nürnberg 11 Mimea	Tokyo
1721.	M	Tokyo 1	Altai	30. V. 1988	1160. Bern 11 Leo	899. London 58 Jovanka	Tokyo
635.	F	York 15	Selenga	2. VII. 1975	381. Catskill 38 Bertland	373. Catskill 36 Rockann	Topeka (N. Y. Zool. Soc.)

Číslo karty	Pohlaví Sex	Číslo evidenční Studbook name	Jméno House name	Datum narození Date of birth	Otec Father	Matka Mother	Stanoviště Site
822.	F	S. Diego 25	Belda	19. V. 1979	469. Catskill 44 Jeanhold	458. San Diego 2 Belaya	Topeka (San Diego)
841.	F	S. Diego 27	Botania	6. VI. 1979	469. Catskill 44 Jeanhold	504. San Diego 5 Bogatka	Topeka (San Diego)
1084.	M	York 32	Boxer	31. VII. 1982	685. San Diego 14 Borkas	380. Catskill 37 Roxy	Topeka (N. Y. Zool. Soc.)
1130.	M	Topeka 8	Coltar	18. V. 1983	568. Catskill 61 Rolmar	549. Brook. 3 Colleen	Topeka
1232.	F	Topeka 9	Shalimar	17. V. 1984	568. Catskill 61 Rolmar	841. S. Diego 27 Botania	Topeka
1249.	M	Topeka 10	Bryansk	7. VI. 1984	568. Catskill 61 Rolmar	822. S. Diego 25 Belda	Topeka
1287.	F	Minnesota 20		9. IX. 1984	688. York 17 George	668. London 34 Anuschka	Topeka (N. Y. Zool. Soc.)
1364.	M	Topeka 11	Bevin	9. VI. 1985	568. Catskill 61 Rolmar	822. S. Diego 25 Belda	Topeka (S. Diego)
1370.	F	Topeka 12	Boyd	14. VI. 1985	568. Catskill 61 Rolmar	841. S. Diego 27 Botania	Topeka (S. Diego)
1458.	F	Topeka 13	Raimee	30. V. 1986	568. Catskill 61 Rolmar	822. S. Diego 25 Belda	Topeka

Figure 4.3. Pages from the Official Register of Living Przewalski's Horses in the Pedigree Book (studbook).

In the U.S.A. the International Species Inventory System (ISIS) developed computer programs for the application of demographic and genetics techniques. In Germany, Gruenerwald sponsored the development of the Local Species Inventory System (LOSIS) and published the "Analysis of the Studbook for the Przewalski Horse" in 1982. Further, in England "The Status and Conservation of the British Population of Przewalski's Horse" was published (Amos 1987). We consider it advantageous that everyone interested may obtain all the basic information from a single source. Therefore, in 1991 we prepared the third General Pedigree Book in which almost 2000 Przewalski's horses are listed.

At present it is evident that the worldwide record of Przewalski's horses in the form of the Pedigree Book played a highly positive role in the protection of this endangered species. Because of it, wild horses came to the attention of specialists of many countries. Individual breeders are in mutual contact, exchange their experiences and supplement their breeding herds to have the highest possible number and quality of offspring. Przewalski's horses are also the concern of several international protection programs such as the Species Survival Plan (SSP) of the American Association of Zoological Parks and Aquariums and the Europäisches Erhaltungszucht-programm (EEP, The European Breeding Programme). Regional coordinators advise the breeders directly and cooperate closely with the studbook keeper. Coordinators are Dr. Oliver Ryder of the San Diego Zoo for the U.S.A., Dr. Waltraut Zimmermann of the Cologne Zoo for central and western Europe and Stanislav Kudrjavcev of the Moscow Zoo for Russia. However, it appears that additional coordinators will be required, i.e., for the Australian region, for Great Britain and for China.

The number of Przewalski's horses kept in captivity has more or less regularly increased (Figure 4.4). During the last thirty-five years (1956–1990) their number has increased more than twenty-three times. By January 1, 1990, a total of 960 Przewalski's horses have lived at 130 locations all over the world. The largest herds are owned by (in alphabetical order): Adelaide (Australia), Askania Nova (Ukraine), Bekesbourne (U.K.), Tierpark Berlin (Germany), Dubbo (Australia), Cologne (Germany), Lelystad (The Netherlands), Marwell (U.K.), Minnesota (U.S.A.), Moscow (Russia), Munich (Germany), National Zoological Park (U.S.A.), New York (U.S.A.), Noorderheide (The Netherlands), Prague (Czechoslovakia), San Diego (U.S.A.), Springe (Germany), and

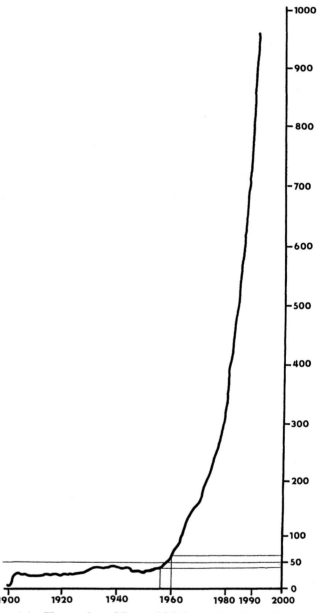

Figure 4.4. The number of Przewalski's horses kept in captivity over time. The creation of an international studbook intensified the interest in breeding Przewalski's horses. On the graph, the year the first questionnaire was distributed (1956) and the year of first publication of the studbook (1960) are marked.

Urumqi (China). It is a significant and stimulating success in the international protection of an endangered animal species.

The present number of Przewalski's horses makes it possible to be optimistic with respect to the future of this species in captivity and also realistic to consider a gradual reintroduction of a part of the population to the wild. This will be the main task during the next decade.

5

Genetic Studies of Przewalski's Horses and their Impact on Conservation

Oliver A. Ryder

INTRODUCTION

Several significant aspects of the biology and conservation of Przewalski's horses involve genetic considerations. The fact that there is little, if any, likelihood that pure Przewalski's horses survive in the wild only emphasizes the concern that must be accorded to genetic issues, including gene pool management.

From the evolutionary perspective, a question of interest is the relationship between the wild horses that once inhabited the Dzungarian basin that we call today *Equus przewalskii* and other populations of wild horses that were extant prior to the domestication of horses. The cave paintings at Lascaux depict animals with many of the morphological attributes distinctive for Przewalski's horses, but were they the same? Are Przewalski's horses the direct progenitors of today's domestic horses? Opinions exist concerning these questions, to be sure. However, is there a strong factual basis for these assertions, and is it possible today to gather new information that will shed additional light on these questions?

A related question concerns the taxonomic status of Przewalski's horses and their hybridization with domestic horses, both in the Dzungarian Gobi and in captivity. Should Przewalski's horses be considered a "good" species and are there any Przewalski's horses that can be considered "pure" given what information exists concerning interbreeding between Przewalski's horses and herds of domestic animals? The introduction of domestic Mongolian pony genes into the captive population is thoroughly documented. To what extent should this information influence present and future management action, including reintroduction efforts?

To the extent that current investigations seeking to characterize the species' gene pool may provide a retrospective view of the genetic diversity of the wild-born founders and, by inference, the populations from which they were derived, the results of genetics research programs offer the opportunity to gain additional insights into a species of intrinsic interest, significance and one of conservation concern.

Inevitably, the continued conservation management of the surviving species' gene pool and the re-establishment of the gene pool in free-ranging populations in their natural habitat involves genetic considerations. A genetic bottleneck that conclusively defined the extent of the surviving gene pool occurred as a result of the capture, transfer to captivity, and variable reproductive rates of individuals removed from the wild. Further loss of gene pool resources occurred, notably due to poor initial breeding successes and a resulting slow rate of population growth. Inbreeding depression also played a role, albeit a small one, in the diminution of the gene pool. The reintroduction of Przewalski's horses into habitats within the historical range of the species will also involve genetic bottlenecks and, unless specific programs of ongoing research are designed and implemented, the re-established populations will lack the gene pool resources available for the species.

GENETIC VARIATION, GENETIC DIFFERENTIATION, HYBRIDIZATION, AND THE SYSTEMATICS OF CABALLINE HORSES

From the earliest moments following the recognition by European zoologists that a wild horse existed in the Dzungarian Gobi (Anonymous 1884), the question of the similarities and differences of these horses with domestic breeds arose. Initial comparisons of Przewalski's horses and domestic horses were centered on conformational data and data on other phenotypic traits (Salensky 1907). However, it was not long thereafter that the capacity of Przewalski's horse to hybridize and produce fertile offspring with domestic horses was tested independently at Halle and elsewhere.

Morphological Variation

The species *Equus przewalskii* was named by the Russian zoologist Poliakov in 1881 based on a holotype and a paratype specimen. Both of these specimens are mounted and may be seen today in the same museum where they were deposited and described, the Zoological Museum of the Academy of Science in St. Petersburg. Also mounted and on display is the skin of a third non-neonatal animal, a mare, #2 Kobdo B, that died in the stables of Czar Nicholas. (Her companion there, the stallion #1 Kobdo A, Waska, was later transferred to Askania Nova in the Ukraine.) These three specimens are remarkable for their diversity, the extent of which is not obscured by the fact that the holotype is in winter coat and the paratype is in summer coat. In his classic and influential treatment of the phenotype of Przewalski's horse, Heinz Heck of Tierpark Hellabrunn presented a series of color drawings in the journal *Equus* that depict traits that typify pure Przewalski's horses and those traits that provide evidence, Heck asserted, of the influence of domestic horse genetic input (Heck 1967). Examination of the preserved skins in the Zoological Museum in Leningrad revealed that pelage variation in *Equus przewalskii* is more extensive than generally recognized and includes animals with dark noses, animals lacking a white underbelly and animals lacking black pigmentation. These observations were based on inspection of all skins and mounted specimens obtained directly from wild populations present in the Museum's collections.

Although more variable morphologically than is generally recognized, the pattern of coat color variation in Przewalski's horses obtained from the wild is still far less diverse than the variation in coat color observed in domestic horse breeds.

One of the nineteen Przewalski's horse skins in the Zoological Museum in Leningrad obtained from Mongolia lacked dark pigmentation and conformed to the fox or chestnut coat color phenotype. This skin is described in the Museum catalog (#37123) as having been received on February 7, 1903. The animal, a juvenile female, was born in the wild in 1902 and was captured near the cities of Oschka and Bulun-Tochoia. Garutt et al. (1965) also mention this skin but do not indicate that it is from a fox-colored individual. Fox-colored Przewalski's horses are known in the studbook population, even from the very early generations of breeding. (#123 Washington 4, lacked dark pigmentation and is thought to have been a fox-colored horse.) The number of fox-colored individuals in the rapidly expanding captive population is currently increasing, allowing the identification of carriers of the fox trait. By analogy to the extension locus (E) which extends the expression of dark pigment in domestic horses, the fox trait is thought be an autosomal recessive trait although this has never been systematically investigated in Przewalski's horse (Bowling, personal communication; Seal et al. 1990). Pedigree analysis of the occurrence of fox-colored individuals assuming an autosomal recessive mode of inheritance requires that the fox allele enter the studbook pedigree at least two times independently. At least two of the founders must have carried the fox allele; one would have been derived from the #11, #12 domestic mare founder group and another would have derived from the #17, #18, #39, #40 founder group.

Thus, documentation exists that at least some of the characteristics Heck (1967) asserted were indicative of domestic horse ancestry (dark nose and dark underbelly), as well as the chestnut or fox coat color, existed in Przewalski's horses obtained from the wild.

Initially, genetic investigations were limited to considerations of coat color and other phenotypic traits. Genetic studies were generally considered peripheral to discussions of Przewalski's horses until the publication of the dramatic finding that Przewalski's horses possessed a different number of chromosomes than did domestic horses (Benirschke et al. 1965).

Chromosomal Variation in Horses

The chromosomal difference between Przewalski's horse and domestic horses was established to have occurred through a mechanism commonly observed in chromosomal evolution and speciation, i.e., centromere-centromere fusion. Mammalian chromosomes have an attachment site for the cellular spindle that ensures that when a cell divides, daughter chromosomes are segregated to each of the two daughter cells. The cellular attachment sites (kinetochores) may be located at or near the chromosome ends (resulting in one-armed chromosomes) or may be located within the chromosomal element itself, resulting in bi-armed chromosomes. Rarely in individuals, chromosomes may fuse (and fission) at the centromere region near the kinetochore. A reduction in chromosome number produced by a chromosomal fusion occurs without a corresponding reduction in the number of chromosome arms. The phenomenon was first described by Roberts in grasshoppers and is frequently called Robertsonian fusion. The same or nearly the same amount of genetic information is packaged in two fewer chromosomes as a result of Robertsonian fusion. Although chromosomal fusions are a rare occurrence among individuals of a species, they rather commonly are noted to differentiate species. Examples of a trend in the reduction of chromosome numbers in the evolution of mammalian chromosomes is well documented, although it is clear that fissions can also occur. Variation in chromosomal number within a species (chromosomal polymorphism) is known to occur. However, it is considered to be a transient phenomenon, often restricted to a population that is or has been isolated from other populations of the same species.

Consequently, the findings of Benirschke et al. (1965) are significant for understanding the relationship between Przewalski's horse and domestic horses. Although apparently interfertile, the existence of $2n = 66$ chromosomes in Przewalski's horse identifies that these animals are more different from their domestic relatives ($2n = 64$) than are any two breeds of domestic horse (Figure 5.1). The chromosomal findings support the notion that *Equus przewalskii* is more like a proper species (even though fertile hybrids with domestic horses are possible), because of the degree of genetic isolation implied by a fixed difference in chromosome number.

The question of hybridization of Przewalski's horses and domestic horses arises repeatedly both in consideration of the populations in Mongolia that survived into the middle of the twentieth century and the particular twelve Przewalski's horses that, with one known domestic Mongolian pony mare, provided the genetic base for the captive population that now constitutes the last survivors of the species.

Additional chromosomal surveys subsequent to those of Benirschke et al. (1965) conducted at the Catskill Game Farm expanded the base of data that could be used in retrospective analysis of pedigrees. No $2n = 65$ chromosome karyotypes were found in any studbook-registered Przewalski's horses in spite of the fact that individuals for all founder lineages have been examined (Benirschke et al. 1965, Matthews and Delhanty 1979, Ryder et al. 1982, Ryder et al. 1978, Ryder unpublished observations). However, the studies of Short et al. (1974) confirmed that the expected $2n = 65$ diploid number of chromosomes was present in a hybrid between a Przewalski's horse stallion (#185 London 9, Tzar) and a Welsh pony mare. That the hybrid was itself also capable of reproduction was confirmed by Short et al. (1974).

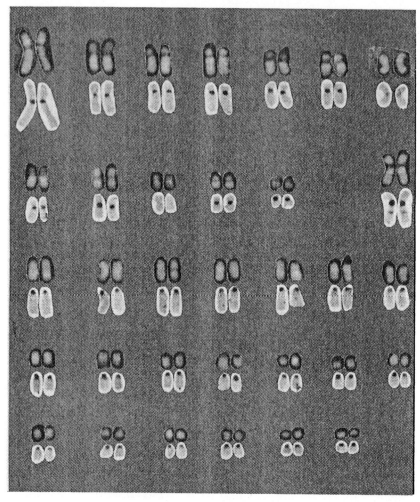

Figure 5.1. Karyotype of *Equus przewalskii* (female, #339 Catskill 29, Bonnette). Sequential Q-banded and C-banded chromosomes. Quinacrine-banded metaphase chromosomes were photographed, destained and subjected to C-banding. Consequently, the pattern of constitutive heterochromatin of the individual elements is displayed (Ryder and Hansen 1979).

In light of the number and founder diversity of individuals whose chromosomal number has been determined, there is no direct genetic evidence that any of the founders of the studbook population were themselves hybrids. In contrast, if most or all of the founders of the studbook population were of hybrid origin, then it is rather likely that a chromosomal polymorphism would have been detectable by the chromosomal studies undertaken.

Dolan (1982) has argued that studbook #18 Bijsk 8, was an F_1 hybrid based on her excessively lengthy mane (see Figure 5.2). Other accounts of travellers in Mongolia and of persons associated with the transfer of animals captured in Mongolia that founded the studbook population also impugn the purity of some of the stock that was transported westward to European and American buyers, e.g., Mohr (1959, 1971).

Genetic variation at the morphological and molecular level may be assessed by a variety of criteria including the frequencies of alleles at discrete loci (including DNA sequence variation) and by variation in quantitative traits (traits that are governed by multiple loci). Although it has been argued that variation in quantitative traits may be most relevant to gene pool conservation management (Hedrick et al. 1986, Arnold in press), relatively few efforts have been undertaken to collect information of this type from large mammals kept in zoological parks (although some information does exist that may be amenable to investigation of quantitative traits in Przewalski's horses). Over the last two decades a variety of investigative approaches have been applied in efforts to assess the level of genetic variability in Przewalski's horses and domestic horses. These data have had practical application to the management of Przewalski's horses and have provided new information concerning the genetic similarities of Przewalski's to domestic horses.

Protein Electrophoretic Markers

Heritable variation in the translation products of genes, i.e., proteins, may be detected on the basis of differences in the net charge of polypeptides in solution and the accompanying differences in mobility in an electric field. Molecular sieving produced by an insoluble matrix through which the proteins in solution migrate may also allow separation on the basis of molecular weight. Staining techniques that identify the catalytic activities of enzymatic proteins and general protein stains serve to allow the simultaneous analysis of homologous proteins from large numbers of individuals. Utilizing this approach, individuals, populations and species may be assayed for the proportion of loci that are variable and for heterozygosity. When Mendelian segregation of loci can be demonstrated or inferred, the analysis of alleles segregating at polymorphic loci can be used for qualifying parents to offspring and vice-versa.

Electrophoretic variation in blood proteins of Przewalski's horses and domestic horses has been investigated for several of the major geographical subdivisions of the studbook population, e.g., Europe (Putt and Fisher 1979, Fisher et al. 1979), North America (Ryder et al. 1979, Ryder et al. 1981, Ryder et al. 1982, Ryder et al. 1984) and the former Soviet Union (Dubrovskaya et al. 1982a, 1982b).

Protein electrophoretic data for horses are often collected in conjunction with serological data, the combination of which is referred to as blood typing. The database of blood typing results provides the most extensive genetic information compiled for Przewalski's horses and also allows comparison to the base bank of information concerning blood typing loci in domestic horses (Bowling and Ryder 1988).

Serological Markers

If red blood cells from one horse are injected into another horse, the recipient animal may produce antibodies to those red cell surface antigens not present on the surface of its own red blood cells. Panels of antibodies produced in this fashion from a genetically diverse array of individuals may be utilized to detect and characterize allelic variation at the multiple loci that specify red blood cell surface antigens. Such immuno-reagent panels have provided a convenient and reliable means of assessing genetic variation and, through analysis of segregation of these markers, qualification or exclusion of direct ancestry (parentage) or descent (progeny). Typically employed in domestic horse breed registries in order to preclude errors in breed pedigree data, these same immuno-reagent panels detect heritable variation in the red blood cell surface antigens of Przewalski's horses and may be utilized for the same purposes (Podliachouk and Kaminski 1971, Ryder et al. 1979, Scott 1979, Smith et al. 1980, Bowling and Ryder 1987). The most recently published study (Bowling and Ryder 1987) included data from 96 Przewalski's horses and included analysis of 14 presumptive loci and 38 different allelic variants.

Although four alleles at four discrete loci have been identified in Przewalski's horses that have not been detected in the domestic horse breeds examined, the large proportion of shared genetic characters demonstrates a close evolutionary relationship between Przewalski's horses and domestic horses. However, blood typing data comparing domestic animals with a small and inbred population of a wild relative are of questionable value for resolving the question as to whether Przewalski's horses are the direct progenitors of domestic horses, especially in light of the fact that there may have been an extinction of the putative sister taxon of wild horse from which domestic horses might have been derived. Alternative possibilities for origin or origins of domestic horses, for example from an extinct species of wild horse related to but not identical with Przewalski's horse (such as the tarpan, *Equus gmelini* or forest horse of Europe), can be tested if reliable estimates of the length of time since divergence from a common ancestor can be obtained. Horses are thought to have been domesticated 5,000 years ago (Clutton-Brock 1981, Zeuner 1963) or possibly earlier (Anthony et al. 1991) but probably not earlier than 10,000 years ago (Bahn 1980).

Mitochondrial DNA Variation

If Przewalski's horse was the progenitor of domestic horses, then the estimated time of genetic divergence should be consistent with a common ancestry of the two lineages approximately 5,000–10,000 years ago. On the other hand, if the estimated genetic divergence of the two lineages is greatly in excess of this amount of time, a direct ancestral relationship of domestic horses and Przewalski's horses would not be supported.

Recent findings suggest that the most appropriate and sensitive assay for genetic divergence of lineages over these, relatively brief, periods of evolutionary time involves the comparison of mitochondrial DNA (mtDNA) molecules (Brown et al. 1979, Avise et al. 1987, Avise 1989). George and Ryder (1986) reported mtDNA restriction maps for *Equus przewalskii*, *E. caballus*, and six other equid taxa. Comparison of mtDNA from one individual each of *E. hemionus onager* and *E. hemionus kulan* identified only a single mtDNA haplotype.

Based upon analysis of matrilines in the studbook population of Przewalski's horse, there are four surviving mtDNA lineages (i.e., maternal clones). These surviving maternal clones are derived from founders #231, Orlitza III; #52 Staraja 2; #12 Bijsk 2; and #40 Bijsk B. The mtDNA analysis of George and Ryder (1986) utilized purified mtDNA and detection of end-labeled cleavage products, an approach that provides a robust data set but which is labor intensive and requires relatively greater amounts of mtDNA than are necessary for detection of cleavage products with hybridization probes.

The three *E. przewalskii* maternal lineages examined (representing three of the potential four surviving mtDNA haplotypes in Przewalski's horse) were identical but differed by 0.05–0.5% estimated nucleotide sequence divergence from four different *E. caballus* mtDNA haplotypes. Although the extent of the observed mtDNA differences between *E. caballus* and *E. przewalskii* would appear to support a relatively more ancient genetic divergence of the two taxa than could be reconciled with a direct progenitor role for Przewalski's horse with domestic horse breeds, additional considerations and investigations are required before conclusions can be drawn.

It would be desirable to undertake a more thorough investigation of the mtDNA differences between *E. przewalskii* and *E. caballus*, including analysis of all the surviving mtDNA maternal clones derived from the studbook population in comparison with mtDNA clones from diverse breeds of domestic horses. Technological improvements make it possible now to collect a larger amount of data from individual mtDNA clones through DNA sequence analysis, allowing a more robust quantification of genetic divergences. Furthermore, the application of primer-directed DNA amplification of equid mtDNA sequences (utilizing PCR, the polymerase chain reaction technique) might allow the collection of mtDNA sequence data from preserved skin specimens. National history museums in the U.S.A., U.K. and the former U.S.S.R. have in their collections skins of Przewalski's horses derived from wild populations. These skins represent a significant addition to the resources for genetic investigations.

Nuclear DNA Markers

Nuclear DNA sequences have also been investigated in efforts to further understand the evolution of genome organization in horses. Highly repetitious tandemly repeated DNA sequences, often called satellite DNAs, have been suggested to play a role in chromosomal evolution and speciation (Singer 1982). Satellite DNA sequences have been purified from *E. przewalskii* and, through *in situ* hybridization to metaphase chromosomes, homologous chromosomal DNA sequences have been localized in *E. przewalskii* and *E. caballus* (Ryder and Hansen 1979, Ryder et al. 1984). Overall, the abundance and distribution of the satellite DNA sequences were similar in individuals of the two taxa differing by a Robertsonian fusion. That the rearrangement event was a fusion rather than a fission is clear, because domestic horses are recently derived. A notable difference in hybridization of the satellite DNA probe on chromosomes of the two taxa involved a site on the short arm telomere of chromosome 1 in *E. caballus* that was absent in *E. przewalskii*. This finding reinforces the generally accepted notion that tandemly repetitious highly reiterated DNA sequences display mobility in mammalian chromosomes (Dover et al. 1982).

Basic genetic maps of restriction cleavage sites in nuclear ribosomal gene units have been prepared from nine equid taxa (Tong and Ryder 1983). In this study, eight restriction endonucleases identified forty-one cleavage sites in the ribosomal gene repeat and flanking sequences. The transcribed regions of the ribosomal genes displayed few cleavage site differences; only one difference, the absence of a Sal I cleavage site in *E. zebra hartmannae*, was noted among the fifteen restriction cleavage sites mapped to the transcribed regions of the 18S and 28S ribosomal genes. The non-transcribed regions of the ribosomal gene repeats displayed considerably more variation. The 18S genes of *E. caballus* are contained in Bgl II fragments of 23 kilobases (kb), 18 kb, and 15 kb, while those of two different *E. przewalskii* individuals were contained in fragments of 18 kb and 15 kb (#1107 San Diego 37, Vargo) or in fragments of 17 kb and 15 kb (#686 San Diego 15, Hedar). Thus, a restriction site difference between *E. przewalskii* and *E. caballus* as well as polymorphism of a different restriction site in *E. przewalskii* are demonstrated. Both the polymorphism within the studbook population of *E. przewalskii* and the difference between the two horse taxa merit further investigation. The *E. przewalskii* site polymorphism could be examined for patterns of Mendelian inheritance and ancestral states inferred. Additional domestic horse individuals derived from a diversity of breeds could be examined to better assess the incidence of the site resulting in a 23 kb Sal I fragment containing the 18S gene. However, the possibility exists that the 23 kb Sal I fragment could represent a diagnostic marker for *E. caballus*.

THE PEDIGREE OF A SPECIES

Extinct in its natural habitat, the Przewalski's horse survives as a biological species due to captive breeding. In captivity, it is possible, even necessary, to identify animals as individuals and to record their vital data: name or other identification, sex, date of birth, identification of sire, identification of dam, and their dates of death. For Przewalski's horse, these data were first collected and published by Erna Mohr (1959, 1971). The International Studbook of the Przewalski's Horse was kept by the Prague Zoo with Jiri Volf as studbook keeper. Annual editions containing information on all living horses were published from 1962 until 1990 when Dr. Volf retired. Those concerned with the conservation of this species acknowledge a special debt to Dr. Jiri Volf and the Prague Zoo. In 1991, the International Studbook was published again by the Prague Zoo with Dr. Evzen Kus as studbook keeper.

The unique Przewalski's horse studbook records the pedigree of a species. From the twelve Przewalski's horse founders and the domestic Mongolian mare to the over one thousand living descendants in 1991, this record provides the basis for our understanding of gene survival in the studbook population as well as such demographic features as age-specific mortality and fertility.

With only thirteen founder animals, inbreeding is an inevitable consequence. However, as others have shown, the consequences of inbreeding in the studbook population of Przewalski's horses, while clearly present and quantifiable, now prognosticate only a small diminution in the current population growth rate (Ballou, chapter 6).

The more serious threat to the retention in the studbook population of heritable variation and the propensity for adaptation in response to the dynamics of selection is the loss of founder genes (see Figure 5.2). The thirteen founders of the studbook population represent a maximum of twenty-six unique gene sequences (called here unique genes or, simply, genes). In the early history of the studbook population, not all individuals reproduced; many of the fifty-four individuals removed from wild populations and brought into captivity at the turn of the century failed to reproduce. Some of the founders left only one offspring that itself reproduced and passed genes on to the next generation. These bottlenecks in the Przewalski's horse pedigree resulted in a sharp decline in the number of surviving founder genes. For example, the entire genetic stock of the Przewalski's horse herd at Woburn Abbey assembled and successfully propagated by the Duke of Bedford is represented in the studbook population only by the descendants of #182 London 6, Neville. Whatever were the details of the Woburn Abbey Przewalski's horse stud, only two alleles for each trait, at most, can survive from this remarkable group that experienced early breeding success. Excellent documentary photographs of the Przewal-

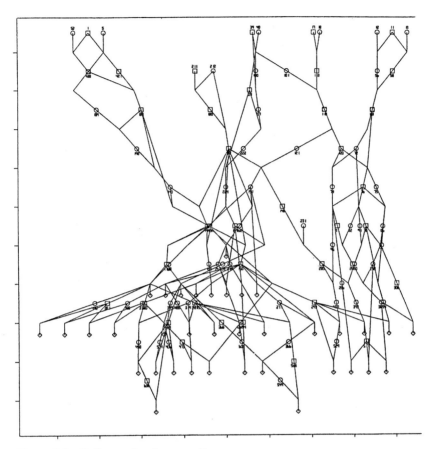

Figure 5.2.   Pedigree of early generations.

ski's horses at Woburn Abbey taken by the Duchess of Bedford depict groups of six or seven horses, including mares with foals at
their sides. But the genes of all except those passed on through
Neville were lost to future generations.

The earliest reproduction of Przewalski's horses in the United
States took place at Cincinnati and New York. These two founder
lines were crossed in the breeding at Philadelphia and Washington, so that the important stallion, #120 Washington 6, Horymir,
received 25% of his genes from each of the four founders, #17 Bijsk
7, #18 Bijsk 8, #39 Bijsk A and #40 Bijsk B. #120 Washington 6,
Horymir, played a formative role in the breeding of Przewalski's
horses in Europe in the 1930s. As the herd stallion in Prague, he
sired numerous important offspring and he brought to the breeding

effort in Prague the genetic input of four founders. However, four founders represent eight possible unique genes as any single individual carries at maximum two unique genes at a locus. Pedigrees which combine representation of more than two founders in a single individual can lead to intuitive overestimates of surviving gene diversity when gene diversity is estimated on founder representation alone.

The number of founder genes surviving in the complicated pedigree that describes the breeding of the studbook population has been estimated by simulation (MacCluer et al. 1986) and by calculation of exact joint probability distributions (Geyer and Thompson 1988, Geyer et al. 1989). The results of these investigations have had significant influence on breeding programs at the national and international level. For example, the results of the investigation into gene survival in population subgroups were decisive in the revision of the Asian Wild Horse Species Survival Plan for North America (Ryder et al. 1989). Similarly, as the studbook population has expanded and reintroduction programs are getting underway, the global management of the residual species' gene pool is recognized as a necessity and will involve calculations not previously undertaken of gene survival in certain population subgroups (Ryder 1991a, 1991b).

Of the twenty-six unique founder genes that represent the potential extent of the genetic diversity of the studbook population, the results of the joint probability calculations indicate that 10.48 genes survive in the studbook population (Geyer et al. 1989). Therefore, approximately 60% of the unique genes of the studbook population have been lost. This statistic emphasizes the genetic vulnerability over time of small populations that derive from small numbers of founders and experience slow rates of population increase.

Estimates based on founder representation or other methods that fail to consider explicitly gene survival deserve careful scrutiny. For example, Lacy has calculated that as much as 0.84 of gene diversity of the population (expected proportion of wild heterozygosity retained) is present in subgroups of the Przewalski's horse studbook population (Seal et al. 1990). Thus, loss of only 16% of wild heterozygosity can accompany a 60% loss of unique founder genes. Losses of founder genes are irretrievable. In any gene pool conservation program for small populations derived from a limited number of founders, prudent management indicates that founder gene loss should be minimized.

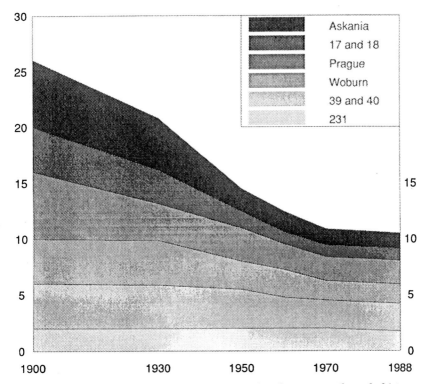

Figure 5.3. Number of surviving genes from founder groups through history. (From Geyer et al. 1989, reprinted with permission of A.R. Liss, Publishers.)

An analysis of the loss of genes from the studbook population over time is shown in Figure 5.3. The first dramatic gene losses were due to the deaths of founders that left one or a small number of offspring. As long as the studbook population remained small, the loss of genes continued at a rapid rate. The studbook population grew to only forty-six individuals in 1939, then declined and did not reach this number again until 1957. Relatively little gene loss has occurred since the 1970s due to the rapid growth of the population. The development of gene pool management programs will help to minimize future losses.

That not all genes in the studbook population are *Equus prze-walskii* genes is documented in the International Studbook itself. The dam of #56 Halle 1, is listed as a domestic Mongolian mare. This mare was one among the group that were utilized for nursing the newly-captured Przewalski's horse foals and transported with the foals to Europe (Mohr 1959, 1971). Numerous anecdotes address the possibility that genes of domestic Mongolian stock introgressed into the declining wild horse population. The excessive mane length of one founder mare (#18 Bijsk 8) has led to the suggestion that this animal is an F_1 hybrid with a domestic horse. The small likelihood that significant numbers of the founders were F_1 hybrids has been alluded to above.

It is possible to assess the number of surviving genes derived from the known domestic Mongolian mare as well as from #18 Bijsk 8 (assuming her hybrid status). 0.57 domestic horse genes survive in the studbook population from the domestic Mongolian mare. 0.27 additional domestic horse genes survive in the studbook population assuming that #18 Bijsk 8 was an F_1 hybrid (Geyer et al. 1989, Seal et al. 1990). Of the 10.48 surviving genes in the studbook population, 9.91 are from founders other than the domestic Mongolian mare; 9.64 surviving genes are non-domestic horse genes assuming that sources of domestic horse genes are the dam of #56 and one of the parents of #18.

Examination of the total number of surviving genes in comparison to the surviving number of non-domestic horse genes in population subgroups reveals that significant numbers of non-domestic horse genes that are not present in the approximately one-third of the studbook population that lack genetic input from the domestic Mongolian mare genes are present in the approximately two-thirds of the studbook population that include the domestic Mongolian mare in their ancestry (Geyer et al. 1989). In the subgroup of living horses in the studbook that do not trace ancestry to the domestic Mongolian mare, Thompson calculated that 7.30 genes survive (Seal et al. 1990). Thus, 2.34 non-domestic horse genes (9.64–7.30) are present only in the subgroup that has ancestry from the domestic Mongolian mare.

As is evident in Figure 5.2, the contributions of the domestic Mongolian mare are inherited with genes from #11 Bijsk 1 and #12 Bijsk 2. However, only 1.55 of the 2.34 non-domestic genes present in the studbook population subgroup tracing ancestry to the domestic Mongolian mare derive from #11 Bijsk 1 and #12 Bijsk 2. Thus, 0.79 (2.34–1.55) non-domestic horse genes (which amounts to 8% of the surviving gene pool resources) are wild horse genes that do not derive from #11 Bijsk 1 and #12 Bijsk 2. The 2.34 non-domestic horse genes that survive in the studbook population subgroup that include the domestic Mongolian mare in their pedigrees account for 22% of all surviving genes.

MANAGING FOR GENE SURVIVAL

Analyses of the data contained in the International Studbook and consideration of the data on gene survival in the whole studbook population and in population subgroups have led to the adoption of a breeding strategy that preserves options for the future.

By 1991, the world population had grown to nearly 1000 animals. Significant advances have been made in the scientific knowledge of the species and the management of its gene pool. Specific projects to re-establish the species within its former range have begun in Xinjiang-Uygur Autonomous Region of the People's Republic of China, in Gansu Province, People's Republic of China, in the Mongolian People's Republic and in the former Soviet Union.

At the 5th International Symposium on the Preservation of the Przewalski's Horse, held in Leipzig, Germany, May 1990, a mechanism was agreed upon whereby the captive breeding community offered its experience and animal resources in order to promote well-designed programs for reintroduction. A Global Management Plan Working Group (GMPWG) was formulated and a steering committee created to organize and administer the Group's activities in coordinating efforts to link the global management of the captive population with efforts to re-establish the species within its historic range.

Among the stated objectives of the GMPWG is the organization and implementation of a captive management program to provide animals as needed for the acclimatization and reintroduction programs while ensuring that the genetic variation and demographic security of the captive population is not compromised. The rudiments of such a program are outlined in the Draft Global Conservation Plan that was prepared by the participants at a technical meeting prior to the 5th International Symposium on the Preservation of the Przewalski's Horse (Seal et al. 1990).

A paramount principle of the Global Conservation Program will be to preserve future options. This requires that the implementation of the plan does not further reduce the number of surviving genes. In this regard, calculations of gene survival in population subgroups initiated by Geyer and Thompson (1988, Geyer et al. 1989) will be continued. Genetically important individuals (those with relatively high proportions of unique genes, i.e., genes not available in other living individuals) will be identified within the relevant population subgroups and their reproductive contributions closely managed. Cohorts of young animals with genetic and demographic characteristics appropriate for reintroduction stock will be removed from the captive population (providing they do not include genetically important individuals) for participation in the reintroduction program.

Increasing cooperation among institutions breeding Przewalski's horses now ensures that gene pool preservation goals will shape the design of captive breeding programs in the future (Ryder and Wedemeyer 1982, Ryder et al. 1989, Ryder 1991a). Regional cooperative management programs are in place in North America (through the Species Survival Plans of the American Association of Zoological Parks and Aquariums), Europe including Great Britain and Askania Nova (through the Europäisches Erhaltungszucht Program), and in the former Soviet Union (through the All-Union Federation of Zoological Parks). These organizations, combined as they are under the aegis of the GMPWG, represent the total surviving gene diversity of the species. No single collection of horses or other group of collections encompasses a similar extent of the species' genetic diversity. All regional efforts are coordinated by the International Studbook keeper of the Przewalski's horse (Prague Zoo, Czechoslovakia).

A great opportunity exists to move forward with plans to implement a world-wide plan for management of the species' gene pool and to participate in the re-establishment of breeding groups of the species within its historic range resulting in free-ranging populations of the species.

ACKNOWLEDGMENTS

Financial support from the Caesar Kleberg Wildlife Foundation, the Zoological Society of San Diego and the John and Beverly Stauffer Foundation is gratefully acknowledged.

6

Population Biology

Jonathan D. Ballou

INTRODUCTION

The captive population of Przewalski's horse is one of the most intensely managed exotic species in captivity (Bouman 1977, Bouman et al. 1982). Bouman et al. (1982 and this volume) present a detailed history of the population. Although the studbook was first published in 1959, individual life-history data as well as data on ancestry and relationships of individuals in the population has been maintained since the original founders entered the population in the late nineteenth century. This truly unique data set reflects the intent of those involved in the management of the Przewalski's horse population to focus not only on individuals but also on the population as a whole. The studbook has proven to be a model for other species and will continue to provide the basis for developing population management decisions for the population. The past and present studbook keepers should be well acknowledged for the detail and care taken in maintaining and publishing this critical database (Mohr 1971, Volf this volume).

The primary objective of the management of the captive population of Przewalski's horse is to maintain a captive population of sufficient size and genetic character to protect the species from extinction. Specifically, consideration must be given to the demographic stability and retention of genetic variation. Management programs to accomplish this goal necessitate careful analyses of the past, current and future demographic and genetic trends of the population. This chapter describes the current genetic and demographic status of the captive population as of 1989 and presents the results of an up-to-date analysis of the effects of inbreeding on early survival in the Przewalski's horse. Population management of the Przewalski's horse is complicated by the introgression of domestic horse genes in 1906 by a domestic mare. The proposed global management plan and the North American Species Survival Plan (Seal et al. 1990) call for management of two sub-populations—the Prague line consisting of descendants of the domestic mare, and the Munich line consisting of animals without genes from the domestic mare—with gene flow from the Munich animals to the Prague line, but not visa-versa. Geyer and Thompson (1988) and Geyer et al. (1989) discuss the genetic differences between these lineages in the North American population. This chapter extends this analysis to the world population and presents the results of an analysis of outbreeding depression that examines the pedigree for detrimental effects of the domestic mare's genes on early survival. The implications of these results for the management of the population are discussed.

DATA SOURCE

Data were derived from the 1989 International Studbook for Przewalski's horses (Volf 1989, Volf this volume). They were computerized and generously provided by Lydia Kolter. This data set consisted of animals born into the population through December 31, 1988.

DEMOGRAPHIC ANALYSES

Population Size and Distribution

The 1989 Studbook lists 878 living animals (360 males, 518 females) distributed in 133 institutions across six continents. The average collection size is seven animals; five institutions held more than twenty individuals. The largest collection is at Askania Nova with eighty-nine animals. Twenty-five percent of the collections consisted of single sex, non-breeding groups. The Prague line consists of 649 animals, the Munich line has 229 animals. The age structure of the total population appears relatively stable although

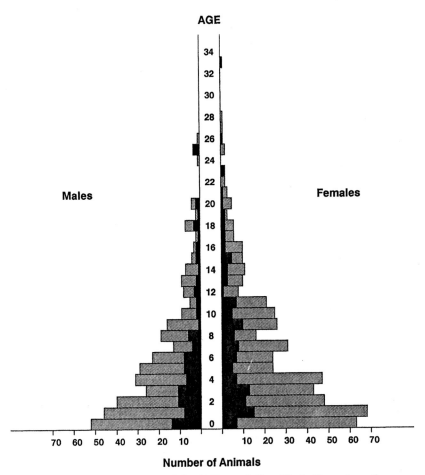

Figure 6.1. The age structure of the 1989 population. Shaded bars show the number of Munich line animals; hatched bars are Prague animals.

the structure of the Munich line is deficient in young animals (Figure 6.1).

Figure 6.2a shows the growth of the captive population between 1910 and 1989. The population remained fairly constant in size until the early 1960s, when the population began to experience significant exponential growth. Figure 6.2b illustrates the annual percent change in population size over the same time period. The period of positive population growth since the 1960s can be clearly seen, as can the population decimation during World War II. As

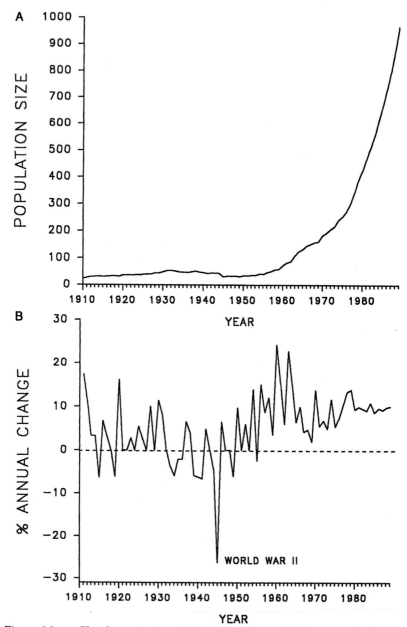

Figure 6.2. a. The change in size of the captive Przewalski's horse population from 1910 to 1989. b. The annual percent change in population size of the captive Przewalski's horse population. The dip in 1945 reflects the population decimation during World War II.

the population grew, the annual population increase became more predictable. By the 1980s, the population experienced a fairly consistent growth rate of about nine percent per year (Figure 6.2b). Bouman (1982) divides the population into three periods: Period I = 1900 to 1945, Period II = 1945 to 1960, and Period III from 1960 to the present. Although these periods are primarily defined on the basis of crosses between genetic lineages, they are also reflected in Figure 6.2 a and b as different stages in the demographic development of the population.

Life-Table Statistics

Demographic analyses were conducted using the PEDDEMO software (Bingaman and Ballou 1986) for analysis of standardized studbook data sets. This software calculates life-tables and provides estimates of generation lengths and population growth rates from the life-table statistics.

Table 6.1 shows summary life-table statistics for different periods in the population's history. The rate of increase calculated from fecundity and survival rates shows a gradual increase over time while the generation length has remained fairly constant. Improvement in population growth rates over time are expected as husbandry and veterinary techniques improve. The rate of increase for the period 1945 to 1989 compare closely to those calculated by Bouman (1982) although the generation lengths presented here are significantly shorter than Bouman's (which ranged from eleven to fourteen years). This is probably because the formula used here corrected for the population growth rate while Bouman did not (Table 6.1). The values for the 1980–1989 period should most accurately reflect current population trends.

Males consistently show lower survival rates than females (Figure 6.3). This difference largely occurs during the first five years of life but small levels of differential mortality occur until the seventeenth year. After this point, females start to suffer higher mortality rates than males, as shown by the converging survivorship curves. Estimates of survival during the older age classes are subject to high rates of error due to small sample sizes.

There were no significant differences in survival rates over different time periods (Mantel-Haenszel chi-square test, Lee 1980). The lack of significant differences since 1945 indicate that differences in generation length and rate of population increase were due to changes in fertility patterns. The Reproductive Value (V_x) represents a convenient way to illustrate the combined effects of

Table 6.1

Life-table summary statistics for various periods during the Przewalski's horse captive history.

Period	Life-Table Rate of Increase[a]		Generation Length (Years)[b]	
	Male	Female	Male	Female
1945–1960	0.081	0.067	9.8	8.2
1960–1980	0.099	0.090	10.2	8.7
1980–1989	0.109	0.092	9.8	8.6
1945–1989	0.102	0.090	9.8	8.7
Prague line (1960–1989)	0.115	0.103	9.7	8.4
Munich line (1960–1989)	0.085	0.065	11.1	9.3

[a]Rate of Increase (r) is the exponential growth rate of the population assuming the survival and fecundity rates remain constant over time. r was calculated by solving for r in the Euler equation (Caughley 1977):

$$\Sigma e^{-rx} l_x m_x = 1.0$$

[b]Generation length (T) is the average length of time between the birth of an individual and its offspring. It is calculated as:

$$T = \frac{\Sigma x e^{-rx} l_x m_x}{\Sigma e^{-rx} l_x m_x}$$

where l_x and m_x are the age-specific survival and fecundity rates and r is the rate of increase (Caughley 1977).

survival and fecundity rates as a function of age (Fisher 1930). Figure 6.4a and b illustrate the reproductive values for females and males during different time periods in the history of the captive Przewalski's horse population. Female reproductive values have shifted slightly during the three time periods. Current trends (period 1980–1989) show that peak female reproductive contribution occurs during ages five to seven. Males show a clear lengthening in reproductive life-span (the spike at age class thirty-one reflects the reproductive activity of only one male but does show that reproduction is possible at this age). The peak for male reproductive contributions currently occurs at ages 9 to 10 but continues to remain substantial until the mid-20s. The longer generation lengths and higher rates of increase of males (Table 6.1) is due to

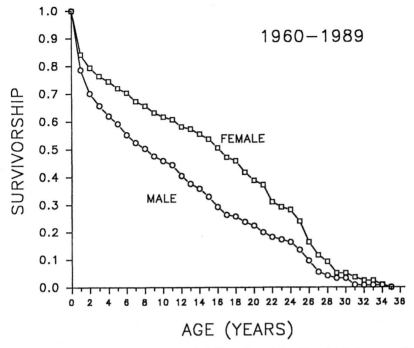

Figure 6.3. Survivorship curves (probability of surviving from birth to a specific age) of male and female Przewalski's horses between 1960 and 1989. Sample sizes used to estimate survivorship (number of animals at risk during each age class) ranged from over 770 in the early age classes to fewer than thirty in age classes beyond the twenty-second year.

the males' higher reproductive values over older age classes than females (Figure 6.4b).

As has been observed by Bouman (1982), there are also significant demographic differences between the Prague and Munich lineages. Figure 6.5a and 6.5b show reproductive values for females and males in both the Prague and Munich lines. The differences between these lines in females is due entirely to fecundity differences. Differences in male values reflect both survival and fecundity differences. Male survivorship differences were only substantial during the second year: second year mortality for Munich males is 2.9% while for Prague males it is 13.9%. Otherwise, all differences in reproductive values of males are due to fecundity. Bouman (1982) also indicates that the primary demographic difference between the Prague and Munich lines is due to fertility. The

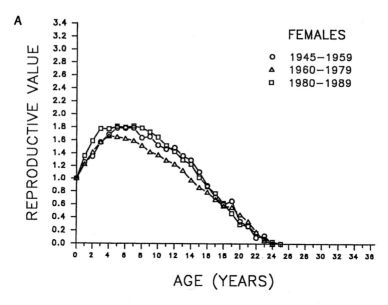

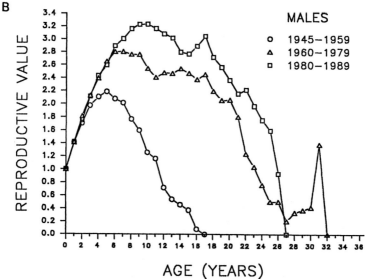

Figure 6.4. Reproductive value (V_x) for females (a) and males (b) calculated for three different time periods during the history of the captive Przewalski's horse population. Reproductive value (V_x) is calculated as:

$$V_x = \frac{\sum\limits_{x}^{n} e^{-rx} l_x m_x}{e^{-rx} l_x}$$

where n is the maximum age class (Fisher 1930), l_x is survivorship and m_x is fecundity for age x.

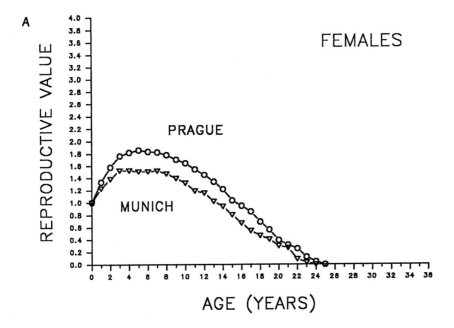

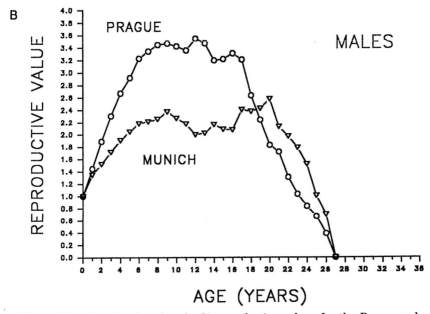

Figure 6.5. Female (a) and male (b) reproductive values for the Prague and Munich lines. See Figure 6.4 for a definition of reproductive value.

higher reproductive values in the Prague line for both males and females of most ages results in the higher rates of population increase for the Prague lineage (Table 6.1).

POPULATION GENETICS

Founder Contribution and Founder Gene Extinction

Genetic management of captive populations usually strives to maximize levels of genetic diversity (Foose 1983). This has continued to be the policy for the genetic management of the Przewalski's horse population (Seal et al. 1990). A decision to manage separate Prague and Munich lineages necessitates a clear understanding of the consequences and benefits of sub-dividing an already small population since one of the clear costs to such subdivision is increased loss of genetic diversity within sub-populations (Lacy 1987). Differences in the genetic composition of the two lineages beyond the contribution of the domestic mare are an important consideration in the genetic management of these sub-populations.

As in many captive populations, disproportionate breeding among founders and their close descendants early in the population's history has resulted in a highly skewed contribution of the founders to the current gene pool. The founder contribution (the proportion of the gene pool descended from each founder) for each founder in the Prague and Munich lineages is shown in Figure 6.6 (Current Founder Contribution).

Founder contribution is more heavily skewed in the Munich line than the Prague lineage. Additionally, and more importantly, founders #11 and #12 are absent from the Munich lineage. As mentioned by Geyer and Thompson (1988), founders #11 and #12 are "linked" to the domestic genes (see Bouman 1982 and Bouman and Bouman, this volume for a discussion of the history relating to these events). Separation of the Prague line from the Munich line forever will result in the exclusion of genes from founders #11 and #12 from the Munich population. Other genetic differences between the lineages relate to the number of original founder alleles surviving in the extant populations. Alleles from the founders can be lost due to pedigree "bottlenecks", which occur when a founder's genome is passed on to a small number of offspring (i.e., a founder pair producing only one offspring will result in the loss of 50% of those founders' genomes). Such bottlenecks throughout a pedigree

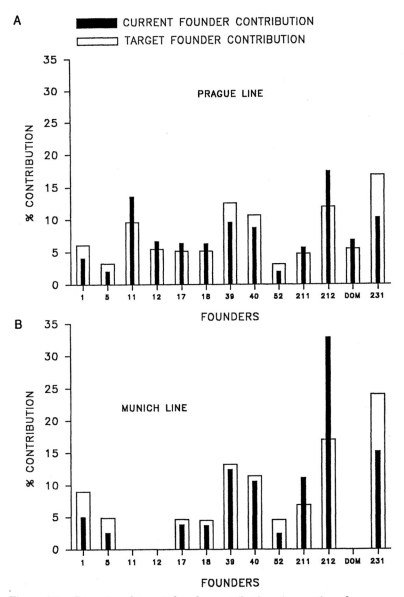

Figure 6.6. Current and target founder contributions (proportion of gene pool descended from each founder) in the Prague (a) and Munich (b) populations. Target founder contribution for a specified founder is calculated as the proportion of the total alleles surviving in the population contributed by that founder.

result in only a proportion of a founders' genes "surviving" to the extant population.

Gene survival for each founder in the total population, and Prague and Munich sub-populations is shown in Table 6.2. In addition to the absence of alleles from founders #11, #12 and the domestic mare, the Munich line also has substantially fewer alleles from founders #17, #18, #39 and #40. The mean number of alleles surviving in these populations, assuming each founder provided two unique alleles at each locus, is 10.37 for the Prague line vs. 7.45 for the Munich line (Table 6.2). The combined effects of skewed founder contribution and gene extinction can be summarized as the Founder Genome Equivalent, which is the number of new founders that would be required to start a new population with levels of genetic diversity currently retained in the existing populations (Lacy 1989). The loss of genetic diversity in the current populations has reduced the genetic effectiveness from the original 13 founders to the current levels of 3.13 and 2.17 founder equivalents for the Prague and Munich lines, respectively. Table 6.2 also shows the levels of gene diversity already lost. These results show that substantial levels of genetic variation have already been lost in these populations. Genetic management should be continued to minimize the future loss of the remaining genetic diversity.

Geyer and Thompson (1988) and Geyer et al. (1989) undertook a number of sophisticated pedigree analyses of the North American Przewalski's horse population that examined the consequences of a management plan to purge selectively the domestic mare's genes from the Prague lineage. Although they only examined the North American population, they found that because of the complete "linkage" between the domestic mare's alleles and the alleles from founders #11 and #12, as well as the differences in allele distribution from founders #17, #18, #39 and #40, any management program that selects against the domestic alleles would also remove substantial levels of genetic variation (30%) from the North American population. Applying the same approach to the world population, the Prague line (without the domestic mare genes) has 31% more founder alleles than the Munich line. As was found in the North American population, selection against Prague animals will significantly reduce the level of genetic variation. These results, and those of Geyer et al. (1989), confirm the need to maintain the Prague lineage despite the presence of domestic mare genes.

Table 6.2

Mean number of founder alleles surviving in the total population, and the Prague and Munich sub-populations. Calculations are based on the Monte Carlo "gene drop" model (MacCluer et al. 1986) using the GENES software (Lacy 1988). These results are the averages of 10,000 Monte Carlo simulations.

FOUNDER	TOTAL	Prague	Munich
1	0.66	0.63	0.66
5	0.35	0.34	0.35
11	0.99	0.99	0
12	0.56	0.56	0
17	0.55	0.53	0.34
18	0.54	0.53	0.49
39	1.32	1.30	0.96
40	1.13	1.10	0.83
52	0.33	0.33	0.33
211	0.49	0.49	0.49
212	1.25	1.24	1.24
231	1.75	1.75	1.75
Domestic Mare	0.57	0.57	0
SUMMARY:			
Number of Founders	13	13	10
Mean No. Alleles Surviving	10.49	10.37	7.45
Founder Genome Equivalents	3.31	3.13	2.17
Gene Diversity Lost	0.17	0.16	0.23
Average Inbreeding	.21	0.18	0.29

Management of Genetic Diversity

The heavy skew in founder contribution reduces the effective population size and consequently reduces retention of genetic diversity. The loss of original founder alleles from genetic drift discussed above causes additional loss of genetic diversity.

Management of genetic diversity can be thought of as the continual process of attempting to rectify the legacies of disproportionate founder contribution and loss of alleles from pedigree "bottlenecks" by selectively breeding individuals that compensate for these discrepancies. Target founder contributions provide a general guideline for selecting these individuals (Ballou and Foose in press). One genetic management strategy might be to select breeding animals to equalize founder contributions. However, this approach ignores the differential rate of gene extinction among founders. Equalizing founder contribution will result in over-representation of founders that have already lost large proportions of their alleles and under-representation of founder whose genomes are still intact. A more appropriate strategy is to manage each founder's genome in proportion to the percent of its genome that has survived to the extant population. This "Target Founder Contribution" for the Prague and Munich lineages is shown in Figure 6.6a and 6.6b. The contribution of each individual towards shifting the current founder contribution towards the target founder contribution provides a basis for selecting priority breeders in the population.

The measure of gene diversity loss (Table 6.2) suggests another approach to mate selection strategies and identifying genetically important animals. Gene diversity lost is the average relationship (as measured by the kinship coefficient) among the living individuals in the population. It can also be defined as the expected inbreeding coefficient of an offspring produced by mating two randomly selected animals from the current population. Measures of gene diversity therefore provide two useful tools for genetic management.

The first application applies to identifying genetically important animals. Since minimizing gene diversity loss (Table 6.2) maximizes the retention of genetic diversity, optimal management of genetic diversity can be accomplished by placing breeding priority on those animals who are the least related to the rest of the animals in the population. For each individual, it is possible to calculate the average relationship between that individual and all animals in the population (including itself). Ranking animals according to this Mean Kinship value provides an efficient way to identify genetically important individuals (Ballou and Foose in press). The software GENES (Lacy 1988) provides algorithms for calculating mean kinship values from studbook pedigrees. Mean kinship should be considered when establishing future pairings of Przewalski's horses.

The second applies to managing inbreeding levels. Mate selection strategies, in addition to attempting to maintain genetic diversity in the population as a whole, should avoid pairing animals with "high" levels of inbreeding. The inherent problem with this guideline is that "high" is a relative term: in some populations an inbreeding coefficient of .01 may be considered high while in others (like the Przewalski's horse) .01 is unrealistically low. Even within a population "high" becomes a relative term since inbreeding levels increase over time. Therefore, recommendations to avoid "high" levels of inbreeding provide no frame of reference. Gene diversity provides such a reference. As the expected level of inbreeding in the next generation (assuming random mating), gene diversity defines the scale for realistic levels of inbreeding among newly selected pairings. A general rule-of-thumb suggests that the relationship between new mates (as measured by coefficient of kinship) should be comparable or less than (but no higher than) the gene diversity of the current population (Ballou and Foose in press). In the Przewalski's horse population, current levels of inbreeding are approximately 25% (Table 6.2). Gene diversity lost indicates that new pairings should be between animals whose relationships are at or below about 23%. This suggests that inbreeding can still be reduced in the population through careful mate selection strategies.

INBREEDING DEPRESSION

Inbreeding and Early Survival

Inbreeding depression is the detrimental genetic effects of breeding animals too closely related to each other. Inbreeding has been associated with reduced survival and reproduction in numerous laboratory and domestic as well as exotic species (Ralls and Ballou 1983). Previous studies by Bouman and Bos (1979) and Bouman (1982) indicate that inbreeding is associated with reduced early survival and shorter life-span in the Przewalski's horse population. We update those reports with an analysis of the current levels of inbreeding depression in the population. The methods of Morton et al. (1956) and Templeton and Read (1984) were used to calculate the severity of inbreeding depression by regressing the log of survival against the inbreeding coefficient,

$$\text{in (Survival)} = -(A + Bf)$$

or, equivalently,

$$\text{Survival} = e^{-(A + Bf)}$$

where f is the inbreeding coefficient and A and B the least squares estimates of the intercept and slope, respectively. Inbreeding coefficients were calculated using the additive relationship method (Ballou 1983). Survival rates for each level of inbreeding were calculated as the percent of animals surviving to thirty days with a correction for small sample sizes (Templeton and Read 1984). The severity of inbreeding depression is reflected in the magnitude of parameter B.

Figure 6.7 shows the plot of survival against inbreeding coefficients with the resulting fitted equation. There were 258 different levels of inbreeding in the pedigree and the log slope of −.295 is significant at the .001 level. On a linear scale, this slope corresponds to an approximate 2% to 3% decrease in survival for each 10% increase in inbreeding. Although statistically significant, this severity of inbreeding depression is substantially less than that found for many other mammalian species. Ralls et al. (1988) found an average slope of −2.33 in their survey of 40 captive mammal populations. Inbreeding depression only becomes a significant mortality factor in extremely inbred (f > .4) Przewalski's horses. These results confirm those of Bouman (1982).

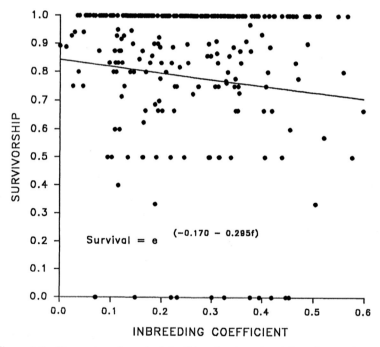

Figure 6.7.   Regression of survival (to thirty days) against inbreeding coefficient in captive Przewalski's horses.

Species vary in their susceptibility to inbreeding depression for many reasons. Species which inbreed naturally would be expected to show very little, if any, inbreeding depression when inbred in captivity. Although this may be the reason for the low susceptibility in the Przewalski's horse, Buisman and van Weeren (1982) believe, on the basis of the mating systems of other equids, that Przewalski's horse did not have a system of close inbreeding in the wild. Naturally outbreeding species would be expected to show higher levels of depression when inbred. However, outbreeding species would be expected to vary in their susceptibility to inbreeding due to the stochastic sampling of founders: by chance alone the founders of a captive population may be individuals who are free of the deleterious alleles causing inbreeding depression. This may be the case with the Przewalski's horse.

Founder Specific Inbreeding Effects

The inbreeding coefficient calculates the probability of an individual receiving a pair of alleles that are identical by descent from a common ancestor. It is also possible to calculate the probability that an individual receives alleles that are identical by descent from a particular founder. These "founder inbreeding coefficients" (f_i) can then be used to identify which founder(s) is(are) responsible for the observed inbreeding depression. Founder inbreeding coefficients were calculated for each of the 13 founders and used in a multiple logistic regression using "1" or "0" for whether the descendant survived or did not survive to thirty days, respectively, as the dependent variable and the founder inbreeding coefficients as the multiple independent variables. Multiple logistic regression allows regression analyses to be performed on the 0/1 dichotomous survival variable (Harrell 1985). The results of the multiple logistic regression are shown in Table 6.3.

The effects of founders #1, #5, #18 and #52 had to be removed from the model because the degree of inbreeding from these founders was insufficient for statistical analysis. The only founder that shows a significant inbreeding depression effect is #211 Woburn 6. Inbreeding through any other founder does not appear to reduce survival. Inbreeding through founder #212 Woburn 7 appears to be positively correlated with survival. These results indicate that the inbreeding depression observed in the population is due primarily to inbreeding of founder #211's genes and suggests that, if desirable, inbreeding depression can be mitigated by avoid-

Table 6.3

Results of the multiple logistic regression[a] of survival (to 30 days) on founder inbreeding coefficients in Przewalski's horses. The regression was performed using the SAS LOGIST procedure (Harrell 1985).

FOUNDER	Effect	SE	p[b]
231	3.94	2.36	0.086
17	0.57	11.05	0.999
11	3.07	10.15	0.764
12	−54.41	161.89	0.146
39	−3.38	5.18	0.549
40	11.90	10.11	0.258
211	−132.59	45.75	0.003*
212	34.25	12.97	0.005*
Domestic Mare	36.23	162.27	0.566

[a]Logistic Model:

$$\text{Probability of Survival} = \frac{1}{1 + \exp[-(A + \Sigma BfP_i)]}$$

Where A is the intercept value, the B are the effects associated with each founder inbreeding coefficient and the summation is across all founders. Negative founder inbreeding effects indicate reduced survival with increased inbreeding (Lee 1980).

[b]Significance calculated from log likelihood for logistic model with all effects included compared to log likelihood with founder inbreeding effect removed from the model.

*Effect is significant at the .01 level.

ing pairings of animals that share a high proportion of genes from founder #211. However, selection against animals who carry genes from #211 is not recommended. To do so would be to only further reduce the levels of genetic variation in the population.

OUTBREEDING DEPRESSION

Outbreeding depression is the potential detrimental effects of breeding conspecifics too distantly related to each other (Templeton and Read 1984, Templeton et al. 1986). Shields (1982) suggests that outbreeding depression can occur in zoo populations when founders are acquired from geographically different sources. These founders may be adapted to their local environments and crosses between founders and their descendants may result in genetic problems in the offspring. One genetic basis for outbreeding depression is the disruption of coadapted gene complexes (a set of genes that require the presence of all genes in the set to function properly). Recombination among chromosomes from founders from different sources can disrupt existing coadapted gene complexes resulting in fitness depression. This occurs in the F_2 and later generations and can be confused with inbreeding depression, which also begins in the F_2 generation (Templeton and Read 1984).

The degree of outbreeding in a pedigree can be calculated using the hybridity coefficient, a measure of the "proportion of an individual's genome that was subjected to genetic recombination between founding ancestors during the formation of the gametes that fused to form the individual" (Templeton and Read 1984:185). The source of the founders needs to be specified when calculating hybridity coefficients. Founders should be grouped according to their source in order to reflect accurately hybridization events that could disrupt potential coadapted gene complexes.

The possibility of outbreeding depression resulting from disrupting coadapted gene complexes has not previously been examined in the Przewalski's horse population. In this species, the potential for outbreeding depression results from several sources. The genes brought into the population by the domestic mare are the most likely source. Hybridization between the domestic mare's genes and known Przewalski's horse genes could result in disruption of gene complexes present in both the domestic genome and the Przewalski's horse genome. A second consideration is founder #18 Bijsk 8, who is suspected of carrying domestic horse genes on the basis of her phenotype (Dolan 1982). Geyer et al. (1989) assume that she was an F1 domestic/Przewalski's horse hybrid for the purposes of their analyses. A third possibility is founder #231 Orlitza III. Although this animal is assumed to be a pure Przewalski's horse, she entered the population much later than the other founders (1957). Coadapted gene complexes are more likely to arise in highly inbred populations. The captive population was already fairly inbred by the time #231 entered and there could be coadapted gene complex differences between the captive population and #231.

To examine the pedigree for possible outbreeding depression, hybridity coefficients were calculated for all individuals in the population for each of the three scenarios described above. It was assumed, in turn, that each of the three founders was the only

Table 6.4

Results of simple logistic regression of survival (to thirty days) on hybridity coefficients (Templeton and Read 1984) assuming the domestic mare, founder #18 (as a suspected F1 domestic/Przewalski's horse hybrid), and #231 were sources of potential outbreeding depression. The regression was performed using the SAS LOGIST procedure (Harrell 1985). See Table 6.3 for a description of the logistic regression method.

OUTBREEDING DEPRESSION SOURCE	Model Parameters			
	Intercept (A)	Effect (B)	SE	p
231	1.16	1.49	0.59	0.009*
18	1.39	1.08	0.87	0.189
Domestic Mare	1.49	0.81	0.79	0.289

*Significant at the .01 level.

founder carrying a different set of coadapted gene complexes into the population. Founder #18 was assumed to be an F1 hybrid. Simple logistic regression was used to regress the hybridity coefficient calculated from each scenario against thirty day survival. The results are shown in Table 6.4.

As none of the outbreeding effects were negative, it does not appear that there has been any outbreeding depression caused by either the domestic mare, founder #18 or #231. However, there was a significant *positive* effect of hybridity from founder #231 on survival. This result reflects the beneficial effects of a new founder being brought into an inbred population.

CONCLUSIONS

Management of the Przewalski's horse population in captivity necessitates continuous and careful analyses of the genetic and demographic status of the population. This chapter presents a brief summary of the population biology of the 1989 population. The population has the capacity to continue to grow rapidly (9%/year). However, the age distribution of the Munich line shows low numbers of young, suggesting a possible decrease in the future growth rate of this sub-population. Management intervention will eventually be required to control the overall population growth. The size of such a controlled population will depend on the capacity of the world zoos to continue to house the population and the status of the reintroduction program, which will either utilize surplus animals or necessitate additional production for the supply of animals to be released (Seal et al. 1990). Demographic analyses can be easily used to estimate the reproductive and survival rates necessary to maintain a captive population at levels deemed necessary for population survival.

Genetic management should continue to focus on the maintenance of genetic diversity as the primary objective. Although electrophoretic analyses indicate the presence of typical levels of heterozygosity (compared to domestic horses; Bowling and Ryder 1987), pedigree analyses indicate that levels of allelic diversity are likely to be low and show significant differences between the Prague and Munich lines (Geyer et al. 1989). Mate selection strategies based on such techniques as target founder contribution and mean kinship can continue to be used to maintain maximum levels of genetic diversity. Inbreeding depression is present at low levels and is a serious consideration only for highly inbred animals. This could become a population-wide concern as the population inevitably becomes increasingly inbred. The inbreeding depression that is present appears to be due primarily to inbreeding of founder #211's genes. Outbreeding depression in survival due to disrupting coadapted gene complexes is not a concern although its effects on reproduction could not be examined using the available studbook data.

Additional data on breeding opportunities vs. breeding successes are needed to examine the important effects of both inbreeding and outbreeding on reproductive components of fitness. Such records should be routinely maintained by the institutions holding the animals and regularly compiled by the studbook keeper for such analyses.

ACKNOWLEDGMENTS

The author thanks the studbook keeper for maintaining the Przewalski's Horse Studbook, as well as those institutions that regularly provide the studbook keeper with annual updates on the status of their collections. The computerized data were provided by Lydia Kolter. The author also thanks the editors for their heroic patience and the reviewers for many useful clarifying comments. Kathy Cooper assisted in preparing the manuscript.

7

Nutrition and Feeding

Harold F. Hintz

DIGESTIVE PHYSIOLOGY

All equids are non-ruminant herbivores. They can utilize feeds containing high levels of fiber because bacteria in the cecum and colon (Figure 7.1) have enzymes that can break down dietary fiber such as hemicellulose and cellulose. The end-products of fiber digestion are primarily short chain volatile fatty acids (acetate, propionate and butyrate) which can be absorbed from the large intestine and utilized for energy. Because the site of fermentation is beyond the small intestine, which is the primary site of digestion and absorption of many nutrients, other products of fermentation such as bacterial protein and water soluble vitamins are not efficiently utilized and therefore amino acids and vitamins are needed in the diet.

Equids do not utilize fibrous feeds as efficiently as do ruminants. For example, Udén and Van Soest (1982) reported that heifers digested 52% of the neutral detergent fiber of timothy hay whereas horses digested only 33%. Sheep digested the fiber of grass hay 30% more efficiently than horses (Martin-Rosset and Dulphy 1987). The reason for lower fiber digestibility by equids is probably because digesta moves more rapidly through their intestinal tract. Thus the bacteria have less time to digest the fiber in horses than in ruminants. Udén et al. (1982) reported that the mean retention time of solids in the digestive tract of horses fed timothy hay was twenty-three hours compared to sixty-five hours for heifers. But a

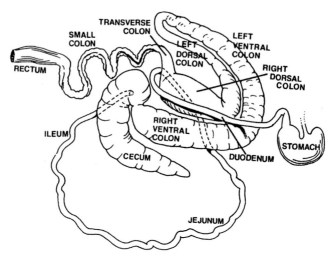

Figure 7.1. The digestive tract of the equid.

faster rate of digesta passage does have some advantages. When feeds containing a high fiber content are consumed by ruminants, the long-term retention results in a full rumen and thus limits intake, whereas the equid utilizes the digestible fraction and more quickly passes the less digestible fraction therefore intake is less limited. Janis (1976) concluded that zebras, wild asses, onagers, feral horses and Przewalski's horses could live in areas with sparse, low quality vegetation that could not support ruminants because their daily intake of digestible fractions could be greater than ruminants.

Digestion coefficients for feeds obtained with domestic horses can probably be reasonably applied to Przewalski's horses. Further studies comparing digestive efficiency among equids are needed but we found no differences in digestive efficiency between zebras and ponies fed timothy hay nor did we find differences in digestive efficiency between zebras and Przewalski's horses fed a complete pelleted diet (Hintz et al. 1976).

Maintenance of a viable bacterial population is an important aspect of equine nutrition. Two diseases that are of great concern to horse owners are colic and founder. Colic (abdominal pain) is considered to be the number one cause of mortality in domestic horses. Colic can be caused by parasite damage to the blood vessels and intestinal tract. Colic can also be caused by a rapid increase in fermentable feed. When this occurs, lactic acid is produced, which increases the acidity of the cecum and colon. With this increased acidity, lactic acid producing bacteria begin to predominate, gram-negative bacteria are killed, endotoxins are released and are absorbed and colic and/or founder can result (see chapter 9).

Changes in the bacterial population of the digestive tract can lead to colic caused by excessive accumulation of gas or decreased motility leading to intestinal impaction (impactive colic). Furthermore, the absorbed endotoxins may cause founder or laminitis (separation of the insensitive and sensitive laminae) in the hoof so that the hoof no longer adequately supports the horse's weight resulting in the bone being pushed downward toward the sole. Lameness can be so severe the horse may need to be humanely destroyed.

Management Practices to Maintain Normal Digestive Function

1. Have an effective parasite control program.
2. Clean palatable water should always be easily available. Inadequate water intake can decrease the moisture content of the intestinal contents leading to impactive colic.
3. Make changes in feed gradually. Rapid changes in feed such as switching from a coarse timothy hay to a leafy alfalfa hay, from hay to lush green pasture, or rapidly increasing the amount of grain can lead to founder and/or a more rapid rate of fermentation and increased gas production leading to gaseous colic. It is suggested that feed changes should take place gradually over four or five days.
4. The diet should provide adequate fiber. The fiber requirement is not established for domestic horses but it is often recommended that horses be fed at least 0.5 kg of roughage equivalent per 100 kg of body weight daily. This level of fiber should maintain normal digestive function and help prevent oral problems such as wood chewing and hair chewing. Although complete pelleted feeds contain fiber, the fiber content is usually not adequate to prevent oral behavior problems probably because the feed is finely ground. One zoo reported that when only complete pelleted feeds were fed to Przewalski's horses, hair chewing was so extensive the animals had to be separated. The addition of hay alleviated the problem. In the digestion trial with Przewalski's horses and zebras mentioned above in which the animals were fed only pellets, their feces contained 8 to 22% silica which indicated that the animals were ingesting significant amounts of sand and dirt. Analysis of random fecal samples taken when these same animals were each fed 4 kg of hay daily in addition to pellets indicated that their silica intake was decreased. Thus, feeding roughage such as hay in addition to a

pelleted feed is desirable not only to maintain bacterial population but also to prevent abnormal feeding behavior.

5. The diet should not contain excessive levels of fiber. Feeding large amounts of high-fiber, poor-quality feeds such as late-cut grass hay or cereal straw can increase the incidence of intestinal impaction because the material is so indigestible.

6. When feeding high amounts of grain, horses should be fed at least three times per day. A consistent supply of fermentable carbohydrate will prevent radical changes in the bacterial population.

7. Do not feed on sandy ground. Ingestion of sand can cause colic because of retention of sand, particularly in the right dorsal colon.

8. Do not feed above shoulder level. When the hay rack is too high, dust inhalation and respiratory problems increase.

9. Maintain dental health. In domestic horses, dental problems can lead to poorly chewed food and hence an increased incidence of impaction. Signs of dental problems include excessive slobbering and dropping of food from the mouth when chewing, loss of weight and larger than normal particle sizes in the feces.

10. Place feed in a large circle or several areas in a pen if it is necessary to feed horses in a group. This helps horses low in the group's dominance hierarchy to obtain their share of feed. It may be necessary to separate particularly aggressive or subordinate horses for feeding.

NUTRIENT REQUIREMENTS

Water

Clean, palatable water should always be easily available. Signs of water deprivation include decreased feed intake and "tucked up" appearance in the abdomen or flanks. Reduced water intake can also lead to intestinal impaction and colic. For example, the incidence of impactive colic may increase during periods of cold weather when voluntary intake of unheated water is decreased. The amount of water that must be supplied depends upon factors such as water content of the feed (pasture vs. hay), dry matter intake, function of the animal, i.e., lactating vs. maintenance, and environmental temperature and humidity. A general rule-of-thumb is two to three liters of water/kg of dry matter intake for non-lactating animals in a comfortable environment.

Unless the Przewalski's horse has developed methods to better conserve water than those found in the domestic horse, the estimated water needs for a 350 kg horse would be fifteen to eighteen liters daily. Water conservation could not be ruled out because the Przewalski's horses occupied arid environments and other desert equids, such as the donkey, are known to be more efficient utilizers of water than the domestic horse.

Energy

To estimate the horse's energy requirement for maintenance, the National Research Council (NRC) (1989) uses the equation DE (Mcal/day) = 1.4 + 0.03W, where DE is digestible energy and W is body weight in kg. Maintenance is defined as zero weight change plus energy for normal voluntary activity. Thus, a horse at maintenance weighing 350 kg would require 11.9 Mcal of DE daily (Table 7.1). Most hay provides 1.65 to 2.0 Mcal of DE per kg. Therefore, the 350 kg horse would require 6.0 to 7.2 kg of hay daily (11.9 ÷ 2.0 or 1.65). There is probably little difference in voluntary activity between a domestic horse and a Przewalski's horse at maintenance

Table 7.1

Estimates of the daily nutrient requirements of horses.[a]

Class	DE (Mcal)	Prot. (g)	Ca (g)	P (g)	Hay[b] (kg)	Grain[b] (kg)
		Mature Wt. 300 kg				
Maintenance	10.4	416	12	8	5.5	—
Gestation, late	12.5	550	24	18	5.0	1.0
Lactation, early	17.6	774	35	21	5.0	2.7
Lactation, late	15.1	664	22	13	5.0	1.9
		Mature Wt. 350 kg				
Maintenance	11.9	476	14	10	6.3	—
Gestation, late	14.3	629	27	21	5.5	1.3
Lactation, early	20.2	889	40	25	6.0	3.0
Lactation, late	17.4	766	21	16	6.0	2.0
		Mature Wt. 400 kg				
Maintenance	13.4	536	16	11	7.0	—
Gestation, late	16.1	708	31	23	6.3	1.4
Lactation, early	22.9	1141	45	29	6.5	3.5
Lactation, late	19.7	839	29	18	6.5	2.5

[a]Based on equations developed by NRC (1989) for domestic horses.

[b]Assuming 1.9 and 3.0 Mcal of DE for hay and grain (90% dry matter), respectively.

(Boyd et al. 1988). Another method to estimate the amount of hay needed is to use the thumb rule that horses at maintenance require 1.6 to 2.0 kg of hay per 100 kg of body weight (Hintz 1983). The use of this thumb rule would result in values of 5.6 to 7.0 kg of hay daily for a horse weighing 350 kg. In either case the amount of hay wasted must be considered. That is, the above values are for hay consumed, not hay fed. Unfortunately, the amount that is wasted, trampled upon and not eaten is often significant. Feeding hay in racks rather than from the ground will reduce wastage by trampling, but may lead to more aggression among the horses.

Although the above methods are useful in estimating the amount of feed needed, they are only guidelines. The body condition of the animals must be monitored in order to evaluate the energy adequacy of their diet. If the animals cannot be weighed, a body score system such as that developed by Hennecke et al. (1981) and shown in Table 7.2 is useful.

The energy requirements for pregnant mares during the 9, 10 and 11th months of gestation can be estimated by multiplying the maintenance requirements by 1.11, 1.13 and 1.20, respectively (NRC 1989). It is assumed that pregnancy does not significantly increase energy requirements prior to the 9th month (NRC 1989).

When calculating the energy requirements for lactating domestic horses, the NRC (1989) estimated that mares produce amounts of milk equivalent to 3% of body weight per day during early lactation (1 to 12 weeks) and 2% of body weight during late lactation (13 to 24 weeks). Furthermore it was estimated that each kg of milk requires 792 kcal of DE. A 350 kg mare requires 11.9 Mcal DE for maintenance. If she produced 10.5 kg of milk (350 × 0.3), she would require an additional 8.3 Mcal of DE or a total of 20.2 Mcal per day. This would be equivalent to 6 kg of average quality hay and 3 kg of grain. I am not aware of any studies in which milk production by Przewalski's horses has been measured. However, early growth rate of Przewalski's foals appears to be similar to that of domestic foals suggesting that Przewalski's and domestic mares produced a similar amount of milk as a percentage of their body weight. Przewalski's foals' birth weight may double by forty-five days of age (Mohr 1971). Data provided by NRC (1989) suggest that domestic foals can double their birth weight by forty to fifty days of age. Przewalski foals usually nurse longer than the four to six months which is typical for weaning of domestic foals. But again it must be stressed that monitoring body condition is an important management practice and is the most effective method of determining energy adequacy for both the mare and foal.

Table 7.2

Condition score for horses.[a]

SCORE	
1	*Poor.* Animal extremely emaciated. Spinous processes, ribs, tailhead projecting prominently. Bone structure of withers, shoulders and neck easily noticeable. No fatty tissues can be felt.
2	*Very Thin.* Animal emaciated. Slight fat covering over base of spinous processes; transverse processes of lumbar vertebrae feel rounder. Spinous processes, ribs, tailhead prominent. Withers, shoulders and neck structures faintly discernable.
3	*Thin.* Fat build up about halfway on spinous processes, transverse processes cannot be felt. Slight fat cover over ribs. Spinous processes and ribs easily discernable. Tailhead prominent, but individual vertebrae cannot be visually identified. Withers, shoulders and neck accentuated.
4	*Moderately Thin.* Slight ridge along back. Faint outline of ribs discernable. Tailhead prominence depends on conformation, fat can be felt around it. Withers, shoulders and neck not obviously thin.
5	*Moderate.* Back level. Ribs cannot be visually distinguished but can be easily felt. Fat around tailhead beginning to feel spongy. Withers appear rounded over spinous processes. Shoulders and neck blend smoothly into body.
6	*Moderate to Fleshy.* Slight crease down back. Fat over ribs feels spongy. Fat around tailhead feels soft. Fat beginning to be deposited along the sides of the withers, behind the shoulders and along the sides of the neck.
7	*Fleshy.* Crease down back. Individual ribs can be felt, but noticeable filling between ribs with fat. Fat around tailhead is soft. Fat deposited along withers, behind shoulders and along the neck.
8	*Fat.* Prominent crease down back. Difficult to feel ribs. Fat around tailhead very soft. Area along withers filled with fat. Area behind shoulder filled in flush. Noticeable thickening of neck. Fat deposited along inner buttocks.
9	*Extremely Fat.* Extremely obvious crease down back. Patchy fat appearing over ribs. Bulging fat around tailhead, along withers, behind shoulders and along neck. Fat along inner buttocks may rub together. Flank filled in flush.

[a]Hennecke et al. 1981.

The energy requirements for growing animals depend upon the desired rate of growth. Studies with several species indicate that skeletal diseases are more common when the animals are growing very rapidly compared to those growing slowly. Other studies with animals such as rats have demonstrated that animals with a lower growth rate, but fed a balanced diet, have greater longevity than animals fed to grow rapidly. As there is no need for Przewalski's horses to grow rapidly to prepare them for yearling sales or shows, there is no apparent reason to have these foals grow rapidly.

Data on the growth rate of Przewalski's horses were not found. Perhaps the thumb rule of 6 to 7 Mcal per 100 kg of body weight daily could be used as a guide. If the expected mature weight was 400 kg, a six-month-old weanling might be expected to weigh 170 kg, gain 0.5 kg daily and need 10 to 11 Mcal/day. An intake of 2 kg of hay and 2 kg of grain daily could supply 10.5 Mcal.

Protein

The NRC (1989) suggests that the total diet of domestic horses at maintenance contains at least 7.2% protein (90% dry matter basis). This would also seem reasonable for Przewalski's horses. As shown in Table 7.3, most feeds contain more than this amount of protein. Feeding concentrations of proteins greater than this would not be likely to be harmful to the horse, but may increase feeding costs. Domestic weanlings are thought to need diets containing at least 13% protein, yearlings 11%, pregnant mares 10% and lactating mares 12% protein (NRC 1989). These values demonstrate horses do not need to be fed diets containing high concentrations of protein. However, if their diet does not contain at least these amounts of protein, a small amount (generally less than 0.5 to 1 kg/horse/day) of protein supplement (Table 7.3) may be fed.

Indications of protein deficiency include reduced feed intake, reduced growth rate, weight loss in mature animals, rough appearing hair coat, and, perhaps, increased coprophagy.

Minerals

The horse requires at least seven major or macrominerals (calcium, chloride, magnesium, sodium, phosphorus, potassium, sulfur) and eight microminerals or trace minerals (cobalt, copper, fluorine, iodine, iron, manganese, selenium, zinc). Macrominerals are so

Table 7.3

Composition of feedstuffs.[a]

	Dry Matter (%)	DE (Mcal/ kg)	Crude Protein (%)	Ca (%)	P (%)
Cereal Hays					
Barley	89	1.75	8.0	0.21	0.20
Oat	90	1.70	8.5	0.29	0.23
Grass Hays					
Brome	90	1.90	9.0	0.32	0.22
Orchard Grass	89	1.85	8.9	0.33	0.25
Timothy	90	1.85	9.5	0.35	0.20
Legume Hays					
Alfalfa	91	2.00	15.0	1.25	0.22
Birdsfoot Trefoil	91	2.00	14.4	1.30	0.21
Clover, Red	89	2.00	14.0	1.25	0.21
Grains					
Barley	89	3.20	12.0	0.04	0.35
Corn	89	3.40	9.0	0.03	0.30
Oats	89	2.85	11.5	0.09	0.34
Protein Supplements					
Cottonseed Meal	91	2.75	41.0	0.17	1.10
Soybean Meal	90	3.15	44.0	0.35	0.65

[a]Composition of hays can vary greatly depending on stage of maturity at harvest and amount of weather damage. The above values are considered to be representative of average quality hay.

named because they are required in larger amounts than microminerals. They are not larger size nor are they more important.

Calcium is important for bone structure but also has many other functions such as key roles in muscle contraction, blood clotting, and transmission of nerve impulses. Inadequate calcium intake can cause rickets in foals and osteomalacia in mature horses. These diseases are characterized by poor mineralization of the osteoid tissue. Thus, enlarged joints and crooked long bones may result.

Grains such as corn and oats are very poor sources of calcium (Table 7.3). Grasses such as timothy, orchard grass and blue grass contain a moderate amount of calcium and legumes such as clover and alfalfa are excellent sources of calcium (Table 7.3). When expressed as percent of diet, the diets of young horses should contain at least 0.5% to 0.6% calcium. The diets of late gestation and lactating mares should contain at least 0.4% calcium. Other mature horses need only 0.2% calcium.

Most commercial grain mixes contain added calcium. Thus, for the mature horse calcium deficiency is unlikely when such feeds comprise a significant portion of the ration or the roughage consumed is a legume such as alfalfa. Calcium deficiency is most likely to happen when the diet consists of mostly grains such as corn, oats or wheat bran (which has a low calcium, high phosphorus content) and some grass hay or pasture. In such cases limestone should be added at a rate of at least 1% of the grain mixture. When legumes comprise a significant fraction of the diet, calcium intake will usually be adequate.

High phosphorus intakes decrease calcium utilization. Thus, it is often recommended that the amount of calcium in the diet equal or exceed the amount of phosphorus, that is that the Ca:P ratio be at least 1:1. Higher calcium ratios can be tolerated. Young animals can be fed diets containing 2:1, perhaps even 3:1 or higher and mature animals at least 4:1 and probably as high as 8:1, but only if adequate amounts of phosphorus are available.

Phosphorus is also necessary for healthy bone. A deficiency in phosphorus, like calcium, also results in poor bone mineralization. It may also cause a depraved appetite (pica). Mares during late gestation and lactation as well as young horses need at least 0.3% dietary phosphorus. Other horses need only 0.15% phosphorus.

Grains usually contain 0.3 to 0.4% phosphorus, whereas the phosphorus content of hay can vary from 0.15 to 0.30% (Table 7.3). As with calcium most commercial feeds contain added phosphorus. The need for phosphorus supplementation can be best ascertained by feed analyses.

Sodium and chloride needs can usually be provided by allowing free access to salt licks.

Adequate potassium intake is not usually a problem if the diet contains at least fifty percent hay or pasture.

Forages may be deficient in trace minerals such as iodine, copper, zinc and selenium as their trace mineral content depends somewhat on the mineral content of the soil in which they are grown. Iodine should be supplied by allowing free access to iodized or trace mineralized salt as the only salt available. A deficiency of iodine in a mare can result in stillborn or weak foals. Affected foals may have goiter (enlarged thyroid). Excessive intake of iodine by the mare can also cause problems in the foal. Pregnant mares fed more than 35 mg of iodine daily could give birth to foals with weakened skeletal systems and enlarged thyroids.

Selenium deficiency is a regional problem. Crops grown in some parts of the United States such as the Northeast, Eastern Coast, or Northwest are likely to be deficient in selenium. In some areas such as parts of Colorado, Wyoming, Montana, Nebraska and North and South Dakota, the crops may contain toxic levels of selenium.

Selenium deficiency causes nutritional myopathy (white-muscle disease). Affected foals are weak, have impaired locomotion, difficulty in suckling and swallowing and impaired cardiac function. The NRC (1989) recommends that the diets of horses contain at least 0.1 ppm (0.1 mg/kg of diet) selenium. Selenium deficiency has been reported in equids in zoos in those areas where the soil is low in selenium. The deficiency can be prevented by having selenium added to the grain mixture, or less effectively by having selenium containing trace mineralized salt as the only salt available. If the forage contains less than 0.1 ppm selenium, it is suggested that a grain mixture or supplement that provides at least 0.5 mg per day be fed.

Excessive selenium is harmful. The maximum tolerable level of selenium for horses has been estimated to be 2 ppm (2 mg/kg of diet). Chronic toxicity is characterized by listlessness, weight loss, a rough, coarse, dry brittle hair coat, loss of hair from the mane and tail, and cracking of the hooves. Affected animals may walk stiff-legged with tenderness or with pronounced lameness. Acute toxicity can cause respiratory failure, brain damage, blindness, and death.

Copper and zinc are required for many functions including proper skeletal development. The NRC (1989) suggests that horse rations contain at least 10 ppm copper and 50 ppm zinc. Other authorities recommend higher levels for broodmares and foals. Most forages contain levels lower than the NRC recommended levels. Therefore, copper and zinc fortification to result in levels of 50 ppm copper and 100 ppm zinc in the grain mixture may be a good safeguard against a possible deficiency.

Vitamins

Equids require both fat soluble and water soluble vitamins in the diet. The need for vitamin supplementation in addition to that in the feed usually depends on the vitamin content of the forage, as grains are lacking in many vitamins. Because it is expensive to monitor the vitamin content of the forage and because many forages contain low levels of vitamins, most commercial grain mixtures contain added vitamins. If the grain mixture is fortified, other vitamin supplements are usually not needed. However, if grains such as oats and barley are fed without fortification, a vitamin supplement could be beneficial.

Vitamin A is required for many functions. Thus, a deficiency can result in a wide range of signs such as nightblindness, excessive lacrimation, reduced intake, respiratory infections, convulsive seizures and spontaneous bone fractures. Excessive intake of vitamin A can cause bone fragility, rough hair coats, loss of hair, poor muscle tone and depression. The NRC (1989) recommends that pregnant and lactating mares receive at least 3000 IU of vitamin A activity per kg of feed and that growing horses and horses at maintenance receive at least 2000 IU per kg.

It was also suggested that the diet should not contain more than 16,000 IU of vitamin A per kg. Feeds such as alfalfa could provide more than 16,000 IU of vitamin A activity, however, it is in the form of the vitamin A precursor carotene. Carotene toxicity has never been demonstrated in horses fed large amounts of alfalfa.

Vitamin D is required for calcium utilization and bone formation. However, vitamin D deficiency has never been demonstrated in horses that are exposed to sunshine. The ultraviolet rays convert compounds formed by the animals into vitamin D. Excessive intakes of vitamin D cause soft tissue calcification. The NRC (1989) suggested that the maximum tolerable dietary level of vitamin D_3 is 2,200 IU/kg of feed.

Vitamin E has been the subject of many studies in recent years. The NRC (1989) increased the recommended level from the 15 IU per kg of feed in the 1978 publication to 50 IU per kg for maintenance and 80 IU per kg of feed for working, breeding or growing horses. Brood mares should get about 500 IU of vitamin E daily; assuming a body weight of 350 kg. The increase in the amount of vitamin E recommended was based on studies which suggested the immune response was improved at the higher level. Vitamin E interacts with selenium in the prevention of nutritional myopathy. Vitamin E deficiency has also been implicated in the development of degenerative myelopathy. Six Przewalski horses at the Bronx Zoo were diagnosed with the condition (Liu et al. 1983).

Ataxia characterized by uncoordinated movement of the hindlimbs and an abnormally wide-based gait and stance was noted. Histological lesions were found in the neural tissues. Low plasma levels of vitamin E and low concentrations of vitamin E in the feed led to the conclusions that a chronic vitamin E deficiency was present. Thus the horses at the Bronx Zoo are now given a vitamin E supplement. Mayhew et al. (1987) suggested that degenerative myelopathy might be caused by vitamin E deficiency in certain bloodlines of domestic horses. That is, there was a vitamin E-genetic interaction. Reports from Oregon State University (Forfa 1987) indicated that massive doses of vitamin E (6,000 IU/day) could be used to treat some cases of degenerative myelopathy in domestic horses. Further studies are needed to evaluate the effectiveness of vitamin E. Fortunately vitamin E appears to be relatively nontoxic. I am not aware of any reports of vitamin E toxicity in the horse.

Biotin has often been advocated for treatment of horses with poor quality (shelly, flaky) hooves. Clinical reports indicated that affected horses treated with 15 mg of biotin daily showed improvement in hardness, integrity and conformation of the hoof horn (Comben et al. 1984). NRC (1989) concluded that there was not sufficient evidence to establish a requirement for biotin.

Requirements have not been established for vitamin C, niacin, pantothenic acid, pyridoxine and vitamin B_{12} as they are not known to be needed in the horse's diet. Thiamin and riboflavin requirements were estimated to be 3 and 2 mg per kg of diet, respectively.

FEEDS

I am not aware of any studies which indicate that Przewalski's horses cannot be fed the feeds conventionally fed to domestic horses. Boyd (1988a) surveyed feeding practices at seven zoos. Przewalski's horses were fed alfalfa hay, timothy hay, oat hay, brome grass hay, pelleted concentrates, commercial grain mixtures, high fiber pellets, and pasture plus a variety of treats such as apples, carrots, and chewing tobacco. The choice of hay usually depends on the quality and price. Grass hays such as timothy and brome, and cereal hays such as oat hay contain less protein, calcium, and vitamins than alfalfa but contain more fiber. Representative analysis of various feedstuffs are shown in Table 7.3. High

Table 7.4

Feeding of Przewalski's horses in eight zoos.

Zoo	Roughage	Amount per Horse	Location	Other	Amount per Horse	Location	Keeper Visits/day
Catskill	timothy	ad lib	ground	mixed grain	1 kg	trough	4–5
Bronx	timothy	5 kg		Pacer[a]	2.5 kg		2
Front Royal	pasture hay in winter	ad lib		Purina Herbivore Zoo Chow[b]	4–6 kg	hay-rack	1
Denver	grass hay	ad lib	trough	Purina Balance Blend[b]	3 kg	wall-feeder	2–3
Toronto	hay	3 kg		monogastric cubes	5 kg		several
San Diego	oat hay and alfalfa	3 kg	trough	alfalfa pellets	5 kg	trough	1–2
Topeka	pasture brome hay	4 kg	manger	pellets	2 kg	tubs	1–2
Los Angeles	alfalfa	4 kg ad lib	manger	bran	0.7 kg	manger	2–3

[a]Blue Seal Feeds, Webster, MA

[b]Purina Mills, St. Louis, MO

quality commercial grain mixtures are recommended over grains such as oats and corn because the feed manufacturer can usually add the micronutrients (minerals and vitamins) more efficiently and effectively than can be done at most zoos, unless excellent mixing facilities are available. Proper mixing is essential. When using commercial feeds, use only those especially designed for horses. Rations formulated for other species might not have the proper balance of nutrients, but more importantly could contain toxic materials. For example, rations for beef steers and chickens often contain ionophores which are beneficial to those animals but are toxic to horses. The LD50 (lethal dose for 50% of those treated) for monensin, a commonly added ionophore, is 2–5 mg per kg of body weight for the horse compared to 200 mg per kg for chickens.

Inappropriate use of feed or contamination of horse feed with feeds designed for other species has caused many deaths of domestic horses. I am not aware of losses of Przewalski's horses but monensin toxicosis has been reported in Stone sheep, blesbok and a camel (Miller et al. 1990).

All seven zoos that responded to the survey used a commercial grain mixture or a complete herbivore pellet (Boyd 1988a). The amount given varied from 1 to 3 kg per day per animal. Most zoos tried to provide some pasture. Five used a grass hay, one used alfalfa and one used both alfalfa and grass hay. Three zoos used a supplement other than salt blocks (Table 7.4).

8

Husbandry

Michael D. LaRue

Husbandry of the Przewalski's horse is much the same as for many of the exotic equines. They adapt very well to a variety of situations and have been kept successfully in rather small pens or in large pastures (Table 8.1).

ENCLOSURES

The most common barrier used to contain horses is fencing of one type or another. However, moats have been used successfully (Figure 8.1) and natural barriers such as canyon walls hold promise for animals in that environment.

Fencing materials are varied but 9-gauge chain link fence fabric with a height of 2.4 meters is probably the most popular. This fabric is made of heavy wire woven in a diamond pattern about 5 cm in size. Horses have been known to jump a 1.8 meter fence. Field fence of woven or welded wire made with a much lighter gauge wire and with openings of 5 cm by 10 cm has also been used. Field fence can be an appropriate barrier if it is properly constructed and reinforced.

It is important in constructing a fence that fence fabric be attached to the enclosure side (inside) of the fence posts. This prevents the horses from contacting the posts. There have been instances where an animal ran a fence line and broke a leg hitting it on a fence post. Horses rubbing on the fence or otherwise pushing

Table 8.1

Enclosure characteristics in eight zoos.

Zoo	No. of Horses	Type of Herd	Enclosure Size (hectare)	Fence	Access to Shelter	Trees	Adjacent Species
A	9	harem	28.3	chain link—2.4 m	100%	1–5	Domestic horses
A	2	bachelor	0.06	chain link—2.4 m	night	0	Plains zebra
A	1	solitary	0.05	chain link—2.4 m	100%	1–5	Sitatunga
B	10	harem	5.3	chain link—2.4 m	100%	1–5	Camels
B	4	bachelor	0.8	chain link—3 m	100%	0	Cheetahs
B	5	harem	0.07	chain link—2.4 m	100%	0	Eld's deer, Oryx
C	4	harem	0.2	chain link—2.4 m	night	1–5	Goose
D	2	harem	0.14	chain link—1.8 m	100%	1–5	Eland, Pere David's deer
E	3	harem	0.2	chain link—1.8 m	100%	1–5	Lesser kudu, Nyala
E	3	juveniles	0.007	chain link—1.8 m	100%	0	Elk, Musk ox
F	1	solitary	4.0	chain link—2.4 m	100%	>20	Oryx, P. horse
F	8	harem	12.0	chain link—2.4 m	100%	>20	Oryx, P. horse
G	1	solitary	0.02	chain link—2.4 m	100%	1–5	Antelope
G	1	solitary	0.02	chain link—2.4 m	100%	1–5	Donkey
G	1	solitary	0.02	chain link—2.4 m	100%	1–5	Donkey
G	1	solitary	0.02	chain link—2.4 m	100%	1–5	Camelids, Equids, Deer
G	9	harem	0.4	chain link—2.4 m	100%	5–20	Camelids, Equids, Deer
G	3	harem	0.2	chain link—2.1 m	100%	1–5	Equids
H	21	harem	0.8	chain link—3 m	night	5–20	Pere David's deer
							Wisent

Figure 8.1. An enclosure at the London Zoo in which moats form the barrier on two sides. The stallion Haldo (#517) is not drinking from the moat but foraging for leaves. Photograph by Katherine A. Houpt.

the fence will push the fabric onto the posts rather than away from them.

The type of substrate is often mandated by the size of the enclosure and the number of horses kept in the enclosure. The substrate recommended is a natural grass pasture. This substrate has been suggested as the best for enhancing appropriate social and behavioral activities (Boyd 1988a, Bouman 1982). The pasture should contain grasses that are high in fiber content and less rich than grasses used for hay such as brome or timothy. Horses can founder on rich grasses especially when the grass is in its spring growth (Simerson 1988). This problem was experienced at the Topeka Zoo where two horses foundered from grazing on a fertilized brome field. However, other horses in the herd did not experience serious problems. The two affected horses were removed to a barren pen, and with repeated hoof trimmings, the hoof problems were corrected. Most of the horses on this pasture must have their hooves trimmed annually. Other zoos have also reported troubles with hoof maintenance.

It is difficult to recommend an appropriate density of horses on pasture. If one ignores the optimal herd size based on appropriate social organization and behaviors, two variables stand out: the type of soil and types of grasses. Pastures with very tough grasses and stable soil will most likely support a larger number of horses.

The Topeka Zoo maintained from three to six horses on 1.6 ha of prairie grasses with moderate success. There was, however, degradation of the pasture as the number of horses increased. The herd was moved to a pasture of 28.3 ha of primarily brome grass and the herd increased to nine animals. No major damage has occurred to the pasture and enough brome is grown to allow harvesting even with grazing. Some guidelines for domestic horses indicate that 2–2.8 ha of prairie grass pasture per horse is required to provide year round nutrition. The space needed can be reduced by supplemental feeding and pasture rotation. The space necessary to prevent physical damage to the pasture depends a great deal on the area and climate in which the pasture is located. Arid regions will require more space per horse.

One of the problems encountered in soft soils is overgrown hooves. In these situations hoof wear may be increased by placing an abrasive substrate around watering and feeding areas (such as rough concrete or rock). This technique may not solve the problem and trimming may be necessary to keep hooves in proper form.

As the size of the enclosure decreases and the concentration of horses increases it is less likely that a natural grass pasture can be maintained. Most zoos have limited space and must hold their horses in relatively small enclosures. The substrate of choice in these small enclosures is generally gravel. Dirt enclosures must have areas that allow the horses to get out of the mud. In the United States this is required by the United States Department of Agriculture under regulations of the Animal Welfare Act (USDA 1973).

Many types of gravel are used including crushed stone and river gravel both washed and unwashed. Gravel size also varies greatly. There have been cases in which a horse's foot became bruised by gravel. This may have been due to the large size of the gravel. Type and size of gravel used may be dictated by what is available in the area. Sand should not be used because its ingestion may cause colic (see chapter 7). On the other hand a grassless area free of gravel is desirable to permit the horses to roll for dustbathing.

Przewalski's horses require very little shelter. A wind break is often sufficient even in the worst weather. On cold winter days with heavy winds and snows, horses are often observed out in the pasture away from shelter with their tails to the wind. Frail or injured animals should have shelter with supportive heat if necessary, but healthy animals do quite well with minimal shelter. In open pasture areas natural shelters such as a grove of trees seems to offer sufficient shelter both in winter and in summer. Wet, cold weather causes more thermal stress than dry cold so consideration should be given to providing dry areas.

On very hot, sunny days, horses will often seek shade, and it is important that provisions are made for shade. Several areas and/ or a large area should be provided so the animals can disperse and not be concentrated in a small area. This reduces aggression among the horses in the shaded area.

Horses can injure themselves in unpredictable ways as evidenced by a couple of incidents with the Topeka herd. At one pasture there were earth-covered concrete bunkers that were once munitions' storage areas. The horses used these bunkers as observation areas in the yards. While the sides of the bunkers sloped to grade level permitting the horses to ascend the slope, the front of the bunker was a concrete wall with large steel doors and a concrete patio. This wall was about five meters high. One morning a mare was found standing but badly injured on the patio. Evidence pointed to activity on top of the bunker that resulted in the mare falling from the top onto the top edge of the steel door, and then onto the concrete patio. Unfortunately, the mare died a few hours after discovery.

After the herd was moved to a new location they had access to a small pen in which grain was fed daily. This pen also had an adjacent shelter with floor-level wooden hay mangers that were once used to feed cattle. One day a mare was found upside down in a hay manger. She was exhausted and had many abrasions but after a period of recovery was fine. It is still not known what occurred that induced the mare to jump or climb into the manger but modifications were made to the hay mangers to prevent a reoccurrence. It is vital, especially when dealing with an endangered species, that managers be keenly aware of all aspects of the enclosures in which horses are to be kept and plan for the worst case.

FEEDING

Horses kept on pasture of good grass will not need supplemental feed. However, supplemental feed is useful for bringing a herd into a corral for daily examination, or to lure them for special procedures. Horses kept in a small pen in which grass is not available must be given hay and, usually, grain for dietary supplementation (see chapter 7).

Good clean water is necessary for all animals and Przewalski's horses are no exception. Open water is important in the winter. However, when available, horses have been observed eating snow. Availability of snow does not preclude the necessity of providing open water. Eating snow will increase the danger of hypothermia by requiring the body to expend energy to melt the snow and warm it to body temperature.

REMOVAL OF JUVENILES

Appropriate horse behavior is learned in the herd at a fairly young age. Young males should be removed from the natal herd at one to two years of age. This is about the time the stallion begins to become very aggressive with the youngster. Young males should be placed in a group of similarly aged males for several years. This time is necessary for the male to develop skills in sparring with other males and in developing dominance. If other young males are not available, a small domestic horse such as a Shetland pony may help develop the necessary social skills. Although not as appropriate as a same-species group, a pony can act as a mentor and provide companionship for the young male. This training and socialization process will provide the male with the necessary knowledge to lead a herd as an adult (see chapter 12).

Fillies can be left with the natal herd for several years until ready for breeding. If the filly's sire is still the herd stallion the female should be moved to another herd to avoid either consanguineous mating or stress to the filly when the stallion attempts to drive her away (see chapter 12). Stallions may show interest in females as young as two or three years of age. Mares can come into estrus as young as two years of age (Boyd 1988a, see chapter 10).

MULTIPLE HERDS

The question of housing several herds of Przewalski's horses adjacent to one another has not been answered completely. Observations of current situations indicate that a herd stallion may attempt to gather mares from another herd or may try to spar with the other herd stallion through the fence.

In one situation where a Przewalski's horse herd was adjacent to a herd of domestic Morgan horses several interesting things were observed. The horses were separated by two fences installed three meters apart. The Przewalski's horse stallion did not try to recruit the Morgan mares. However, when the Morgan stallion was present the Przewalski's horse stallion marked the fence line with feces and kept his herd well away from the fence line adjacent to the Morgans. He also ran along the fence line when the Morgan stallion was in view and was observed to leave his herd and travel several hundred meters to the fence to do this.

It is likely that two or more herds of Przewalski's horses can be kept in adjacent pastures. Those pastures should be large enough for the stallions to keep the herds apart. The fences separating the herds should be of sufficient construction to prevent them from being breached. Use of a common fence to separate herds is not recommended. Two fences with sufficient distance between them should be used. This distance should be at least three to six meters. This area of separation would be more effective with visual barriers.

Establishing all male groups may be important if the breeding herd produces males that cannot be placed. Various methods have been used to form these all male groups (Tilson et al. 1988). The San Diego Wild Animal Park has successfully kept a stallion herd consisting of eight males ranging from two to four years of age. They are isolated from any contact with other equines.

Occasionally, one or more horses will form a subgroup that stays some distance from the main group. When this happens it is usually due to a dominant mare that keeps them away from the main group. In one case a stallion tried to get the whole herd together while at the same time the dominant mare was chasing one of the ostracized mares away from the group.

An ostracized animal may have to be removed from the herd to reduce stress in the herd and stress on the affected animal. Moving a single animal from a herd situation to a solitary pen may replace one stress with another. Consideration should be given to reduce the stress on the moved animal by providing companion animals.

TRANSPORT

Przewalski's horses can be transported much the same way as domestic horses, either in modified horse trailers or crates. The main modification to the horse trailer is to cover the openings to prevent injury from a horse trying to go through the openings.

Many zoos move horses in shipping crates with a door in both the front and the back. This allows the horse to be unloaded as easily as loading it. The shipping crate should either be just wide enough to fit the horse and prevent the animal from turning around, or made wide enough so the horse can turn around easily. An intermediate size invites trouble because the horse may try to turn but become wedged in the crate.

Przewalski's horses can be herded into a trailer or crate with some effort but they are often at least partially sedated first. If no tests or examinations are necessary prior to loading, a light dose of an immobilizing drug may be given. This will allow the horse to be physically guided but still move under its own power. However, the type of drug used may determine if this is possible. A successful drug used in the past to move horses was etorphine hydrochloride (M99). When a light dose was given and before the drug took full effect, slings were placed under the horse to keep it from falling. With people holding these slings and others to guide and push from behind, a horse could be walked just about anywhere. Walking over rough terrain or stepping into a trailer requires some care and assistance, however. Complete immobilization is necessary for blood drawing or other medical tests. These procedures must be done under the guidance of a veterinarian.

INTRODUCTIONS

Introducing one horse to another, or to a group, can be a challenge. Normally, there is a slow, planned introduction often called a "howdy" period. This may consist of placing the new horse in an area adjacent to the animals currently being held. The area may allow sight or sound but no physical contact. Depending on the sex of the animals involved and the breeding situation, this period may be without incident or the horses may be very active, running fence lines, etc. The next step is generally to move the new animal closer, possibly allowing some physical contact through the fence fabric. If all goes well the new animal can join the others. If all does not go well introduction may take place the hard way, by removing the barrier between them. When the horses do get together there will probably be a period of fighting and roughness while the horses establish and re-establish their dominance hierarchy. The severity of the fighting may look awesome but injuries are generally not life-threatening.

The Minnesota Zoo has made videotapes of introductions of males to bachelor herds (Reindl and Tilson 1985a). The behaviors exhibited were extremely rough with much running, biting, kicking, etc. At the Topeka Zoo some horses have had to be removed from the group to recuperate after a particularly difficult introduction. For the most part though, introductions work out well after the initial fighting. The horses find their place within the herd and things are peaceful most of the time.

IDENTIFICATION

Przewalski's horses are often identified by visual cues noted by their keeper. However, the pelage changes due to seasons and/or age, and these cues may not always work. Keepers also change and pertinent information may be lost. More than once an animal has been misidentified where proper marking techniques could have prevented the mistake (Bowling and Ryder 1988).

More permanent identification should be used to mark horses. Some techniques for permanent identification that have been used include ear notching, lip tattoos, heat branding and freeze branding. Photographs or drawings with keys to identification are also helpful but do not substitute for permanent marking.

The latest marking technique is the use of an implanted microchip. Microchips are programmed with an identification number of a horse, and a wand can read the identification from a distance of fifteen centimeters. The Captive Breeding Specialist Group (CBSG) of the IUCN has endorsed this marking technique. Protocols are being developed for the implant procedures and location for many species including horses (CBSG 1991).

RECORD KEEPING

One of the most important aspects of husbandry of the Przewalski's horse is the keeping of accurate records. There are two types of data that should be kept on each horse: (1) basic demographic and pedigree data and (2) life-history data. Basic demographic and pedigree data include: (a) date of birth or acquisition, (b) date of disposition or death, (c) cause of death, (d) place of birth, if wild, or previous owner, (e) parents, (f) location acquired from, (g) location sent to, and (h) accession number.

Life-history data is really open-ended but usually includes narratives about behaviors, reproductive activity, introductions, movements within an institution, notes on acquisitions or dispositions, etc.

It is fortunate that this information can be recorded with microcomputers in a logical and consistent way. Increasingly, institutions worldwide are adopting the software package Animal Records Keeping System (ARKS) available from the International Species Information System (ISIS).[1] ARKS can record all the data necessary for Przewalski's horse husbandry. In addition, it provides data to ISIS for international record keeping.

While ARKS can provide inventory information, another software package can analyze the pedigree and demographic data that can help to make breeding recommendations and other population management decisions. This package is known as the Single Population Analysis and Record Keeping System (SPARKS) and is also available from ISIS. There is a need to standardize the information recorded within each institution. Such a standardization process should greatly enhance the husbandry and medical management of these animals.

Veterinary data can be considered life history data but often veterinarians keep this type of data themselves. Another software package from ISIS helps to ensure that veterinary data can be integrated with the inventory data provided by ARKS. This package is known as the Medical Animal Records Keeping System (MEDARKS). MEDARKS can record such data as: record or schedule of routine parasite exams and treatments, vaccinations, anesthesia records, drugs administered, blood and urine test results, etc. In addition, physiological norm data from all participating institutions and from the holding institution can be used to compare blood values for making diagnoses.

SUMMARY

Husbandry can be defined in degrees of intensity of management and it is sometimes difficult to choose which degree should be

---

[1] International Species Information System, 12101 Johnny Cake Ridge Road, Apple Valley, MN 55124–8199, U.S.A.

used. Optimal husbandry strives to provide the best quality and quantity of everything needed for maintaining appropriate nutrition, social structure, reproduction and behaviors. Many husbandry needs can be provided with management and facilities that are less than optimal. For example, it seems optimal to keep Przewalski's horses in a herd situation on natural pasture. But if room is not available it is possible to place a group in a day pasture and move them to a much smaller paddock or barn at night. The animals can even be separated into individual stalls at night. The horses are nutritionally fit and reproduce well.

It is not practical in many situations to be able to provide optimal husbandry. There is a question about what is lost by not providing optimal husbandry. Are behaviors necessary for surviving in a wild or semi-wild situation lost? Will social structures that allow for changes in herd composition be lost? Can we identify things that might be lost? Can we determine if they are necessary for the long term survival of the Przewalski's horse? What minimal criteria must a zoo meet if they are to house Przewalski's horses? Husbandry needs are refined all the time as we learn more about the species we care for. There is not yet a final answer to providing the best husbandry for maintaining the Przewalski's horse in captive or managed situations. Provision of optimal husbandry is important as a conservation and an animal welfare issue.

9

Veterinary Care

Katherine A. Houpt

The purpose of this chapter is to present the veterinary procedures that are frequently performed on Przewalski's horses and to discuss the diseases that affect the species, including those for which there are vaccinations.

VETERINARY PROCEDURES

The goal of veterinarians in well-run zoos is to prevent injury and disease rather than to treat injuries and illnesses. The health of a herd of Przewalski's horses depends on parasite control, vaccination and, most importantly, supervision of management so that injuries from fences, feeders and conspecifics is kept to a minimum. Organization of preventative measures so that immobilizations can be minimized is also important.

Immobilization

Because they are wild animals, many routine procedures such as hoof trimming and wound treatment cannot be performed without chemical restraint. Therefore, the most important veterinary procedure performed on Przewalski's horses is immobilization. This can also be a life-threatening procedure although the risk is probably low given that most Przewalski's horses are immobilized no more than once a year. Reasons for immobilizations can be elective

143

or emergency situations. The most common elective procedures are hoof trimming or transport. Most emergencies are treatments of wounds, but may include treatment of other illnesses or dystocias.

Etorphine. Etorphine is an opiate so that its effects can be reversed rapidly with an opiate antagonist. The antagonist, diprenorphine at a dose twice that of etorphine, is administered intravenously. The central nervous effects of etorphine are reversed within one to twenty minutes of diprenorphine administration. Heretofore, etorphine (M99) was the drug of choice for equid immobilization. To achieve light anesthesia, 1000 mg of xylazine is administered twenty minutes before 0.016–0.13 mg/kg etorphine. Within twelve to twenty minutes after administration, the horse will be sedated enough to be pulled into lateral recumbency. There will still be a fair amount of muscle rigidity, but the depth of anesthesia is adequate for hoof trimming, vaccination, blood sampling and minor surgery. If greater muscle relaxation is needed 10–20 mg diazepam can be administered intravenously. Two hundred immobilizations have been performed with this dosage with no fatalities (Dr. Peregrine Wolff, Minnesota Zoo, personal communication). The Przewalski's horse is less sensitive to etorphine than domestic horses. If too low a dose is administered the horse may become over-excited and injure itself. Side effects of etorphine are tachycardia, increased blood pressure, respiratory depression, muscle tremors or rigidity, myopathy and hyperthermia. If the weight of the horse is unknown an adult may be given 3–6 mg/horse in combination with 10–20 mg of acepromazine or 50–100 mg xylazine to immobilize horses in one to fifteen minutes. Juveniles are given 2.5–3 mg etorphine and 5–15 mg acepromazine.

Great care must be taken when using etorphine because humans are much more sensitive to it than horses. Veterinarians have been killed when accidentally injected with the drug. A human dose of the antidote always should be available in a syringe before the etorphine is prepared.

Drug delivery is another problem. Few Przewalski's horses can be hand held for an injection. A Capchur gun usually is used to deliver the immobilizing drugs, although a blow gun or pole syringe can be used if the horse has been premedicated or restrained (Fowler 1986). Just as important as the dosage of drug is the condition of the animal prior to immobilization. The following rules were developed at the San Diego Zoo (Oosterhuis 1979).

1. Prepare people and equipment for procedure to be done.

2. Each immobilization should be carried out at the coolest part of the day in most seasons except during cold weather.
3. Keep the animal to be immobilized as calm as possible.
4. Take the utmost care in administering the immobilizing drugs. A good complete injection is extremely important.
5. Have the animal go down in a safe level location. Most horses can be safely approached, roped or haltered, and led to a safe place several minutes before they become recumbent.
6. When the animal is recumbent cover the eyes and remove ropes to prevent facial paralysis.
7. Limit total time to one hour from injection to reversal.
8. Prepare area for reversal by removing excess equipment and personnel.
9. Administer any necessary medication such as antibiotics or anthelmintics followed by antagonist.
10. Allow the animal to arise on its own in as quiet an environment as possible without prodding or slapping.

In order to insure that the horse's respiratory efforts are producing adequate oxygenation, pulse oximetry should be used to measure oxygen saturation of the hemoglobin by means of light passed through thin tissue such as the tongue, ear or vulva; supplemental oxygen should be available to administer if needed. Rectal temperature should also be monitored frequently, especially on warm days. Hyperthermia can develop rapidly, particularly when muscle relaxation is poor.

Etorphine and a variety of other drugs have been used to improve muscle relaxation. Those include xylazine, acepromazine, and diazepam. Anticholinergic drugs may be used to prevent bradycardia and excessive salivation or respiratory tract secretion. A suitable anticholinergic is glyceryl guaiacolate. The dose of glyceryl guaiacolate is 27 to 110 mg/kg (0.25 to 1 ml/kg of a 5% solution) administered intravenously as soon as the animal is restrained sufficiently to insert a large catheter or needle (Janssen and Oosterhuis 1984).

A mortality rate as high as 3% has been reported following immobilization. Table 9.1 lists the horses that died secondary to immobilization procedures. Some deaths during immobilization were the result of injury sustained as the drugs took effect or while the animal was recovering; other deaths were of animals that were

Table 9.1

Deaths associated with immobilization procedures in two zoos.

I.D.	Sex	Age	Cause
#319 Bellina	F	7 yr.	immobilized for shipment
#530 Vashka	M	13 yr.	fracture 4th cervical vertebra while recovering from etorphine anesthesia for wound treatment
#669 Bondari	F	8 yr.	recovering from etorphine plus halothane for neurectomy (for laminitis)
#1210 Viktor	M	4 yr.	euthanized after suffered comminuted fracture during immobilization
#1453 Beka	F	1 yr.	immobilized for treatment of *Coccidioides*

already compromised by illness. Immobilization can also cause morbidity, usually by infection at the injection site.

Other immobilization agents. The use of opioids in Przewalski's horses and other species has been reviewed by Haigh (1990). Allen (1992) immobilized eighteen Przewalski's horses with 0.02 mg/kg carfentanil. Immobilization success depended on dart placement; the best sites were the highly muscled areas of the neck, shoulder or thigh. The time from dart injection to recumbency was 9 ± 3 min. Antagonism with naltrexone at fifty times the carfentanil dose resulted in standing within two minutes. Renarcotization (reappearance of sedation after the antagonist is metabolized) was not a problem.

Detomidine is also used alone or in combination with carfentanil or butorphanol (Taylor et al. 1988, Short et al. 1989). It is most unfortunate that etorphine is no longer available because injuries and even deaths during immobilization will probably rise until the optimum dose of the best drug or combination of available drugs is determined. For example, Kock et al. (1988) reported on the use of detomidine 0.12 or 0.18 mg/kg and butorphanol 0.06–0.1 mg/kg. The first sign of sedation was seen in 11 ± 7 minutes, the time of restraint was 20 ± 7 min and the first sign of recovery was 39 ± 21 min. One Przewalski's horse died of severe pulmonary hemorrhage after she had been given an additional dose after incomplete injection of the first dose, so that a total of 80 mg detomidine and 50 mg butorphanol were administered. An alpha-2-antagonist and a narcotic antagonist were also administered when signs of distress were noted. The combination of detomidine (0.029–0.046 mg/kg) with carfentanil also gives variable results. Medetomidine-ketamine has been used successfully in five Przewalski's horses (Jalanka and Roeken 1990).

PREVENTIVE MEASURES

There are illnesses and injuries that are rarely fatal, but which require attention from keepers, curators and veterinarians. Table 9.2 lists the medical problems reported by keepers at one zoo. Most bite wounds did not need treatment. Wounds caused by retained darts used for drug delivery often resulted in another immobilization to remove the dart and treat the wound. Most lamenesses that were not caused by laminitis resolved without treatment. Vaccinations and hoof trims were usually done at the same time to minimize the frequency of immobilization. Anthelmintic treatment was administered regularly. Table 9.3 lists the medical interventions for one horse during the first five years of her life as an example of normal medical care.

Diseases for Which Przewalski's Horses May Be Vaccinated

Most horses are vaccinated with a four-way vaccine for tetanus, influenza and eastern and western equine encephalitis. Some zoos also vaccinate for rhinopneumonitis. All horses should be vaccinated for rabies.

Tetanus. All horses should be vaccinated with tetanus toxoid. This will not only protect the individuals but also their foals who will obtain antibodies in the colostrum. Ideally, foals should be vaccinated with tetanus toxoid at 2, 3 and 6 months of age. If a horse of unknown vaccination status is injured, it should be given 15,000 I.U. antitoxin.

Encephalitis. The commercially available 3-way vaccine which is administered to Przewalski's horses in many zoos contains killed virus of eastern and western equine encephalitis as well as tetanus toxoid. Both of these diseases are caused by arthropod-borne RNA viruses called alphaviruses. Mosquitoes are the usual vector and birds are the reservoir. These are zoonoses, but horses are "dead end" hosts. The virus can be passed from a bird to a person, from a bird to a horse, but not from a horse to a person or a horse to a horse. The signs of the disease are an altered state of consciousness

Table 9.2

Summary of veterinary procedures at one zoo.

Year	Number of Horses	Lame	Wounds	Wormed	Immobilization
1984	21	3 (1 treated)	7	4x	5
1985	23	4 (2 treated) (1 dart)	3 (1 treated)	4x	18 (1 7x) (1 3x) (3 2x)
1986	25	5	12—1 fracture 5 bites (3 treated) 2 dart 2 freeze brand 1 kick	4x	30 (1 3x)
1987	25	4 (1 treated)	8—2 bites 1 death	3x	24
1988	25	3 (1 treated)	6 bites (1 self-induced)	4x	17 (1 4x) (1 2x)
1989		7 (1 treated)	10—3 treated 1 bite 1 feeder 2 darts		13 (1 3x) (1 2x)

Table 9.3

*Medical record of an individual Przewalski's mare, Maggie
(#1287 Minnesota 20).*

09/09/84	Born
11/01/84	Oral treatment 2.4 g mebendazole (Telmin anthelmintic) x 3 days
02/09/85	Oral treatment 6.0 g mebendazole (Telmin) x 3 days
05/23/85	Immobilized 500 mg xylazine, 25 mg diazepam and 2 mg etorphine (M99) i.m. over 15 min. 175 mg ketamine i.v. over 10 min. Hoof trim, tissue biopsy, freeze brand, blood sample for equine infectious anemia test and for Dr. Ryder. Vaccinated against rabies (IM Rab), eastern and western encephalitis and tetanus (Encevac-T). Given 5.5 cc vit E (E-Se) and 7 cc penicillin (Flocillin i.m.). 4 mg diprenorphine (M5050) to reverse etorphine.
07/15/85	Oral treatment Telmin x 3 days
10/15/85	Oral treatment 14.4 g Telmin x 3 days
11/13/85	Immobilized 25 mg diazepam, 500 mg xylazine (Rompun) and 2 mg etorphine (M99). Hooves trimmed, blood for blood count and equine infectious anemia test. Reversed with 4 mg diprenorphine.
11/19/85	Vaccinated for encephalitis (Encevac) and 5 cc penicillin (Flocillin) for cut on left foreleg from striking stall.
11/25/85	5 cc penicillin (Flocillin)
03/20/86	Immobilized to move. 4.5 mg etorphine (M99) followed by 200 mg xylazine (Rompun)
10/14/87	Immobilzied to move. 7 mg etorphine (M99) plus 200 mg xylazine (Rompun). Hooves trimmed. Floated teeth 8 cc penicillin-streptomycin combination (PennStrep). Biopsy for Dr. Ryder.
01/11/88	Fecal examination, ivermectin (Eqvalan anthelmintic)
02/16/88	Oral treatment ivermectin (Eqvalan)
05/27/88	Immobilized to treat wound acquired when she was caught in manager. 7 mg etorphine (M99) plus 200 mg xylazine (Rompun), 600 mg corticosteroid (Soludelta Cortef) 100 cc penicillin-streptomycin combination (PennStrep); 6 cc penicillin (Flocillin). Tetanus antitoxin 1500 U. Reversed with 7 cc diprenorphine (M5050).
06/11/88	Oral treatment ivermectin (Eqvalan)
08/30/88	Oral treatment ivermectin (Eqvalan)
01/24/89	Oral treatment ivermectin (Eqvalan)
04/08/89	Oral treatment ivermectin (Eqvalan)
04/19/89	Immobilized for move. 7 mg etorphine (M99), 200 mg xylazine (Rompun) plus 3 more cc etorphine. Vaccinated for encephalitis (Encevac) and Strepvax. 8 cc penicillin-streptomycin combination (PennStrep).

preceded by a fever. After a period of excitability, the horse will become somnolent. The vaccination should be given a month before mosquitoes become active in the spring (Wilson 1987).

Rabies. Rabies is caused by a rhabdovirus that affects all mammals. Therefore, all animals should be vaccinated against rabies because it is possible for a wild rabies-infected animal such as a coyote, raccoon, skunk, fox, or bat to bite a Przewalski's horse. The signs are usually neurologic, but the only sign may be lameness or colic. Because rabies in horses is usually the "dumb" form, that is they are stuperous rather than aggressive, an incorrect diagnosis could be made and several humans exposed. Brains of horses dying from neurological disease in rabies endemic areas should be submitted to a public health laboratory for examination for the rabies antigen. Horses should be vaccinated with an inactivated virus vaccine administered in the muscles of the rump.

Parasites

The internal parasites most likely to cause clinical disease in horses are: 1) the large strongyles, *Strongylus vulgaris, S. edentatus,* and *S. equinus*; 2) ascarids, *Parascarus equorum*; 3) bots, *Gastrophilus*; and 4) pinworms, *Oxyuris equi*. Strongyles can cause colic or ischemia of any tissue supplied by blood vessels obstructed with migrating larvae. Thus, thromboembolic consequence of strongyle infestation is much more serious than the presence of the adult worm in the intestine. Ascarids are mainly a problem in foals in whom they can cause failure to thrive, diarrhea, coughing and colic. The major problem with bots is the irritation of the horses by the adult flies, but gastric rupture can occur if too many of the larval form are present in the stomach. Pinworms can cause pruritus of the perineal region.

Anthelmintics. Treatment for internal parasites is particularly important for zoo animals because they are kept in confined spaces where the number of infective parasite ova can build up. Feces should be removed frequently from all the areas where the horses are kept, not just from exhibit areas, because removing feces twice a week from paddocks and pastures can be as effective as chemical anthelmintics. Frequent cleaning is effective because parasite ova are usually not infective when first eliminated from the host, so that even if they are ingested they will not cause disease. However, after a week, depending on the particular parasite, temperature and humidity, they are infective.

Most zoos are now using ivermectin (Eqvalan; Merck, Rahway, NJ) which is 90 to 100% effective against large strongyles, ascarids, bots and pinworms. To avoid resistance occurring, anthelmintics should be rotated on a yearly basis. Benzimidazole drugs such as thiabendazole are nearly as effective as ivermectin and would be a good choice for alternate years. Dichlorvos is also used. Fecal flotations should be done before and after worming to check that the anthelmintic used has actually decreased the number of eggs shed by the horses.

Drug Delivery

Delivery of drugs is also a problem in Przewalski's horses. Powdered wormers can be mixed with grain; powdered gelatin desserts or soft drink mix can be added to increase the sweetness and, therefore, the palatability. Molasses can also be used. Molasses has the added advantage of sticking the medication to the grain. Nine out of ten domestic horses prefer sweetened feeds (Hawkes et al. 1985) so presumably a similar proportion of Przewalski's horses do too. Paste wormers may simply be mixed with the feed despite the directions which imply that the horse's mouth should be empty when the paste is administered. Paste wormers may also be administered as the last procedure during an immobilization. Administer the reversal agent (opiate antagonist) and then administer the paste orally.

Delivery of intramuscular injections can be given by hand in very tame animals, by using a pole syringe or a projectile delivery system such as a blow pipe or CO_2 powered system. Dart guns may be used, but the darts should not be barbed. Collared darts work well; non-collared darts tend to bounce out before all the medication is delivered.

Hoof Care

One of the more controversial subjects in veterinary care of Przewalski's horses is how often hooves should be trimmed. Some zoos in the United States trim hooves as frequently as once a month. Most zoos trim hooves twice a year and some do not trim at all. The question is whether the risks of immobilization are greater than the risk of mechanical founder. If horses have to be immobilized for other procedures, their hooves should be trimmed at the same time.

Normal Values for Blood Constituents

The normal values for a variety of blood constituents are presented in Table 9.4. Domestic horse values can also be used, if information is not available for that particular constituent for Przewalski's horses. Kuttner and Wiesner (1987) found that blood

Table 9.4

Hemogram and serum chemistries on Przewalski's horse (Equus przewalskii). [a]

HEMATOLOGY	WBC	RBC	HGB	HCT	NUC.RBC	MCV	MCH	MCHC
	$10^3/\mu l$	$10^6/\mu l$	g/dl	%	%	fl	%	%
Mean ± S.D.	8.6 ± 2.5	13.7 ± 18.3	14.6 ± 2.2	41.5 ± 5.7	.0 ± .0	41.6 ± 13.9	15.3 ± 5.1	35.2 ± 3.2
#Samples (#Horses)	268 (110)	108 (69)	253 (114)	274 (117)	59 (37)	113 (71)	111 (69)	250 ± 113

DIFFERENTIAL	SEGS	BANDS	LYMP	MONO	EOSIN	BASO	RETICS	PLATELETS
	$10^3/\mu l$	$10^3/\mu l$	$10^3/\mu l$	$/\mu l$	$/\mu l$	$/\mu l$	%	$10^3/\mu l$
Mean ± S.D.	4.3 ± 1.5	.0 ± .1	3.6 ± 1.8	232 ± 182	156 ± 145	8.4 ± 24.8	.0 ± .0	201 ± 73.9
#Samples (#Horses)	199 (94)	156 (69)	197 (92)	191 (88)	185 (87)	154 (66)	84 (40)	30 (29)

CHEMISTRY	CA	PHOS	GLUCOSE	BUN	URIC ACID	CHOLEST	T.BIL	D.BIL
	mg/dl	mg/dl	mg/dl	mg/dl	mg/dl	mg/dl	mg/dl	mg/dl
Mean ± S.D.	11.2 ± 0.6	4.5 ± 1.3	168 ± 49.8	3.8 ± 0.7	0.7 ± 0.3	85.4 ± 21.5	1.2 ± 0.8	0.2 ± 0.1
#Samples (#Horses)	176 (100)	174 (98)	174 (100)	173 (98)	110 (62)	146 (88)	178 (102)	23 (15)

	I.BIL	ALK PTASE	CREAT	NA	K	CL	MG	HCO$_3$
	mg/dl	IU/l	mg/dl	mEq/l	mEq/l	mEq/l	mg/dl	mEq/l
Mean ± S.D.	0.7 ± 0.2	220 ± 129	1.2 ± 0.2	137 ± 3.2	4.7 ± 0.7	96.7 ± 4.0	1.6 ± 0.3	30.1 ± 2.7
#Samples (#Horses)	22 (15)	174 (99)	174 (99)	169 (95)	172 (98)	155 (96)	10 (7)	88 (45)

	LDH IU/l	AST IU/l	SGPT IU/l	CPK IU/l
Mean ± S.D.	485 ± 151	340 ± 98.4	15.1 ± 12.8	435 ± 238
#Samples (#Horses)	134 (77)	172 (100)	168 (96)	94 (53)

ELECTROPHORESIS

	T. PROT g/dl	GAMMA GLOB g/dl	ALBUMIN g/dl
Mean ± S.D.	6.6 ± 0.6	3.3 ± 0.6	3.4 ± 0.4
#Samples (#Horses)	155 (97)	101 (62)	143 (86)

[a] data provided by ISIS

glucose rose and hematocrit fell 30 min after immobilization with an etorphine-acepromazine combination.

CAUSES OF MORTALITY

In general, the same problems that result in morbidity-trauma and lameness result in mortality. The causes of death fall into roughly nine categories discussed below: 1) abortions, stillbirths and neonatal mortality, 2) gastrointestinal problems such as torsions (twisting of the organ), volvulus (twisting of the blood vessel), and intussusception (telescoping of one part of the intestine into another), 3) traumatic injuries, 4) problems associated with immobilization, 5) infectious diseases, 6) euthanasia for geriatric problems, 7) euthanasia because of lameness, 8) neuromuscular disorders, and 9) miscellaneous causes. The causes of death of Przewalski's horses in seven zoos are given in Tables 9.5–9.12.

Prenatal and Neonatal Causes of Death

Abortion and stillbirths. Abortion is defined as expulsion of the fetus before 300 days gestation. The fetus need not be dead at delivery and may survive for hours. Prematurity is defined as birth between 300 and 325 days. Stillbirth is expulsion of a term or near term dead fetus. Table 9.5a lists the number of births, deaths,

Table 9.5a

Abortions and stillbirths in Przewalski's horses over a ten-year-period.

Year	Total[a]	Births	Abortion (%)	Stillbirth (%)	Born But Died Within 1 week (%)[b]
1980	421	72	1 (1.3)	5 (6.9)	11 (15.3)
1981	464	81	2 (2.5)	1 (1.2)	12 (14.8)
1982	500	73	8 (11.0)	1 (1.4)	6 (8.2)
1983	552	86	2 (2.3)	5 (5.8)	13 (15.1)
1984	614	112	5 (4.5)	5 (4.5)	8 (7.1)
1985	660	103	2 (1.9)	2 (1.9)	6 (5.8)
1986	723	123	2 (1.6)	6 (4.9)	9 (7.3)
1987	797	130	9 (6.9)	12 (9.2)	5 (3.9)
1988	873	135	3 (2.2)	7 (5.2)	15 (11.1)
1989	961	154	8 (5.2)	12 (7.8)	8 (5.2)

[a]Total = total Przewalski's horse population

[b]% = % of live births

abortions, and stillbirths of Przewalski's horses from 1980 through 1989. The percentage of abortions is similar to or lower than the rate in domestic horses which varies from 4% to 20% (Rossdale and Ricketts 1980). However, the percentage of aborted Przewalski fetuses is compared to the number of live births and might be higher if early pregnancy diagnosis were made, as many early abortions may go undetected, especially in herds housed in large enclosures. Table 9.5b lists causes of neonatal mortality from six zoos and includes abortion and stillbirths.

There are many causes of abortion: primary infections with bacteria, fungi or virus, or secondary damage to the fetoplacental unit after trauma or disease. The fungi, *Mucor aspergillus* or *Allocheiria*, may cause abortion. Bacterial causes in domestic horses are *Streptococcus pyogenes var equi*, *Escherichia coli*, *Klebsiella pneumonia*, *Staphylococcus aureus* and, rarely *Salmonella abortoequina*.

Contagious equine metritis, a recently discovered disease, may also cause abortion. Contagious equine metritis is a venereally transmitted equine disease caused by a microaerophilic coccobacillus *Haemophilus equigentalis*. A severe diffuse endometritis and cervicitis occurs and the organism can usually be cultured from the clitoral fossa. No clinical signs are seen in stallions, but mares have a vaginal discharge and are at least temporarily infertile. Mares can be asymptomatic carriers. Strict measures have been instituted to control spread of the disease, particularly to prevent establishment in other countries. Both mares and stallions of domestic breeds must have negative cultures before being released from quarantine. Contagious metritis has not been diagnosed in Przewalski's horses, but it would be a serious threat to the species if it were.

The viral diseases rhinopneumonitis and viral arteritis can cause abortion in horses. Rhinopneumonitis is discussed below under infectious diseases. Clinical signs indicated that it was the cause of several abortions and stillbirths in at least one zoo. The mares that aborted had signs of pneumonia and neurological problems. Liver and lung tissue from an aborted fetus should be submitted for pathological examination so that the appropriate steps, in this case vaccination of mares, can be taken.

The signs of viral arteritis are high fever, congestion and swelling of the mucous membranes, especially those of the eyes, edema of the lower limbs and, in stallions, the scrotum and sheath. A high percentage of pregnant mares abort. This disease can be transmitted sexually from stallion to mare or vice-versa and from mare to mare by direct contact; therefore, the results could be disastrous for a zoo population if an infected animal of either sex were introduced.

There are several miscellaneous causes of abortion including the stress of immobilization. Another cause of abortions that probably goes undetected is copulation with a newly introduced stallion. This has been shown to occur in feral *E. caballus* (Berger 1983), and is one reason why pregnancy diagnosis should be performed on mares before a stallion is added. Developmental abnormalities of the fetus may also cause abortion as can endocrinological dysfunction or malnutrition in the mare. Twinning was a cause of abortion in one Przewalski's horse in 1966 (Volf 1982). The two placentae compete resulting in one fetal death and, often, abortion of both fetuses.

There are a variety of causes of death of neonatal foals (see Table 9.5b). Because these represent the highest percentage of loss, it is important to try to minimize these deaths. Hypothermia, in-

Table 9.5b

Causes of death of neonate Przewalski's horses in six zoos.

Date	I.D.	Sex	Age or wt	Cause
1981	#958 premature	F	15.5 kg	lungs expanded, but very weak died in 30 min; no significant bacterial or viral growth.
1981		M	8.1 kg	stillbirth.
1981	#969 neonate	M	27.5 kg	no diagnosis; no sign of infection.
1981		F	33.4 kg	stillbirth, *Aeromonas*, *Enterobacteria* and *Streptococcus* cultured from placenta.
1983	neonate	F	1 day	death associated with inclement weather conditions.
1983	neonate	F	1 day	neonatal weakness, maternal condition not optimal for preparturient period; vitamin E deficiency.
1983	neonate	F	3 days	hypothermia and acute shock associated with stormy night.
1984	neonate	?	27 kg	suffocation; wrapped in fetal membranes.
04/05/87	#1537	M	33 kg	presumed chilling; born in poor weather conditions.

Date	I.D.	Sex	Age or wt	Cause
08/07/87	#1624	F	2 days	?
09/18/82	#718 × #667[a]	F	7.6 kg	?
05/30/86	#1446	M	9 days	?
05/06/87	#1556	M	2 days	attacked by stallion.
09/19/90				cleft palate.
10/17/81	#568 × #549[a]	?	4.5 mos. gestation	?
05/19/81	#975	F	1 day	?
09/26/81	#278 × #505[a]	M	0	stillborn.
06/08/86	#1470	F	0	stillborn.
06/14/86	#1479	F	1 day	kicked in fight between mares.
03/06/87	#921 × #470[a]	F	0	stillborn.
04/01/87	#917 × #470[a]	F	0	stillborn.
04/29/88	#917 × #470[a]	F	0	stillborn.
03/29/83	#1107 Vargo	M	2 days	trauma inflicted by stallion.
05/21/84	#1226 Bolkhov	M	5 days	osteopetrosis, bacteremia.
06/14/86	#1476 Borella	F	4 days	failure to nurse.
07/07/87	#? × #568[a]	?	0	stillborn; 4 days after dam immobilized 3 days in a row.
02/27/88	#1665 Bokova	F	3 days	enteritis and sand.
04/04/88	#1670 Boykeva	F	5 days	hemorrhagic enteritis *Citrobacter*.
12/29/88	#? × #568[a]	?	0	stillborn.
06/25/80	#906	F	2 weeks	bronchopneumonia, *Pseudomonas*, cholangiohepatitis.
02/22/83		?	abortion	12 kg, myodegeneration of cardiac and skeletal muscle; axonal degeneration of spinal cord.
05/13/85	#1327 Valor	M	7 days	foreign body pneumonia, esophagitis, hepatitis, omphalitis.
10/06/85	#1399	F	1 day	omphalitis, septicemia, gastric ulcers, lymphoid hyperplasia.
09/18/88	#1777	F	4 days	omphalitis, pneumonia.
06/06/88	#1726	M	5 days	euthanized due to curvature of spine.

[a]No studbook number assigned; foal identified by parents.

fectious disease and injury inflicted by other horses are the most common problems. Vitamin E deficiency caused two deaths and can now be prevented by supplementation of the dam's diet.

Colic. Colic is a common cause of morbidity and mortality in domestic horses, but has only been reported a few times in Przewal-

Table 9.6

Deaths of Przewalski's horses caused by gastrointestinal problems.

Date	I.D.	Sex	Age	Cause
08/05/82	#1082	F	2 wks.	intussception
01/13/89	#909 Adolph	M	9 yr.	volvulus
03/15/88	#616 Roccol	M	13 yr.	torsion

ski's horses. This is probably because Przewalski's horses are fed high roughage diets or kept on pasture and wormed frequently.

Table 9.6 lists gastrointestinal causes of death. One problem was of a young foal. Neonatal foals may also have gastrointestinal problems (see Table 9.5b). For example, a foal Bokova (#1665 San Diego 59), ate sand, a common problem in domestic horses in grassless sandy enclosures. The foal may not have been nursing and therefore "grazed" sand instead because it was hungry.

Trauma as a Cause of Death

The causes of death related to trauma are given in Table 9.7. The incident that led to trauma severe enough to kill the horse or

Table 9.7

Traumatic causes of death in five zoos.

Date	I.D.	Sex	Age	Cause
06/27/88	#697 Tanya	F	11 yr.	euthanzied, leg caught in feeder.
06/23/85	#532 Burton	M	13 yr.	broken neck in pen with second stallion and mares.
01/31/88	#921 Sicca	F	8 yr.	drowned.
08/29/84	#504 Bogatka	F	13 yr.	perforated rectum following rectal examination.
03/04/86	#606 Vulkan	M	11 yr.	euthanized after vertebral fracture.
07/23/81	#944 Jr	M	6 months	euthanized, necrosis of lower limb due to wire cut.
06/16/88	#1736	M	1 week	fractured third metatarsal, infection of metatarsal areas under cast; incidental enteritis and myocardial degeneration.
07/30/83	#549 Colleen	F	11 yr.	trauma; fell from bunker.
10/31/88	#368 Bonhold	M	21 yr.	euthanized; foreleg injury.

See also Table 9.5b—#1107 Vargo

necessitate euthanasia is rarely observed; the injured animal is discovered some time after the event. Some accidents have to do with the environment. One horse cut the tendons of its forelegs on a hay feeder. Another drowned after falling through the ice into a stream. Other injuries may be caused by aggression, as discussed below.

Aggression. Bite and kick wounds occur in all groups of horses, but are more common in bachelor groups, especially those containing stallions over the age of five. The rate of aggression increases when horses are confined in smaller areas (Hogan et al. 1988) and this should be borne in mind when moving horses from larger to smaller enclosures.

Mare-Mare. The function of a dominance hierarchy is believed to be reduction of serious injury to group members. Dominance hierarchies have been identified within groups of Przewalski's horses (Boyd 1988a, Hogan et al. 1988), but occasionally there can be serious aggression between mares that have been living together for some time. An example is the case of the mare Colleen (#549 Brookfield 3) who died accidentally when she fell from the top of a former ammunition bunker used as a shelter. The horse frequently grazed on top of the bunker but hoof prints there and observations of aggression between the mares in the preceding few days led to the conclusion that she fell or was driven over while fighting with a mare who had been subordinate to her (Boyd 1986 and chapter 8).

Stallion-Stallion. Adult stallions are rarely kept together because fighting is to be expected. Two stallions, Semari (#392 Catskill 40) and Sembon (#818 Catskill 68), were kept with two mares at the Catskill Game Farm, but one stallion was the son of the other and, therefore, probably never challenged him. The dam (Bonnie Jean, #228 Catskill 2) of the younger stallion (Sembon) was one of the two mares and the son was unlikely to attempt to breed her. The stallions took turns mounting the second aged mare in the enclosure.

The outcome was not so peaceful when mares were added to a pasture containing two adult stallions, Rocky (#470 Catskill 45) and Burton (#532 Catskill 52). Two days after the mares were added, the younger of the two stallions was found dead with a broken neck. He apparently had run into a fence. It is presumed that he ran into the fence while being chased by the other stallion.

The formation of bachelor herds of stallions is advocated for

two purposes: 1) conserving housing space for "surplus" and immature stallions and 2) provision of social experience for immature
stallions that will facilitate their abilities to interact with mares
(Tilson et al. 1988). There has been little serious injury associated
with mixing of immature stallions or even with addition of an
adult stallion to a group of immature stallions. Mixture of adult
stallions does often result in injury as indicated above. The chance
of serious injury is reduced if the area is large enough for victims to avoid the aggressor and especially to avoid being trapped
against a fence or in a corner.

Nevertheless, serious bite wounds do occur even in groups that
have been established for some time. For example, the stallion
Adolph (#909 Minnesota 2) sustained severe injuries, presumably
inflicted by other stallions, to his leg and scrotum during very cold
weather. He was removed from the group and treated for four
months, during which time he was immobilized seven times (see
Table 9.2). Other stallions have had to be medically treated for less
serious wounds. A videotape of stallions' behavior when first introduced indicates the ferocity of intermale aggression even in the
absence of mares (Reindl and Tilson 1985a). It is interesting that
the immature stallions appear to be treated as mares in that they
are herded away from other stallions.

Stallion to Mare. Examples of stallions attacking mares are
Bars (#285 Askania 3) and Sibir (#607 Hellabrunn 70). Keiper
(1988) studied Bars whose aggressive behavior began in 1974. One
of his own foals was kicked to death, presumably in a fight between Bars and the foal's dam Bara (#492 Praha 106). With age
the intensity of his aggression increased, especially after he was
transferred to the Munich Zoo. In 1985, at age 22, he bit a mare
(Sirikit #754 Hellabrunn 75) so badly that she had to be euthanized.

At the Cologne Zoo, Sibir (#607) attacked mares, especially
younger mares and would keep those mares separated from the
rest of the herd (Kolter and Zimmermann 1988). He had been
added to the group when he was only three and for the next five
years was subordinate to some of the mares. Stallions with this
history frequently show abnormal social and sexual behavior later
(Boyd 1986).

Mare to Stallion. Although most sexual aggression is directed
by stallions toward mares, the reverse can also occur. Mare aggression toward stallions is most likely to occur when a stallion, espe-

cially a young stallion, is introduced to an established group of mares. In one case, the stallion received bite wounds to the penis and prepuce.

Mare to Foal. Outright foal rejection, in which the mare attacks the foal, has not been reported in Przewalski's horses, but some mares, especially primiparous mares, may neglect their foals (see Table 9.5b).

A much more common problem than neglect is accidental injury to foals inflicted either by the dam or by another mare. These injuries occur when the foal is caught between mares that are kicking one another. Mare-mare aggression is common after a new foal is born; the other mares approach and the dam tries to drive them away from the foal. Whether the motivation of the other mares is curiosity or attempts to keep the dam from nursing (Rutberg and Greenberg 1990) is unclear. Because foals will follow any animal the first few hours or days after birth the dam attempts to limit access to the foal. An example of a foal killed in a fight between its dam and another mare is #1479 (Table 9.5b). Another example is probably Boneta (#1104 Denver 3), a foal of Benna (#712 San Diego 16), who was removed and reared artificially after she was injured as a neonate while her parents were copulating. She did not die of her injuries but developed diarrhea a few months later, as many artificially reared foals do, and died. This is an example of a death that was an indirect result of social activities.

Stallion to Foal. There are several cases of Przewalski's stallions attacking foals. In the best documented case Basil (#293 Catskill 17), after living with the mares for less than a year, killed a foal (Vargo, #1107 San Diego 37) of Vata's (#826 Askania 47) sired by another stallion (Plunzer, #832 Askania 49) (Boyd 1986, Ryder and Massena 1988). He had probably also killed another foal (#1103 San Diego 36) in the herd. In subsequent years, the stallion showed no aggression toward his own foals including one from the same mare but sired by him. A two-day-old colt was attacked by a stallion at the Minnesota Zoo and died of peritonitis due to colonic rupture. There are reports of Przewalski's stallions attacking their own foals (Kolter and Zimmermann 1988). Most colts are removed from their natal group as yearlings. By the time the colt is two the stallion will aggress against him. The aggression may begin suddenly so it is probably better to remove colts before there is any sign of friction between father and son. Feral *E. caballus* stallions show similar behavior to their male offspring (Keiper and Houpt

Figure 9.1. Self-mutilation. The stallion Sibir (#607) would bite his side in certain environments, particularly when housed with mares, but would stop when placed in another enclosure. Photograph courtesy of Dr. W. Zimmermann, Cologne Zoo.

1984). Stallions also attempt to drive their daughters away; this behavior probably evolved as a means of reducing inbreeding. A mare at Port Lympne lost her tail to her sire and another leaped a fence to escape him.

Self-Mutilation. Self-mutilation by stallions usually takes the form of biting at the flanks or chest. This behavior is usually accompanied by kicking and squealing. It has been reported in a Przewalski's stallion (Kolter and Zimmerman 1988; see Figure 9.1) as well as in domestic stallions (Houpt 1983). Although opiate blockers have been shown to reduce the frequency of self-mutilation in stallions (Dodman et al. 1988), a change in the social environment such as adding or subtracting mares or reducing grain, is more practical for Przewalski's horses.

Infectious Disease

Table 9.8 lists the horses that died of infectious disease. In general Przewalski's horses are not at risk of infectious disease because they are not exposed to other horses. Nevertheless, newly acquired horses should be isolated for several weeks before being placed with resident animals. Equine influenza and rhinopneumonitis have been diagnosed as causes of death. The number of horses that died of infectious disease may be underestimated because not all horses are given a thorough post-mortem which should include culture of tissues for an etiologic agent.

The diseases to which Przewalski's horses are at higher risk are the non-contagious diseases such as tetanus (for example a Przewalski's horse in Europe died of tetanus) and, in the southwestern U.S.A., *Coccidioides*.

Table 9.8

Deaths due to infectious diseases.

Date	I.D.	Sex	Age	Cause
07/13/88	#1492 Vargos	M	2 yr.	*Coccidiodes*; euthanized; had been attacked by other males in group.
08/24/87	#1453 Beka	F	1 yr.	*Coccidioides*; died when immobilized for treatment.
06/25/80		F	14 days	bronchopneumonia *Pseudomonas*.
01/02/86	#1282 Vesuvius	M	18 mos.	meningoencephalitis, enterocolitis, gastric ulcer, pulmonary congestion.

Tetanus. Horses are the species most at risk of contracting tetanus because the etiologic agent, *Clostridium tetani,* is a normal inhabitant of the equine gastrointestinal tract. *C. tetani* is a large gram negative spore-forming bacillus that requires an anaerobic environment; therefore, it is unable to survive in normal tissue; devitalized tissue is a prerequisite. A puncture wound in the hoof is the usual cause, but umbilical infections and metritis associated with retained placenta can also lead to the disease.

The signs of tetanus are classic: spasms of the masseter muscle, "lock-jaw." Prolapse of the third eyelid will occur if the head is raised. The ears will be upright and the nostrils flared. The stance will be stiff and has been likened to a sawhorse. Tetanus must be differentiated from other central nervous system diseases such as rabies or meningitis or metabolic conditions such as hypocalcemia (lactation tetany) or hypomagnesemia (grass tetany).

The toxin, tetanospasmin, localizes in the brain and spinal cord and blocks the release of inhibitory neurotransmitters. Normally trivial stimuli provoke exaggerated responses (Cohen 1983, Johnston 1987). Tetanus is the most easily preventable of the common equine diseases so that all horses should be vaccinated annually.

Coccidioidomycosis. Coccidioidomycosis is a dustborne disease caused by *Coccidioides immitis.* Although it is usually a mild self-limiting respiratory disease, there is a chronic, usually fatal, form characterized by weight loss, accumulation of fluid in the abdominal or thoracic cavity and granulomatous lesions of the lung, spleen, and liver.

Rhinopneumonitis. Rhinopneumonitis is caused by equine herpes virus Type I. It is spread by aerosol droplets. There are three forms of disease: respiratory, abortogenic and neurologic. The respiratory disease is seen most often in young horses. Abortions occur in late pregnancy or a foal is born that survives less than twenty-four hours. The neurological signs are usually hindlimb paresis or paralysis.

Postmortem examination of aborted fetuses reveal jaundice, pulmonary edema, splenic enlargement and white foci of hepatic necrosis. Lung, liver and thymus of the fetus should be submitted for viral isolation (Liu 1983).

The two commercially available vaccines, one live and one killed virus, confer immunity for only a few months and must be administered several times during pregnancy. In some zoos, a pattern of late abortions and neurological signs may indicate that there has been an outbreak of rhinopneumonitis.

Influenza. Influenza in horses is caused by a myxovirus. The virus attacks the ciliated columnar epithelium of the respiratory tract. Uncomplicated cases require three weeks for regeneration of the epithelium. The signs are a high fever and dry cough. Secondary bacterial infection which occurs because of epithelial disruption, causes pneumonia and mucopurulent nasal discharge. Mortality is usually low except in young foals (McAllister 1982).

Przewalski's horses are usually not at risk for this disease because they are not exposed to other horses that could spread the disease to them. The available vaccine confers immunity for less than a year.

Deaths and Euthanasia Associated with Old Age

Old Przewalski's horses may be euthanized either because they are so thin or so lame that zoo visitors express concern, or because they seem to be suffering and euthanasia is the most humane treatment. Przewalski's horses (Table 9.9) can live into their thirties, which is longer than most domestic horses who are often euthanized when they can no longer be ridden. As horses age they are more likely to have sharp points on their premolars and molars that both lacerate their cheeks and prevent efficient mastication. One sign of dental problems is dribbling of food from the mouth. Regular floating of their teeth will help increase weight gain and decrease the risk of choking on imperfectly masticated food. Provision of commercial diets composed of beet pulp, grain, and molasses or equine "senior" diets would help old horses that have lost teeth.

Table 9.9

Deaths and euthanasia associated with old age.

Date	I.D.	Sex	Age	Cause
10/13/87	#278 Rocca	F	25 yr.	died; had been thin and moved slowly
11/01/87	#267 Roxane	F	26 yr.	euthanized
09/19/88	#228 Bonnie Jean	F	30 yr.	euthanized
05/20/89	#168 Rolanda	F	33 yr.	euthanized
08/13/89	#566 Rolox	M	16 yr.	euthanized
08/13/89	#277 Marianna	F	27 yr.	euthanized
08/13/89	#408 Roxie	F	20 yr.	euthanized
07/05/81	#159 Rolf	M	30 yr.	euthanized

Neoplasia is another cause of death or reason for euthanasia in old Przewalski's horses. Even when Przewalski's horses are over twenty years old a post mortem examination is valuable in order to determine what the neoplasms and senile changes affecting them are.

Lameness

Laminitis. Laminitis is the non-infectious disease to which Przewalski's horses are most susceptible. Figure 9.2 illustrates a typical case; with corrective trimming this horse became sound. Laminitis or founder is the condition in which the third phalanx rotates away from the hoof wall. The sensitive and insensitive lamina of the hoof have become separated. The complete pathogenesis of this condition remains obscure, but arteriovenous shunting of blood reduces capillary perfusion which in turn leads to increased permeability of the capillaries. Consequently, exudate builds up between the matrix and the anterior horny wall of the hoof which allows the third phalanx to rotate. The signs of acute laminitis are those of acute pain. The horse will stand with its forelegs more anterior than normal and lift its feet every few seconds. The horse is reluctant to walk and may lie down more than the usual 4% of daylight hours. When the horse is examined the hoof is warm. The warmth indicates an increased blood flow to the hoof, but arteriovenous shunts deprive the lamina of blood. If the third phalanx penetrates the sole, the prognosis is grave. In the chronic phase of the disease the coronary band is smaller. There will be a diverging growth line indicating more growth (wider rings) at the heel than the toe. Eventually, in an untreated case, the toe will curl up anteriorly. When examining a Przewalski's horse one can use the rings to determine how long ago the horse was foundered.

There are two main causes of laminitis in Przewalski's horses: 1) overeating of grain, which usually is due to overfeeding of the palatable material or 2) grazing on lush spring or fall pasture. Overfeeding is easily prevented by instructing all personnel on the dangers inherent in providing too much grain. It is more difficult to limit pasture, but, if possible, time spent grazing on lush pasture should be limited to a few hours for the first two weeks. Horses can graze a given pasture for several years, especially drought years, only to founder when more abundant rain increases the growth rate of the grass. Overweight horses are at more risk.

Absorption of endotoxin through mucosa damaged as a result of excess lactic acid production in the cecum and colon is believed

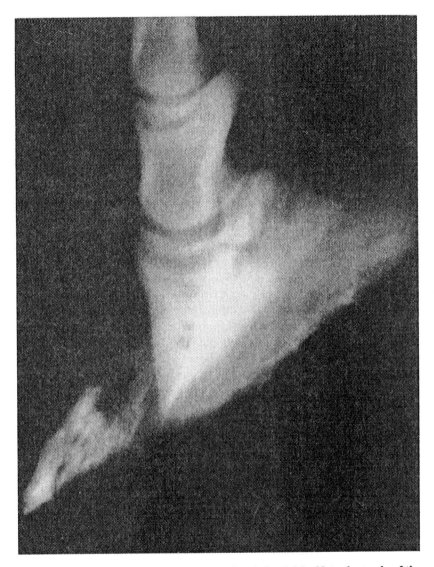

Figure 9.2.   A radiograph of a hoof affected with laminitis. Note the angle of the third phalanx. The mare Boyd (#1370) became lame while grazing on fresh lush pasture. Radiograph courtesy of the Topeka Zoo.

to be the etiology of grain-overload laminitis. The etiology of pasture laminitis is unknown.

The two main goals of treatment of laminitis are to relieve pain and decrease the angle of rotation of the third phalanx. Oral non-steroidal anti-inflammatory drugs such as phenylbutazone (2–4 mg/day) will relieve the pain. Care must be taken not to overdose with this drug as it is ulcerogenic. The hooves should be trimmed so that the heel is lowered, but not to the point where the horse is standing on the frog. The toe should be rasped down over the cranial aspect if the wall is deviated or concave. In severe cases corrective shoeing will be necessary. To further reduce pain, soft footing should be provided.

Salt should be removed from the diet temporarily to help reduce blood pressure. Methionine (10 g/day) may be added to the diet because it is essential for hoof growth (Garner 1980, Moyer 1980). Table 9.10 lists horses that were euthanized for lameness.

Nutritional Problems

Liu et al. (1983) reported eight cases of vitamin E deficiency in Przewalski's horses. The amount of vitamin E required by the horse, *E. caballus* or *E. przewalskii*, 50–80 IU/kg/day, is much higher than originally assumed (compare NRC 1978 and NRC 1989). There apparently is a familial component to the degenerative myeloencephalopathy (Mayhew et al. 1987); some horses require more vitamin E than others. The ataxia and other neurological problems in Przewalski's horses attributed to inbreeding (Ashton and Jones 1979) may have been due to vitamin E deficiency. The problem may indeed be genetic, i.e., a larger than normal requirement for vitamin E, but can be prevented by vitamin E supplementation. Equine degenerative myeloencephalopathy has been associated with a vitamin E concentration lower than 0.8 µg/ml (Craig et al. 1989), but some horses with levels this low are clinically normal and probably lack the familial predisposition. Figure 9.3 illustrates one of the typical lesions associated with vi-

Table 9.10

Deaths as a consequence of lameness in three zoos.

Date	I.D.	Sex	Age	Cause
03/09/87	#818 Sembon	M	8 yr.	euthanized; laminitis.
04/29/86	#781 Boroda	F	7 yr.	euthanized; laminitis; hoof wall necrosis; had done neurectomy.
07/16/87	#268 Henrietta	F	25 yr.	euthanized; laminitis; gastric lesion.
11/09/88	#1361 Valerius	M	3 yr.	euthanized; laminitis; incidental findings: myocardial steatosis, mild diffuse enteritis, chronic interstitial nephritis, testicular atrophy.

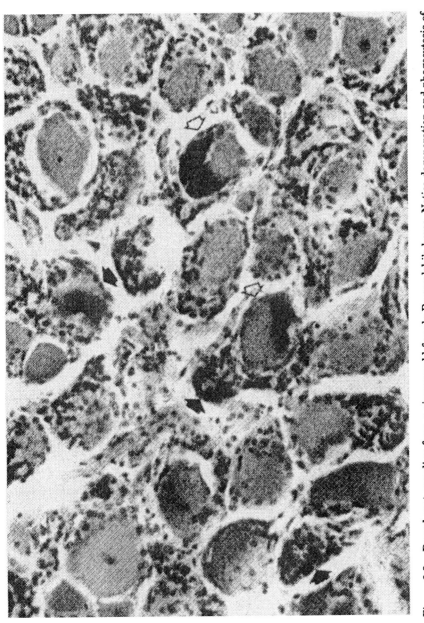

Figure 9.3. Dorsal root ganglion from a six-year-old female Przewalski's horse. Notice degeneration and phagocytosis of neurons (solid arrows), and PAS-positive lipopigment within the neuronal perikarya (open arrows). Luxol fast-blue-periodic acid-Schiff; x130. (From Liu et al. 1983, reprinted with permission of the Journal of the American Veterinary Medical Association).

Table 9.11

Deaths due to myopathy.

Date	I.D.	Sex	Age	Cause
06/23/78	#731 Rockette	F	11 mos.	euthanized, "wobbler"
02/20/81	#858 Gina	F	2.5 yr.	degenerative myelopathy

tamin E deficiency. The incidence of neuromuscular problems and infertility appears to have decreased since supplementation with vitamin E has become routine. See chapter 7 for vitamin E and other nutrient requirements of Przewalski's horses. Table 9.11 shows two cases of myopathy as a cause of death.

Miscellaneous Problems

Cancer, neurological disease, renal disease, and sudden death are the additional causes of death listed in Table 9.12. See Dietz and Wiesner (1984), Mansmann et al. (1982), Robinson (1983, 1987) and Wintzer (1986) for further information on equine diseases.

SUMMARY OF CAUSES OF DEATH

The results presented here, representing the past ten years (1979–1989) at six zoos, differ somewhat from those of Ashton who reported first on 163 Przewalski's horses who died before 1978 (Ashton and Jones 1979) and later included all 210 horses that died between 1943 and 1980 (Ashton 1984) (see Table 9.13). They

Table 9.12

Deaths due to miscellaneous causes.

Date	I.D.	Sex	Age	Cause
10/06/88	#964 Bodena	F	7 yr.	sudden collapse.
09/25/82	#1017 Allegra	F	1 yr.	euthanized due to convulsion.
02/22/83	#683 Martha	F	6 yr.	renotubular necrosis, disseminated intravascular coagulation, neuronal and axonal degeneration.

Table 9.13

Summary of the main findings in 210 Przewalski's horses which died or were destroyed in the 37 years, 1943–1980, and in 79 horses from six zoos from 1981–1989.

Category	1943–1980 No.	(%)	1981–1989 No.	(%)
Injuries	34	(16.2)	9	(11.4)
Neonatal deaths	32	(15.2)	22	(27.8)
Stillborn/Premature	20	(9.5)	14	(17.8)
Senile deaths	18	(8.6)	8	(10.1)
Gastro-intestinal signs/lesions	15	(7.1)	3	(3.8)
Metabolic (Myopathy/Neuropathy/Steatitis)	25	(11.9)	2	(2.5)
Transport accidents	9	(4.3)	7	(8.9)
Poisoning	6	(2.8)	0	
Infections	0		6	(7.6)
Miscellaneous	51	(24.3)	8	(10.1)
	210		79	

found that injuries accounted for most deaths followed by senile deaths and neurological problems. The decrease in neurological problems is probably due to vitamin E supplementation. The increase in the percentage of stillborn/premature and neonatal deaths from 25% to 46% of all deaths indicates that this is an area where improvement should be made.

10

Reproduction in the Przewalski's Horse

S.L. Monfort, N.P. Arthur and D.E. Wildt

INTRODUCTION

Structurally, the reproductive tracts of the Przewalski's (*Equus przewalskii*) and domestic (*Equus caballus*) horse are quite similar (R. Montali, personal communication 1990), as are the durations of the estrous cycle and gestation (Monfort et al. 1991). Strong evidence for the close taxonomic-relatedness of the two species comes from interbreeding studies. The mating of domestic horse stallions or mares with Przewalski's horses can result in pregnancy and the production of fertile offspring (Short 1975). Additionally, the inter-species transfer of Przewalski's horse embryos into the uterus of domestic mares has resulted in the birth of live young (Hearn and Summers 1986, Summers et al. 1987).

Zoological parks throughout North America, Europe, Asia, Australia, and the former Soviet Union have successfully bred Przewalski's horses (Volf 1989). The overall population is increasing by almost 10% per year, and more than 900 Przewalski's horses currently are maintained in captivity (Volf 1989). This suggests that this species does not experience a high rate of sub- or infertility. There is a general consensus that the existing population is physiologically 'normal,' and that instances of failed reproduction likely are related to behavioral incompatibilities (Boyd 1988a). Current management strategies focus little on attempting to improve reproduction rates. Rather, most emphasis has been placed on broadening the genetic base by minimizing inbreeding and maximizing the genetic contribution of offspring from each of the original thirteen founders (Ryder 1988).

Although Przewalski's horses have been maintained in captivity since 1898, there have been few efforts directed at understanding the fundamental reproductive biology of the species. Until recently, most of the available information was the by-product of routine zoo breeding programs. Although some contemporary efforts have been made to examine the endocrinology and embryology of the Przewalski's horse in detail, the data base for the Przewalski's stallion remains rudimentary. In this chapter, we provide an overview of our present understanding of the reproductive biology of both male and female Przewalski's horses.

GENERAL REPRODUCTIVE FEATURES OF THE PRZEWALSKI'S MARE

Age at First Reproduction

Przewalski's mares are physiologically capable of conceiving as early as two years of age, however, most do not breed until the fourth year of life (Groves 1974). Some females demonstrate cyclic ovarian activity but refuse to mate, and at least one breeding pair failed to produce offspring until they were eleven years of age (Mohr 1971). Mares generally remain fertile until about twenty years of age, and one female is known to have foaled at the age of twenty-four years (Veselovsky and Volf 1965, Mohr 1971).

Gestation Length and Seasonal Distribution of Births

A typical gestation lasts approximately eleven months with a reported range of 46 to 50 weeks (Veselovsky and Volf 1965, Mohr 1971, Groves 1974, Summers et al. 1987, Monfort et al. 1991). This variability in pregnancy length is not unusual in the domestic mare and it is not uncommon to observe variations in gestation length between 327 to greater than 357 days (Roberts 1986). Although human error in detecting behavioral estrus may contribute to this marked range, there is strong evidence that pregnancy length among individual females indeed can vary by as much as three weeks. Based on observed copulation dates and urinary estrogen measurements, we have measured gestations to range from 47.3 to 50.5 weeks for the Przewalski's horse (n = 6, mean = 48.6 ± 0.4 weeks; Monfort et al. 1991).

Although births have been observed in all months of the year (Mohr 1971), more than 75% of all foals born in 1988 were born between April and July in the northern hemisphere (Volf 1989). Of thirty-two births ever recorded in the southern hemisphere, 69% have occurred between March and July, and 31% between October and December (Volf 1989). Nothing is known about the seasonal breeding patterns of wild Przewalski's horses while they were in their native habitat. Recent studies (Monfort et al. 1991) indicate that captive Przewalski's mares in North America are seasonally polyestrous with estrous cycles commencing in the early spring. The potential breeding season lasts seven to eight months (Monfort et al. 1991). These data suggest that Przewalski's mares, like domestic horses, may rely on photoperiodic cues (increasing daylength) to re-initiate estrous cyclicity following a period of seasonal anestrus.

Abortions, Perinatal and Neonatal Mortality

The incidence of abortions, perinatal and neonatal mortality in the Przewalski's horse are similar to the domestic horse. For example, in 1988, 3 of 145 (2%) known pregnancies (Volf 1989) ended in abortion after the third month of gestation. By comparison, the incidence of abortion in domestic mares after the third month of gestation is between 2% and 12% (Roberts 1986). Although no information exists describing the incidence of early embryonic loss (during the first ninety days of gestation) in Przewalski's mares, it is estimated that early abortion occurs in 8% to 15% of all domestic horse pregnancies (Roberts 1986). Perinatal mortality refers to deaths of term offspring just before birth or during the first week of life. In domestic horses, these losses are usually attributable to asphyxiation, starvation, hypothermia or congenital abnormalities (Randall 1984). A 15% perinatal mortality rate was observed in Przewalski's horses in 1988 (22 of 145 pregnancies; Volf 1989) which is similar to rates observed in the domestic horse (5% to 15%; Randall 1984). Approximately 3% of neonates (4/145) born in 1988 died between 2–15 weeks of age (Volf 1989).

General Reproductive Concepts for Females in the Genus Equus

The characteristics of the Przewalski's mare estrous cycle and gestation lengths are best described in the general context of our present understanding of domestic mares (Figure 10.1a and b). Domestic mares demonstrate distinct photoperiod-entrained rhythms

S. L. Monfort, et al.

of ovarian activity and estrous behavior in the spring/summer, and ovarian inactivity, anestrus, in the winter. The breeding season lasts approximately five months in the northern hemisphere (May through September; Ginther 1974) with the average estrous cycle duration of twenty-two days in length. Within these cycles (Figure 10.1a), behavioral estrus usually lasts five to eight days with ovulation usually occurring on the last two days of estrus (Ginther 1974; Hughes et al. 1975; Stabenfeldt and Hughes 1977). Estrus duration is shorter during the mid-summer (peak breeding season, about five days) than during the spring (eight to fifteen days), early summer (about seven days) or fall (about eight days) (Ginther 1974). Conception is most likely to occur during the summer months when copulation occurs any time between three days before through the day of ovulation (McDonald 1980).

The onset of estrus (and ovulation) is preceded by an increased pulsatile release of gonadotropin releasing hormone (GnRH) from the hypothalamus. GnRH stimulates pituitary gonadotroph cells to secrete follicle-stimulating hormone (FSH) and luteinizing hormone (LH) into the systemic circulation for delivery to the ovarian target tissues (Figure 10.1a). Together, these hormones activate ovarian thecal (LH) and granulosa (FSH) cells of the preantral follicle which in turn promote antral follicle growth and development (McDonald 1980). Androgens produced by thecal cells are converted to estrogens in granulosa cells, an event which provokes sexual behavior. Increasing pituitary LH secretion induces preovulatory follicle expansion, and a progressive 4–5 day increase (see Figure 10.1a) in LH induces ovulation (expulsion of the oocyte); ovulation usually occurs around the third day of this increase (Stabenfeldt and Hughes 1977). After LH concentrations peak (often 1–2 days after ovulation), levels gradually decline to baseline over a 4–5 day period. After ovulation, the collapsed follicle is converted into a corpus luteum (CL) when granulosa cells (which once secreted estrogens) develop the capacity to secrete progesterone in response to additional LH secretion. Estrogens predominate in the circulation during folliculogenesis (follicular phase, Figure 10.1a) and up until the time of ovulation after which increasing progesterone concentrations reflect active CL function (luteal phase, Figure 10.1a). Therefore, the reproductive status of mares can be monitored by assessing either estrogen and/or progesterone levels in the blood (the actual hormones) or in voided urine (hormonal metabolites).

In a nonpregnant domestic horse, the lifespan of the CL is

Estrous Cycle of the Mare

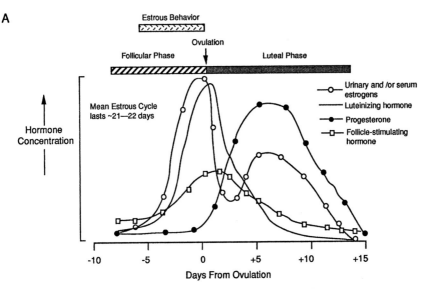

A

Estrous Behavior

Ovulation

Follicular Phase | Luteal Phase

Mean Estrous Cycle
lasts ~21—22 days

Hormone
Concentration

○ Urinary and /or serum estrogens
— Luteinizing hormone
● Progesterone
□ Follicle-stimulating hormone

-10   -5   0   +5   +10   +15

Days From Ovulation

B   The Endocrinology of Pregnancy in the Mare

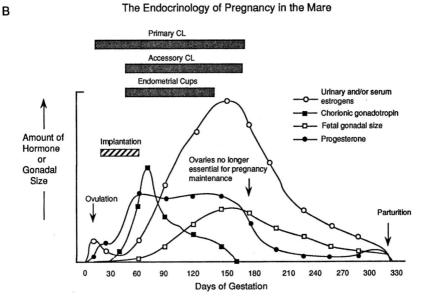

Primary CL

Accessory CL

Endometrial Cups

Amount of
Hormone
or
Gonadal
Size

Implantation

Ovulation

Ovaries no longer
essential for pregnancy
maintenance

Parturition

○ Urinary and/or serum estrogens
■ Chorionic gonadotropin
□ Fetal gonadal size
● Progesterone

0   30   60   90   120   150   180   210   240   270   300   330

Days of Gestation

Figure 10.1.   Schematic representation of the endocrine events associated with the estrous cycle (a) and pregnancy (b) in the domestic mare. (Fig. 1b adapted from Stabenfeldt and Hughes 1977).

about fourteen days, and, if conception does not occur, the CL regresses and a new ovarian cycle ensues (McDonald 1980). However, when fertilization occurs (Figure 10.1b) and an embryo forms, the CL is sustained and continues to produce progesterone for approximately the first two hundred days of gestation. Fertilization of one oocyte (and rarely two or more oocytes) occurs in the proximal end of the oviduct, and the resulting embryo migrates to the uterus during a five day transit period after which implantation is delayed for thirty to fifty-five days (McDonald 1980). The implanting embryo then invades the uterus and forms endometrial cups, which are fetally-derived hormone-producing structures which secrete chorionic gonadotropin (CG) until approximately 120 to 140 days gestation (McDonald 1980). Equine CG in blood commonly is used to diagnose pregnancy after forty days gestation. However, because CG secretion can continue autonomously even after fetal death, this test can lead to false positive pregnancy diagnoses (Lasley et al. 1990). Because it has FSH-like activity, CG induces further follicular development and "accessory" ovulations during early pregnancy (between 60 and 120 days gestation). The CL which result from these accessory ovulations, together with the primary CL (from the conceptive ovulation), continue secreting progesterone until both luteal types begin regressing rapidly between about 180 to 200 days of gestation (McDonald 1980). After 200 days, ovarian progesterone production is not required, and a secondary increase in progestins results from placental biosynthesis which remains active until parturition (McDonald 1980).

During early pregnancy, circulating (and urinary) estrogen concentrations increase markedly by approximately thirty-five days of gestation which is the result of CG stimulation (Lasley et al. 1990). This early rise in ovarian hormone secretion is most easily detected by assessing conjugated urinary estrogens. Lasley et al. (1990) recently have demonstrated that an increase in these metabolites can be used to detect pregnancy efficiently in the domestic mare. A major proportion of this initial increase is of maternal origin; therefore, pregnancy diagnosis (and assessment of fetal well-being) is not definitive until after day seventy of gestation when all estrogens are contributed by fetal tissues (Lasley et al. 1990). After day seventy, estrogen concentrations first increase dramatically (until day 150), and then decrease (until birth) in parallel with an initial growth and subsequent regression in fetal gonad size (Raeside et al. 1973, Pashen and Allen 1979, Pashen et al. 1982). The onset of parturition is accompanied by a precipitous fall in circulating estrogen and progesterone concentrations. Almost all domestic mares demonstrate a post-partum estrus (known as the 'foal heat') 2 to 13 days after foaling (Lovell et al. 1975). A subsequent estrus can occur 18 to 23 days after the onset of foal heat, and conception is possible at both of these times (McDonald 1980).

Reproductive Activity in the Female Przewalski's Horse

To date, three approaches have been used to study the physiological aspects of the reproductive cycle of the Przewalski's horse: 1) ultrasound combined with rectal palpation; 2) milk progesterone analysis; and 3) urinary hormonal metabolites.

Ultrasound/rectal palpation. Real-time B-mode ultrasonography combined with direct rectal palpation of the ovaries has been used to characterize follicular growth patterns and CL formation in the Przewalski's horse (Durrant et al. 1986). In this study, each of two mares was subjected to repeated anesthesia on seven occasions over a three month interval. After anesthesia was induced, each mare was placed in lateral recumbency. A linear-array ultrasound scanner (5 MHz transducer) was used to monitor temporal follicular growth profiles, and these observations were confirmed by simultaneous hand manipulations of ovarian structures. According to these authors, follicle size increased about 3 to 5 mm per day and ovulation occured when follicles reached an overall diameter of 48 to 50 mm (Durrant et al. 1986). These data are similar to the domestic horse which ovulates when follicle diameter is approximately 45 mm (Hughes et al. 1975).

Milk progesterone concentrations. Assessment of milk progesterone in samples collected 3 to 5 times per week has been useful for assessing estrous cyclicity in lactating mares (Zimmermann 1985). The two females used in this study were mated during this lactational ovulatory period. Milk progesterone concentrations increased from a preovulatory level of about 2 ng/ml to between 10 and 20 ng/ml by 8 days post-ovulation. Milk progesterone concentrations declined to approximately 4 ng/ml by 35 days after ovulation, but levels increased again to more than 20 ng/ml by 60 days of the resulting gestation, presumably reflecting accessory CL formation (Zimmermann 1985). Milk progesterone peaked at more than 40 ng/ml by 5 months of gestation and, thereafter, ranged from 15 to 36 ng/ml until parturition when concentrations fell rapidly to below 4 ng/ml. Post-partum ovulation and estrus were observed in both mares 9 and 12 days after foaling (Zimmermann 1985).

Urinary and fecal hormonal metabolites. The ultrasound/rectal palpation and milk progesterone studies (described above) were significant because both demonstrated the possibility of monitoring gonadal activity in the Przewalski's horse via methods used traditionally with domesticated livestock (McDonald 1980). Although few animals were used, both studies revealed some similarities in the reproductive physiology of the domestic versus Przewalski's horse. Of course, the problem with this research strategy is the need for repeatedly anesthetizing mares (for ultrasound/rectal palpation) or having access to tractable lactating individuals (for milk collection). Therefore, as for most wildlife species, there is a need for technology which will allow the analysis of endocrine (and thus reproductive) events without risking animal safety from anesthesia or mandating inordinate amounts of time for taming animals. One of the best non-invasive approaches available for studying the reproductive biology of many wildlife species, including the Przewalski's horse, is the assessment of hormonal metabolites in voided urine or feces.

Estrogen concentrations in the domestic horse traditionally have been determined by collecting blood samples. Unfortunately plasma estrogen levels in the cycling mare are relatively low, and it has not always been possible to accurately monitor ovarian folliculogenesis using this approach (Lasley et al. 1990). An alternative strategy is to exploit the physiological phenomenon that endogenous hormones normally become pooled and concentrated in the urine before excretion. This fact facilitates identifying an 'amplified' estrogen signal. In the domestic horse, the ovarian hormone estrone is excreted almost exclusively in the urine (Velle 1963). Consequently, urinary steroid analysis has been useful for documenting reproductive status in this species (Hillman and Loy 1975, Palmer and Jousset 1975). More recently, radioimmunoassay of conjugated urinary estrogens has been used to assess reproductive activity and diagnose pregnancy in domestic (Evans et al. 1984, Lasley et al. 1990) and feral (Kirkpatrick et al. 1988) horses, Przewalski's horses (Boyd 1988a, Monfort et al. 1991), and zoo-maintained zebras (Czekala et al. 1990). New techniques for monitoring urinary progesterone metabolites in zebras and domestic mares (Kirkpatrick et al. 1990a) also may be applicable to the Przewalski's mare. These simple enzyme assays should permit the assessment of ovulation, luteal function and regression and pregnancy in a diversity of Equidae. Pregnancy diagnosis also is possible in feral horses by evaluating estrogen and/or progesterone metabolites in feces or even from urine-soaked snow (Kirkpatrick et al. 1990b). Recently, fecal estrogen analysis has been demonstrated to be effective for pregnancy determination in captive Przewalski's horses (Chaudhuri, personal communication). Fecal progestagens also have been used to track estrous cyclity in five nonpregnant Przewalski's mares (Schwarzenberger et al. 1992). Although only a small number of estrous cycles were monitored (Schwarzenberger et al. 1992), this report clearly demonstrated the utility of utilizing broad spectrum antisera which detect a variety of 20α or 20β-hydroxygroup-containing fecal progestagens.

To date, the most extensive longitudinal assessment of the reproductive endocrinology of the female Przewalski's horse has been conducted at the National Zoological Park's Conservation and Research Center. In this study (Monfort et al. 1991), voided urine samples were collected from eight mares (two to seven years of age) from May 1987 through November 1988. Mares were maintained with a single stallion in a twelve hectare pasture and observed two to four hours daily for sexual activity. All observed copulations were recorded. After animals urinated, samples (1 to 5 ml) were aspirated within one minute from urine pooled on the ground. Each sample was centrifuged to remove particulate matter and stored frozen until assayed. Samples were collected approximately five times/week/female throughout the eighteen month study period. To compensate for changes in fluid balance, all samples were indexed by creatinine (Cr) measurement (Taussky 1954, Monfort et al. 1991), and values were expressed as mass units hormone/mg excreted Cr. Urinary estrogen conjugates were analyzed by a radioimmunoassay procedure described previously (Monfort et al. 1991).

Based on variations in urinary estrogen conjugates, onset of estrous cyclicity coincided with increasing daylengths, and, depending on the animal, the onset occurred between February and April. Representative longitudinal estrogen profiles from three mares sampled from January through June are depicted in Figure 10.2(b–d). Although four mares exhibited cyclic ovarian activity (based on urinary estrogen profiles) and copulated early in the year (February-March), none of these mares conceived until after March. All conceptions (n = 9) occurred in the months of April through November (April, n = 1; May, n = 1; June, n = 1; August, n = 3; September, n = 1; November, n = 2).

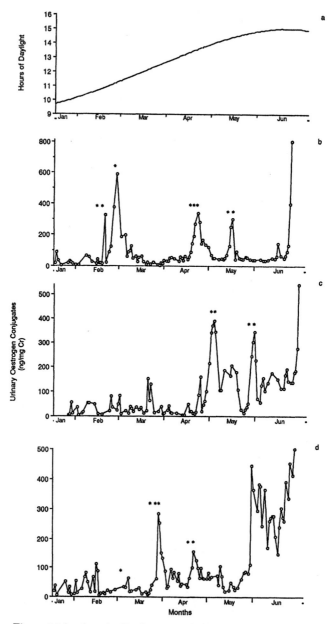

Figure 10.2. Longitudinal urinary estrogen conjugates profiles from 3 Przewalski's mares (b-d) sampled from January to June during increasing daylengths (a). Asterisks indicate observed copulations. (From Monfort et al. 1991, reprinted with permission of Journal of Reproduction and Fertility.)

Daily mean urinary estrogen conjugate concentrations representing seventeen non-conceptive estrous cycles from six mares are
presented in Figure 10.3. All sample data were aligned by the day
of the estrogen conjugates peak (Day 0). Based on the interval between consecutive estrogen conjugates peaks, the mean estrous cycle length was estimated to last twenty-four days. Twenty-nine of
thirty-five (82.9%) observed copulations occurred from Day -4 to

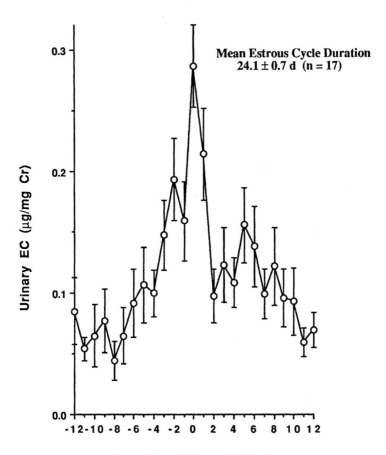

Days From Urinary EC Peak

Figure 10.3. Daily mean urinary estrogen conjugates (EC) representing seventeen estrous cycles from six non-pregnant mares. Hormone
values were aligned to the day of the urinary estrogen conjugates peak.
Vertical bars represent the s.e.m. (From Monfort et al. 1991, reprinted
with permission of Journal of Reproduction and Fertility.)

Day +1. The mean estrous cycle length of twenty-four days was shorter than that reported for the donkey (twenty-five days; Henry et al. 1987), but longer than the domestic horse (~21–22 days, Back et al. 1974, Hillman and Loy 1975, Hughes et al. 1975). However, the temporal relationship between copulatory behavior and the estrogen excretion profile was similar between the Przewalski's and domestic (Munro et al. 1979) mare.

An overall weekly pregnancy composite profile (Figure 10.4) was generated from nine pregnancies aligned to the day of parturition (Day 0). Based on known copulation dates for six mares, the mean gestation length was 48.6 weeks (range, 47–50 weeks), and the mean time of conception was best approximated by Week -49 (Figure 10.4 inset). During early pregnancy, mean estrogen conju-

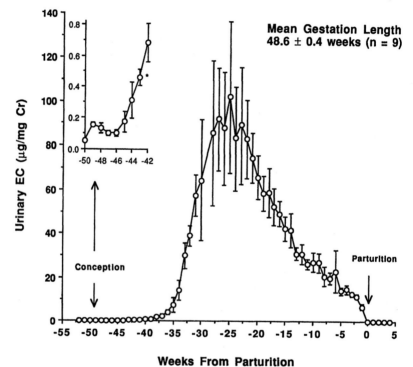

Figure 10.4. Weekly mean (± s.e.m.) urinary estrogen conjugates (EC) representing nine pregnancies monitored in seven mares. Hormone values were aligned to the day of parturition. Inset graph depicts increase in urinary estrogen conjugates around the time of conception. Asterisk indicates significant increase in estrogen conjugates in comparison to non-pregnant concentrations. (From Monfort et al. 1991, reprinted with permission of Journal of Reproduction and Fertility.)

gates declined slightly by Week -46 (Figure 10.4 inset), increased significantly by Week -43 (six weeks after the mid-cycle estrogen conjugate peak; Figure 10.4 inset), rising an additional two hundred-fold to peak pregnancy concentrations of 102 μg/mg Cr by Week -25 (51% gestation). After the mid-pregnancy peak, weekly estrogen conjugate concentrations decreased steadily to 7 μg/mg Cr by Week -1 and were not different than levels in non-pregnant mares by Week +1 post-partum. Urine sampling frequency decreased during the post-partum interval because of nervous behavior by the mares. Nonetheless, there was evidence of increased ovarian activity ten to fourteen days post-partum in three mares based on increased estrogen conjugates excretion. An example is the mare depicted in Figure 10.5 which exhibited two non-conceptive ovarian cycles followed by a conceptive cycle and pregnancy. An irregular excretory pattern of estrogen conjugates was observed

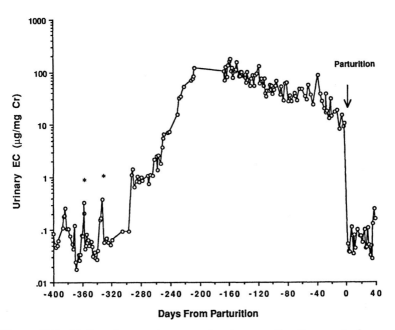

Figure 10.5. Daily urinary estrogen conjugates excretion from a single mare sampled from eleven weeks before conception (-400 days) until six weeks post-partum (+40 days). Hormone values were aligned to the day of parturition. The vertical axis is presented on a logarithmic scale to facilitate identifying cyclic hormonal patterns. Asterisks denote observed copulations. (From Monfort et al. 1991, reprinted with permission of Journal of Reproduction and Fertility.)

post-partum with metabolite concentrations achieving levels measured before conception.

Urinary estrogen conjugate concentrations were elevated by the sixth week of gestation which was the earliest time that a potential pregnancy could be accurately diagnosed. This temporal estrogen excretion profile was comparable to the domestic horse (Evans et al. 1984, Lasley et al. 1990). In the latter species, the sharp increase in urinary estrogen excretion between thirty and forty days of gestation appears to reflect increased ovarian activity in response to CG secreted by the trophoblast. Our observations suggest that similar mechanisms may exist in the Przewalski's horse. Because endometrial cups can produce CG in the absence of a fetus (Cole and Goss 1943), increased urinary estrogen conjugates excretion only indicates an attempt to establish pregnancy. Therefore, concentrations of this metabolite may not reflect actual fetal presence and viability until after endometrial cup production of CG ceases at about ninety days gestation (Lasley et al. 1990).

Our finding of a gestation length of 48.6 weeks agrees well with estimates reported by others (Mohr 1971, 47 weeks; Groves 1974, 48 weeks; Summers et al. 1987, 47 weeks) for this species. The temporal estrogen excretion patterns throughout pregnancy were analogous to the findings of Czekala et al. (1990) who examined composite profiles from different mares sampled once or twice during gestation. Czekala et al. (1990) also diagnosed pregnancy successfully in the Przewalski's horse by assessing estrone sulphate concentrations. These investigators anesthetized mares and collected a blood sample and a single urine sample by catheterizing the urinary bladder. Twenty-three mares were sampled, and pregnancy could be diagnosed accurately within ~3 months of copulation (estimated by back-dating from parturition; breeding dates were unknown). Pregnancy diagnosis was 100% effective (15 of 15) with no false positives. Urinary estrogen conjugates concentrations were correlated significantly with serum estrogen levels in both nonpregnant (r = 0.93) and pregnant (r = 0.67) mares (Czekala et al. 1990). These data validated the urinary approach for this species and indicated that urinary estrogen conjugates accurately reflect circulating estrogen concentrations. Monfort et al. (1991) measured peak urinary estrogen concentrations exceeding 100 μg/mg Cr, and these concentrations were 25% to 50% higher than the maximal levels measured by Czekala et al. (1990). Peak excretion of urinary estrogen conjugates in the domestic horse occurs at six to seven months of gestation (Raeside and Liptrap 1975, Nett et al. 1975), which was about thirty days later than the Przewalski's mare (five to six months). However, both species experience a rapid decline in estrogen excretion after mid-pregnancy with the decrease becoming more gradual with approaching parturition.

These results demonstrate the utility of longitudinal urinary estrogen conjugate profiles for studying reproductive seasonality and the endocrine events associated with cyclicity, pregnancy and parturition in the Przewalski's horse. Specifically, these data confirm that Przewalski's mares in North America are seasonally polyestrous with estrous cycles commencing in the early spring. The failure of all mares to conceive during February and March suggests that the first seasonal estrous periods in the Przewalski's horse may be anovulatory, similar to that observed in the domestic horse (Ginther 1974). The finding that conception only occurred from April to November affirmed that this species has a potential breeding season of seven to eight months, which is similar to the domestic horse (Ginther 1974, Hughes et al. 1975) and donkey (Henry et al. 1987).

From a conservation and management perspective, results indicate that longitudinal reproductive events can be monitored precisely by evaluating urinary estrogen conjugates in samples collected from Przewalski's mares maintained under semi-free-ranging conditions. Long-term assessment of urinary estrogens enables diagnosis of abnormal ovarian activity and/or detection of early embryonic loss. Longitudinal sample collection under field conditions is time-consuming, but provides an effective, non-invasive method for diagnosing pregnancy. Although this approach may not permit tracking fetal viability through the first quarter of gestation, we detected no false positives (n = 9) in our study. For field diagnosis of pregnancy, we speculate that as few as three urine samples collected over a two week interval is necessary to predict pregnancy accurately. When stallions are interchanged in an effort to enhance genetic diversity within breeding herds, information on pregnancy status can be used to help prevent infanticide which is observed in this species (Boyd 1986). We presently perform pregnancy checks before introducing new stallions to the breeding herd, and pregnant mares are removed to a nursery herd for foaling. Finally, longitudinal monitoring of urinary estrogen metabolites, including prediction of ovulation, could be extremely useful in conjunction with artificial insemination, ovulation induction and embryo recovery. These biotechniques could be particularly important for ensuring reproduction between valuable but behaviorally incompatible pairs while eliminating the risks inherent in transporting animals between breeding facilities.

GENERAL REPRODUCTIVE FEATURES OF
THE PRZEWALSKI'S STALLION

Age at First Reproduction

Przewalski's stallions tend to mature later than their domestic horse counterparts. The testes do not descend into the scrotum until 2.5 to 3 years of age (Mohr 1971). This delayed descent also is observed in other wild equids including onagers, wild asses, and zebras (Mohr 1971). It is likely that young stallions are infertile until the testes permanently enter and reside in the scrotum. However, there are other factors that may affect male fertility. For example, immature males (up to four years of age) may be incapable of breeding because they either are subordinate to older stallions/ mares or exhibit incompetent sexual behavior (Boyd 1986). Therefore, most stallions do not begin copulating until five years of age (Groves 1974). Although the precise age of reproductive senility is unknown for the Przewalski's stallion, given the opportunity, most will copulate with estrual females well into their third decade of life (Mohr 1971). The oldest known stallion to sire offspring was thirty-six years old (Veselovsky and Volf 1965).

General Concepts for the Genus Equus

Since very little information exists describing the reproductive physiology of the Przewalski's stallion, general reproductive characteristics are best described with respect to our understanding of the physiology of the domestic stallion. Stallions exhibit seasonal changes in sperm production and sexual behavior (Clay et al. 1987), however, semen can be obtained year-round from both domestic and Przewalski's horses (Durrant 1990). Although the increased sexual behavior exhibited by stallions during the peak breeding season (spring and summer) corresponds to increased blood androgen hormone levels (McDonald 1980), Przewalski's stallions can sire offspring during all months of the year (Volf 1989). In the domestic horse, the hormonal signals which modulate reproductive function are similar for both the stallion and mare. In the stallion, GnRH (from the hypothalamus) stimulates LH and FSH production and release (from the pituitary) into the bloodstream for delivery to the testis. These gonadotropins induce a cascade of intracellular events within the testes including testosterone production by Leydig cells (LH) and sperm production and maturation (testosterone and FSH) in Sertoli cells, the site of spermatogenesis. Because very little information exists describing the reproductive physiology of the Przewalski's stallion, presently, we can only speculate that similar physiological mechanisms control spermatogenesis and reproductive behavior in this species.

There are no reports detailing reproductive/endocrine rhythms in the Przewalski's stallion and only a few reports describe semen characteristics of the species. In one study (Bader et al. 1991), semen from five Przewalski's stallions was evaluated (4 to 20 years of age) to screen for subfertility. Semen was collected either by artificial vagina (n = 30) or by electroejaculation (n = 10) under general anesthesia. Three stallions with histories of poor fertility generally had low sperm counts ($0–2.0 \times 10^6$), decreased sperm motility (0–33%) and a high proportion of morphologically abnormal sperm (53–61%). Histological examination of testicular tissues from these same stallions also revealed degeneration and atrophy of the germinal epithelium and/or perivascular inflammation of the testes (Bader et al. 1991). Durrant (1990) evaluated electroejaculates collected throughout the year from ten males whose ages ranged from 2.5 to 22 years of age. Each stallion was anesthetized using a combination of etorphine (M99), acepromazine and guaifenesen (for muscle relaxation), and a 5 cm lateral electrode rectal probe and an electrostimulator was used to stimulate semen emission. This approach was effective as ejaculates containing sperm were collected on 21 of 29 occasions. Semen volume tended to be greatest in the spring (45.7 ml) whereas percentage sperm motility was higher in the fall and spring months (56.0%; 45.8%, respectively, $P < 0.05$) compared to summer values (15.5%).

Numbers of morphologically abnormal sperm also varied with season and were lowest ($P < 0.05$) in the winter compared to all other seasons. When the author analyzed seminal traits on the basis of animal age (males < ten years versus those ten years and older), there were no differences among seasons within age groups. There also were no differences in seminal traits among males which were proven (offspring produced) and unproven breeders. Although these data demonstrate the feasibility of collecting good quality ejaculates from adult Przewalski's stallions, the reported results are difficult to explain in light of the more definitive data on seasonal reproductive patterns in conspecific females. Logically, it could be expected that optimal semen quality would be achieved coincident with the late spring and summer months when mares are experiencing peak fertility. However, Durrant (1990) reports that both sperm motility and volume were poorest during the summer whereas the incidence of sperm pleiomorphisms was lowest during the winter preceding the breeding season. These observations contrast with studies in the domestic horse which demonstrate that seminal characteristics are optimal during the spring and summer breeding season (Clay et al. 1987). Clearly, more attention needs to be directed towards documenting circannual spermatogenic events and elucidating the mechanisms regulating gonadal function and sexual behavior in the Przewalski's stallion.

INTER-SPECIES EMBRYO TRANSFER

Most reproductive biotechniques, including artificial insemination, sperm/embryo freezing and in vitro fertilization, have considerable promise for facilitating management and sustaining genetic diversity in the Przewalski's horse population. None of these procedures currently are in use, however, because their application depends on a sound understanding of the basic reproductive characteristics of both the female and male. With the advent of more data on seasonality and cyclicity in the mare, and the use of noninvasive approaches like urinary hormone monitoring for predicting ovulation, some of these techniques no doubt will be used to assist in ongoing management plans.

The potential of biotechnology for helping to manage the Przewalski's horse is best-illustrated by a recent inter-species embryo transfer study. Using two Przewalski's mares, Summers et al. (1987) were able to collect embryos non-surgically. Donors were repeatedly subjected to embryo collection attempts over two successive breeding seasons (total number of attempts = 18). Mares were allowed to cycle and breed naturally. A total of eleven embryos were collected between six and ten days after estimated ovulation. The developmental stage of the embryos ranged from blastocysts to expanded blastocysts. Donor embryos were transferred surgically (n = 9) or nonsurgically (n = 2) to Welsh-type pony mares which had ovulated one to three days after the Przewalski's donors. After each embryo collection, the mares were given an injection of a prostaglandin analogue (Estrumate, 373 to 500 µg administered i.m.) to induce premature luteolysis (or a short-cycle) immediately after embryo collection so that another collection attempt could be made in the next cycle.

After embryo transfer, pregnancy status in the domestic horse recipients was monitored by real-time ultrasonography of the uterus through 120 days post-ovulation. Blood samples also were collected three times per week and analyzed for progesterone and CG, and sera were evaluated for cytotoxic antibodies against lymphocytes from the genetic parents. Based on the circulating profiles of progesterone and CG as well as ultrasound criteria, seven pregnancies were established. Not all of these pregnancies produced live young. Four foals were live-born, all resulting from surgical embryo transfer. Gestation ranged from 46 to 48 weeks and the onset of CG secretion (detectable 35 to 44 days from presumed ovulation) was similar to patterns observed for intra-species embryo transfers in domestic horses. The duration of CG secretion, however, was short-lived in comparison to normal domestic horse pregnancies. Lymphocytotoxic assays were used to assess the recipient mares' immune response to the extra-specific embryo. With only a single exception, cytotoxic antibodies first were detected shortly after the expected time of endometrial cup formation (about thirty-five days post-ovulation). The increased antibody responses at the time of endometrial cup formation were similar to those seen when a domestic horse's fetus is of a different lymphocytic antigen type than the mother. The magnitude of the immune response did not closely correspond to pregnancy outcome.

This study demonstrated that inter-species embryo transfer may be a useful technique for enhancing reproductive efficiency in the Przewalski's horse. There have been concerns about the behavioral/developmental outcome of Przewalski's horses produced by inter-species embryo transfer (Gibbons and Durrant 1987) but both of the two surviving embryo-transferred Przewalski horses have been integrated into a larger herd of Przewalski's horses. Both have successfully mated and raised their foals. See chapter 11 for a description of the behavior problem one of them did have. This approach could be used to increase the numbers of offspring from genetically rare individuals. Because six to eight embryos can be collected from a Przewalski's mare in a breeding season, it may be possible to produce two to four offspring from a single female each year (Hearn and Summers 1986). With improvements in cryopreservation technology, these approaches could permit the transport of genetic material between geographically-isolated populations. This strategy also could avoid jeopardizing the health and safety of valuable breeding stock which always is a risk when transporting wild and often stress-susceptible animals.

CONCLUSIONS AND DIRECTIONS FOR THE FUTURE

Recently, major strides in biotechnology have helped improve our understanding of the reproductive biology of the Przewalski's horse. In the mare, it now is possible to evaluate seasonal endocrine profiles and track estrous cyclicity, diagnose pregnancy and monitor fetal viability through the longitudinal assessment of urinary estrogens. There also are very recent data suggesting that it will be possible to monitor progesterone metabolites via non-invasive urinary methods (Kirkpatrick et al. 1990a). It is now possible to monitor reproductive/endocrine status in domestic and feral horses by evaluating estrogen and/or progesterone metabolites in feces and/or urine-soaked snow (Kirkpatrick et al. 1990a,b), and fecal estrogens are useful for diagnosing pregnancy in captive Przewalski's horses (Chaudhuri, personal communication). These techniques may permit evaluating reproductive status in free-living Przewalski's horses released into native habitats. Exciting advances in inter-species embryo transfer also hold promise for improving captive breeding efficiency in rare or behaviorally incompatible horses. Unfortunately, our understanding about fundamental reproductive processes in the Przewalski's stallion is poor and, thus, deserves high research priority. Areas of particular interest include examining how environmental cues mediate male fertility with particular emphasis on evaluating endocrine, morphometric and seminal traits in relation to season. In addition, because of the low numbers of original founders, sperm morphology among males and among populations should be studied. In other wildlife species, there is evidence that a restricted genotype contributes to an increased incidence of sperm pleiomorphisms which can be associated with infertility (see reviews in Wildt 1989, Wildt et al. 1991). Furthermore, there is a need to conduct many more studies in the field of gamete biology and low temperature biology. More emphasis should be placed on developing non-invasive semen collection techniques (such as the use of an artificial vagina) and determining optimal methods for cryopreserving sperm and embryos. The more efficient use of artificial breeding also will require developing new hormone treatments for regulating the estrous cycle and stimulating multiple ovulations. Many of these advanced biotechniques are used routinely and successfully in domestic horses, and there appears to be no physiological reason why these same procedures could not enhance the propagation of the Przewalski's horse. Because reproduction is the key to any successful species survival plan, continued efforts should focus on expanding the fundamental data base, a strategy that will allow both natural and artificial breeding to contribute to the more effective management of this endangered species.

ACKNOWLEDGMENTS

The authors thank Dr. Christen Wemmer, Dr. Mitchell Bush and Larry Collins for advice and logistical support. We especially are indebted to the animal keeper staff including Tracy Kepler, Ken Lang, Caroline Martinet, Pamela Starkey, Lauren Wemmer and the many volunteers at the Conservation and Research Center for assisting in collecting urine samples and performing assay procedures. This research was funded by grants from the Scholarly Studies Program of the Smithsonian Institution, the Friends of the National Zoo, and the Women's Committee of the Smithsonian Associates.

11

Activity Patterns

Lee Boyd and Katherine A. Houpt

ETHOGRAM

Ethogram Development

In any study of animal behavior an ethogram must be developed. The ethogram is an attempt to compile a comprehensive list of the behaviors exhibited by members of that species. Behaviors must be unambiguously described and criteria suggested to distinguish similar behaviors from one another.

Complete guidelines for developing an ethogram are beyond the scope of this work. The development of ethograms is discussed by Lehner (1979). An example of an illustrated ethogram can be found in Beck and Wemmer (1983). The most complete description of equine behavior to date is given by Waring (1983). Feist and McCullough (1976), Crowell-Davis (1983), and Berger (1986) provide limited ethograms for domestic and feral horse behavior. These were used as the initial basis for our Przewalski's horse ethogram.

In general, one should attempt to meld what has already been described in the literature with what is being observed in the field and augment this with further descriptions. Deriving the ethogram, as we did, by watching many populations adds to the validity of the descriptions if the behavior of the species as a whole is under study.

There are at least two strategies in designing ethograms. One method is to define each category of behavior so as to be mutually exclusive of all others. The other method is to define positional (postural and locomotor) behaviors to be recorded in combination with other activities (Prost 1965). The posture of standing, then, could be combined with any other activity with which it is observed to occur, such as eating, pawing or defecating, to give added context. We employed primarily the first method, although many of our mutually exclusive descriptions included postural criteria.

Behaviors presented in an ethogram are usually divided into behavioral states and behavioral events (Altmann 1974). Behavioral states are those behaviors which are typically longer in duration so that it is reasonable to record how long the behavior lasts, if desired. Behavioral events typically are of brief duration so that it is practical only to record that the behavior occurred, without attempting to record its duration.

Because they have a duration, behavioral states are subject to interruption. When collecting data by focal animal sampling (Altmann 1974), the observer must set a criterion for what constitutes a pause (interruption) versus a change in state. For instance, if a grazing horse lifts its head and then resumes grazing, should this be recorded as 'Grazing, Standing, Grazing,' or 'Grazing' throughout (interrupted by a pause which may not be recorded)? Criteria for defining bouts versus interruptions are discussed by Lehner (1979). The most stringent criterion for separating intra- from inter-bout pauses is the log-survivorship method in which a change in slope indicates the boundary. Except where noted otherwise, for the purposes of our study, whenever any behavior defined in the ethogram as a state occurred with a duration of less than three seconds, it was considered too brief to be practical to record, and was ignored (treated as an interruption).

Przewalski's Horse Ethogram

The following ethogram was developed for behavioral observation of Przewalski's horses. Portions of this ethogram have been utilized by at least ten different researchers in over sixteen different zoos (Anvers, Catskill Game Farm, Denver Zoo, London Zoo, Los Angeles Zoo, Memphis Zoo, Minnesota Zoo, Munich Zoo, National Zoo's Conservation and Research Center, Nature Park Lelystad, New York Zoological Park, San Diego Zoo, San Diego Wild Animal Park, Topeka Zoo and Conservation/Propagation Center, Toronto Zoo, and Whipsnade).

The ethogram is presented in outline form. General categories are listed with subheadings for specialized subsets of behavior. It is recommended that abbreviations be used as codes for these behaviors to expedite recording during observations. For time budget analysis it is often expedient to collapse subsets of behaviors (indicated by letters) into the broader (numbered) categories. For example, if one is only interested in the total amount of time spent feeding (behavior #1), there is no need to distinguish the subsets of a) eating hay, b) eating grain, c) grazing, d) browsing, or e) woodchewing from one another.

Behavioral States

1. Feeding—bouts are considered to begin when the animal takes food into its mouth and to end when the animal stops chewing.
   a. Eating Hay—Feeding on hay, either in a rack or in piles on the ground.
   b. Eating Grain—Feeding on grain until it becomes so scarce that it isn't readily visible and horses are having to search for stray kernels.
   c. Grazing—Feeding on material, other than discrete piles of hay or grain, found along the ground. In grassy pastures grazing is assumed to mean consuming grass unless otherwise noted as below in special cases. In dirt-floored enclosures grazing is assumed to mean searching for and consuming edibles unless otherwise noted as a special case.
   Special Cases:
   Grazing hay—searching for scattered wisps of hay.
   Grazing grain—searching area where fed grain for stray bits.
   Eating snow—consuming mouthfuls of snow.
   Eating leaves—consuming fallen leaves (e.g., in autumn).
   Eating feces—noting whose feces, and time of defecation if known.
   Eating dirt—actually consuming soil.
   Eating salt—licking or chewing salt block.
   d. Browsing—Feeding on tall forbs (i.e., sunflowers), shrubs, or trees.
   e. Woodchewing—see behavior problems.
   f. Cribbing or Windsucking—see behavior problems.
   For all of these behaviors, stands are not recorded as occurring unless the animal has stopped chewing. Walks are not recorded during hay or grain consumption unless the ani-

mal has moved more than two meters from the food source
while walking. For example, movement of a horse to a new
location at a hay rack would not be recorded unless it traveled more than two meters away from any part of the rack
while shifting location. Walks of less than ten seconds duration are not recorded while the animal is grazing or browsing as these are considered to be part of the act of foraging.

2. Drinking—Horse has mouth to water (and therefore is assumed to be ingesting it). If one is within a few meters of the
animal it is usually possible to observe swallowing as evidence
that water is being ingested.

3. Nursing—Foal has head under mare's flank and nose to her
udder. Pauses in suckling of more than thirty seconds duration
are considered to separate two nursing bouts.
   a. Blocking—Although not considered part of actual nursing
   bout, blocking is often performed by foals attempting to ini-
   tiate nursing. Foal crosses in front of the mare blocking her
   forward motion so that she will hold still for nursing.
   b. Bunting—a forceful upward thrust of the foal's head
   against the udder; often occurring at the onset of a bout.
   c. Suckling—occurs when the foal has a teat in its mouth and
   is sucking milk from it.

4. Stand—No locomotion, but no resting posture exhibited.
   a. Standing awake—immobile, with no other activity.
   b. Stand sniffing something (nasal contact).
   c. Stand pawing.
   d. Stand stretching—often seen after rest. The horse may pull
   itself stiffly erect with neck extremely arched, or extend its
   neck and forelegs downward so that the forequarters drop
   before pulling back up to a standing position.

5. Standing Resting—No locomotion and two of the following
four criteria must be exhibited. (See Figure 11.1.):
   One hindlimb flexed.
   Lower lip relaxed (drooping).
   Ears to side and partly lowered.
   Eyes partly or completely closed.

6. Locomotion
   a. Walk—Four beat gait with all four feet moved at least once
   sequentially.
   b. Trot—Two beat gait in which one foreleg and the opposite
   hindleg are moved at the same time.

Figure 11.1. The adult mare (#961) is standing resting over her day-old foal (#1275). This response toward young recumbent foals was described by Crowell-Davis (1986) for domestic mares. Both foals are lying sternally. Photographs by Lee Boyd unless otherwise noted.

   c. Run—Canter or gallop. Three and four beat gaits, respectively, characterized by a moment of suspension.

     If desired, one can record whether a focal animal is approaching or leaving another individual while performing one of these categories of locomotion. An additional type of locomotion is the stereotyped behavior of pacing in which the animal repeatedly retraces a path. This is discussed as a behavior problem later, and should not be confused with the gait referred to as pacing in which the hind and foreleg on the same side of the body are moved forward and backward in unison, a gait not yet reported in the Przewalski's horse.

   d. Swimming

7. Recumbency

   a. Lying sternally—Lying on the sternum, usually with head up and legs flexed (see Figure 11.1).

   b. Lying laterally—Lying flat on the side, often with neck and

Figure 11.2.   Four-month-old foal (#1192) lying laterally.

  legs outstretched, and with the head usually contacting the
  ground (see Figure 11.2).
8. Groom Self—Care of its own body by an individual (see Figure
  11.3).
  a. Chewing—using the mouth to groom the body.
  b. Rubbing—rubbing part of the body on an object or rubbing
     the head against another part of the body.
  c. Rolling—rolling on the ground. The horse may stay on one
     side or roll from one side to the other with legs off the
     ground. It may prop itself up on its forelegs as if to begin
     standing but then rub its sternum on the ground. The bout
     ends with the horse propping itself up with its forelegs,
     moving the hindlimbs under the body and using the hind-
     quarters to push itself up. Shaking commonly follows stand-
     ing.
  d. Scratching—use of one part of the body other than the
     mouth to scratch another. Typically one of the hindlimbs is
     used to scratch a more anterior portion of the body.
9. Mutual Groom—Reciprocal coat care in which the partners
  nuzzle and chew one another's coats (see Figure 11.4). Other

Figure 11.3.   The foal on the left (#1249) is grooming itself by chewing. Its mother (#822) is grooming herself by rubbing.

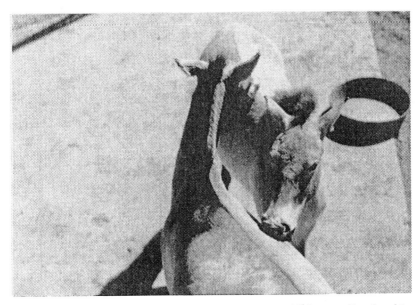

Figure 11.4.   The mare Botania (#841) mutual grooms with her yearling daughter Shalimar (#1232). Close relatives are preferred grooming partners.

information such as the part of the body being groomed may be recorded if desired.

10. Play—Behavior with no other perceived function. In contrast to aggressive behavior, the participant's ears are generally directed forward or laterally rather than flattened posteriorly.
    a. By Self—performed alone. Includes running, bucking, and mouthing objects.
    b. Playing directed at another individual who does not reciprocate—includes biting, pulling mane or tail, kicking, and mounting.
    c. Mutual Play—play which is reciprocated by a partner. Bouts often include nose nips, hock bites, knee bites, crest bites, kicking, mounting, rearing, chasing, etc. (see Figure 11.5a and b).

11. Mating Behavior—Can be treated as a state if the duration from the approach of the stallion until he dismounts or turns away from the mare is recorded. Common events that occur in this context include:
    a. Proceptive Behavior—The mare backs into the stallion, or stands in front of him with tail deviated. She may urinate and evert the clitoris.
    b. Erection of the stallion's penis.
    c. Mounting—the stallion may rest his chin on the mare's back testing her willingness to stand, and then rear and place his forelimbs anterior to the mare's pelvis. Inexperienced stallions or those mares who mount may mount from the side rather than from the mare's rump.
    d. Mating face (Rossigkeitgesicht)—seen in female. Ears turned back but not flattened, lips relaxed.
    e. Intromission of the penis into the vagina.
    f. Pelvic Thrusting by the stallion.
    g. Ejaculation—Cessation of thrusting, marked by tail flagging (raising and lowering of tail).
    h. Dismounting.

Behaviorial Events (can be recorded under whatever state the animal happens to be in at the time)

1. Urination—Typical female stance is for the tail to be elevated and the hindlegs to be spread slightly laterally. Clitoral winking (repeated eversion of the clitoris from its fossa) follows the voiding of the urine, but is prolonged when the mare is in es-

Figure 11.5.   a. The yearling colt Bryansk (#1249) bites the crest of his half-sister Shalimar (#1232) in play. Note that the ears are not flattened back as in aggression. b. The four-month-old colt Vasiliy (#1192) and the mare Belaya (#458) rear while playing together.

trus. Typical male stance is to step the forelegs anteriorly so that both forelegs and hindlegs are extended beyond ninety degrees during penile letdown and voiding of the urine. The hindlegs then are brought forward as voiding is completed.

2. Defecation—The tail of both sexes is elevated.
3. Flatulency—Tail is elevated and expulsion of gas is frequently audible.
4. Marking—Usually performed by stallion after he sniffs urine or feces. He typically steps over the excretion and marks it with urine or feces.
5. Flehmen—Lip is curled dorsally and the head and neck are often outstretched and elevated. Accompanied by inhalation and exhalation. Typically occurs after sniffing urine or feces, or the anogenital region of another individual. May also be shown when encountering unfamiliar substances such as ice or blood.
6. Yawn—The mouth opens widely and the mandible may be shifted laterally; the eyes are partially closed.
7. Dislodging flies
   a. Stamping—Horse may pick up and forcefully put down a limb to dislodge flies.
   b. Kicking at flies—Horse may kick a hindlimb forward to brush flies off the belly.
   c. Swatting flies—with the head or tail. Tail flicks may be too frequent to quantify if the flies are numerous.
   d. Shaking or rubbing on objects to remove flies—May be difficult to determine whether this is fly-induced or simply part of self-grooming not related to the presence of flies.
   e. Twitching skin—Brief contractions of subcutaneous muscles in response to skin irritation.
8. Shying—Response to frightening stimulus. Horse jumps laterally away from the frightening object, then either flees or turns to face it.
9. Masturbation by stallion—Penile letdown and erection, followed by flipping the erect penis against the belly. May be seen in a variety of contexts but most often when the stallion is standing resting (see Figure 11.6).
10. Communication and Additional Sounds (see also chapter 12):
    a. Touch Noses—Two individuals make nose-to-nose contact with one another. Necks may be slightly arched, and squealing and striking may follow.

Figure 11.6.   Masturbation by the stallion Rousseau (#701).

b. Neigh (Whinny)—A long vocalization of high amplitude that varies in frequency. See Figure 12.1.

c. Nicker—Usually quieter than a neigh. Often seen between a mare and foal, or when a stallion courts a mare.

d. Squeal—Usually heard during aggressive interactions.

e. Cough—A response to respiratory tract irritation—frequent coughing may be indicative of respiratory pathology.

f. Snort—Short forceful exhalations from nostrils.

g. Fear Snort or Blow—Explosive snort with nostrils flared and head high. An alarm call.

h. Grunt or Groan—Low pitched vocalization sometimes indicating discomfort.

i. Snores—Raspy sounds while recumbent.

11. Aggression and Related Behaviors (see also chapter 12):

a. Snapping—(Champing, Toothclapping) Usually seen in young animals. Opening and closing mouth with lips retracted. Head and neck may be extended.

b. Supplant—Approach of one horse causes another to move away, without overt aggression.

Figure 11.7.   Bite threat by the mare Loxy (#618).

    c. Bite Threat—Bite intention movement with ears back and neck extended, with no actual contact (see Figure 11.7).

    d. Bite—As above, but with actual contact to another horse's body.

    e. Kick Threat—Intent to kick, performed by swinging rump or backing up, or by waving or stamping hindleg toward another horse (see Figure 11.8).

    f. Kick—One or both legs thrust backward in an attempt to contact another horse.

    g. Strike—One foreleg swiftly and stiffly extended (see Figure 11.9).

    h. Rear—Both forelegs leave the ground, horse rises on hindlimbs.

    i. Chase—One horse runs after another, often involving bite threat by the chaser.

    j. Herding (Snaking, Driving)—Usually used by the stallion to drive mares. Head and neck are usually lowered and extended, with ears back. Leg action is often stiff in appearance. The head and neck alone or the entire body may be moved in a serpentine fashion (see Figure 11.10).

    k. Arched Neck Threat—Two stallions touch noses with ex-

Figure 11.8. Mutual kick threats by the mares Roxina (#480) and Bessah (#961). This incident later escalated into a series of exchanged kicks.

Figure 11.9. The stallion Rolmar (#568) and the mare Botania (#841) simultaneously strike after touching noses.

Figure 11.10.   The stallion Roccol (#616) herding the mare Loxy (#618).

tremely arched necks. Squealing and striking almost always follow.
l. Parallel Display—Two stallions walk or trot in parallel
with one another, often exhibiting arched necks, elevated
tails, and high leg action (prancing).
For additional descriptions and illustrations of these behaviors in
domestic horses (*Equus caballus*) see Waring (1983).

SAMPLING METHODS

Discussions of sampling methods for observing behavior are
provided by Altmann (1974) and Lehner (1979).
To obtain time budgets and frequency of occurrence of particular behaviors, we used fifteen minute focal animal samples (Altmann 1974). Fifteen minutes was chosen as being longer than the
typical duration of any behavioral state, but not so long as to fa-
tigue the observer. The next focal animal to be observed was drawn
randomly without replacement from the list of herd members until
all herd members had been observed once; the process was then
repeated.

During focal observations, instantaneous samples taken at five minute intervals were used to record the area of the enclosure that the animal occupied, its nearest neighbor, distance to the stallion if observing a mare or foal, and distance to the dam if observing a foal, or distance to the foal if observing its dam. For further methodological details see Boyd (1988a) and Boyd et al. (1988).

There are a variety of ways for dealing with periods when a focal animal goes out of sight (Lehner 1979). We chose to either delete the time spent out of sight from the sample and only use the time in sight to calculate the time budget, or assume, if the out of sight period was brief, that the animal continued the behavior it was last seen doing while it was out of sight.

When multiple observers participate in a study, interobserver accuracy becomes important. When we expanded data collection to zoos around the world, we met with prospective observers and provided them with a copy of the ethogram and instructions on how to collect data. They were able to practice recording observations while viewing a continuous sequence of Przewalski's horse behavior on videotape. Their data could then be compared with that recorded by the primary observer (Boyd) who had filmed the videotape. Finally, field trials of interobserver accuracy were periodically conducted by having several observers collect data on the same animal simultaneously and comparing the percentage of agreement between everyone's results (Lehner 1979).

TIME BUDGETS

A knowledge of the amount of time horses spend in various activities can be useful in a variety of ways. The behavior of horses who are thought to be ill can be compared to typical behavior of healthy animals. Time budgets of horses in unnatural settings such as small dirt-floored yards can be compared to those on pasture and the comparison used to suggest ways to make their behavior more closely approximate that in more natural settings. The time budgets of juveniles can be used as an index of their maturation process.

Twenty-four hour time budgets (Bubenik 1961, Boyd et al. 1988), time budgets of adult Przewalski's horses (Boyd 1988b), and time budgets of juvenile Przewalski's horses (Boyd 1988c) have been compiled. Hogan et al. (1988) compared time budgets of the same group of Przewalski's horses in a small versus a large enclosure.

Twenty-four Hour Time Budgets

The horses in the most extensive twenty-four hour study were in a harem housed in a large grassy pasture at the National Zoo's Conservation and Research Center in Front Royal, Virginia (Boyd et al. 1988). On average, the horses spent 46% of their time feeding, 0.5% drinking, 20.5% standing, 16% stand-resting, 2% self-grooming, 2% mutual grooming, 7% in locomotion, 1% playing, and 5% in recumbency.

The percent of time spent in most behaviors varied by time of day. The amount of time spent feeding peaked at night (68.2% of time budget between 2000 and 2400 hours), perhaps because the study was conducted during the warm summer months. Feral horses (Keiper and Keenan 1980, Kaseda 1983) and Przewalski's horses (Bubenik 1961) have previously been reported to forage predominately at night during the summer. The Przewalski's horses also spent most time in recumbency at night, between 0000 and 0400 hours, as has also been reported in feral horses (Keiper and Keenan 1980) and other Przewalski's horses (Bubenik 1961).

During the warmer hours of the day the Przewalski's horses in this study spent more time standing, stand-resting, moving around and drinking. Mutual grooming and rates of aggression also peaked at this time as the horses were standing around in close proximity to one another.

Adult Time Budgets

The study by Boyd (1988b) involved fifteen male and twenty-seven female Przewalski's horses in twelve enclosures at seven zoos. Presently that data set has been expanded to twenty-eight adult males and sixty-nine adult females in twenty-five enclosures at sixteen zoos around the world. Three males and two females were observed in more than one location. Individuals included in the analysis were all more than one year old, and 90% were greater than two years old. The time budgets were tabulated from 1319 hours of focal animal observation (Altmann 1974), with an average of 13.3 ± 1.6 (S.E.M.) hours of observation per horse. Data were collected as described in Boyd (1988b).

All females and 58% of the males were members of harems. Some harems were housed in dirt-floored enclosures and others were on pasture. Two-way analysis of variance was used to compare the effects of gender and enclosure type on the time budgets of harem members (Table 11.1). Harem males spent more time in recumbency than females. They also spent more time defecating and urinating, perhaps because marking behavior was included in these categories for the purposes of this analysis. Males also showed flehmen with greater frequency than did females. Harem members housed in yards spent more time drinking than those horses on pasture, presumably because the hay they fed upon contained less moisture than uncut grass. They also spent more time urinating, and groomed one another less than pastured animals. Horses in yards spent less time standing resting, as was noted in the previous study (Boyd 1988b), or resting in a recumbent position. Most animals in yards are on-exhibit in urban areas and it is

Table 11.1

Time budgets of harem members by gender and enclosure type.

N	All Members 89	By Gender		By Enclosure Type	
		stallions 18	mares 71	yard 58	pasture 31
States (% time)					
Feed	52.5 ± 1.5	50.6 ± 0.9	53.8 ± 1.8	50.5 ± 0.3	53.9 ± 0.6
Coprophagy	0.1 ± 0.0	0.0 ± 0.0	0.1 ± 0.0	0.1 ± 0.0	0.0 ± 0.0
Drink	1.0 ± 0.1	1.0 ± 0.1	0.8 ± 0.0	1.3 ± 0.0	0.5 ± 0.0**
Self-Groom	1.9 ± 0.3	1.4 ± 0.2	2.1 ± 0.0	1.6 ± 0.1	1.2 ± 0.1
Mutual Groom	1.1 ± 0.1	1.2 ± 0.1	1.2 ± 0.0	0.8 ± 0.0	1.7 ± 0.1*
Play	0.4 ± 0.1	0.5 ± 0.1	0.3 ± 0.0	0.6 ± 0.0	0.2 ± 0.0
Standing	22.5 ± 1.2	22.8 ± 0.6	21.1 ± 0.2	24.9 ± 0.2	19.1 ± 0.5
Stand Resting	8.5 ± 0.9	7.4 ± 0.5	9.9 ± 0.1	6.6 ± 0.2	10.8 ± 0.3*
Locomotion	10.4 ± 0.6	11.4 ± 0.3	9.5 ± 0.1	11.4 ± 0.1	9.6 ± 0.2
Recumbency	0.7 ± 0.2	2.0 ± 0.1	0.6 ± 0.0**	0.5 ± 0.0	2.1 ± 0.1**
Defecation	0.2 ± 0.0	0.3 ± 0.0	0.2 ± 0.0*	0.3 ± 0.0	0.2 ± 0.0
Urination	0.2 ± 0.0	0.4 ± 0.0	0.1 ± 0.0**	0.3 ± 0.0	0.2 ± 0.0*
Mate	0.1 ± 0.0	0.1 ± 0.0	0.1 ± 0.0	0.2 ± 0.0	0.0 ± 0.0
Events (per hour)					
Aggressions	2.9 ± 0.2	2.8 ± 0.0	2.8 ± 0.0	2.9 ± 0.1	2.7 ± 0.1
Vocalizations	1.6 ± 0.2	2.0 ± 0.1	1.5 ± 0.0	2.0 ± 0.0	1.5 ± 0.1
Flehmen	0.1 ± 0.0	0.3 ± 0.0	0.1 ± 0.0**	0.2 ± 0.0	0.2 ± 0.0

Values listed are means ± standard error of the mean.
*ANOVA, significant difference at p<0.05
**ANOVA, significant difference at p<0.01

possible that the sights and sounds of visitors and potential predators housed nearby are not conducive to sleep. Pastured horses are
often not on exhibit, or if they are, the pasture is large enough to
prevent the public from approaching the horses too closely if the
horses choose to move away. Although neither the sex of the individual nor the enclosure type seemed to affect the average amount
of time spent eating feces, 29% of the horses in yards exhibited
coprophagy as compared to 10% of those on pasture. The presence
of food ad libitum, i.e., pastures, has been shown to reduce the incidence of coprophagy (Boyd 1986, 1988b). No difference attributable
to sex was observed; 22% of adult males and 22% of adult females
were coprophagous.

   In the analysis of variance one behavior showed an interactive
effect between gender and enclosure type; females in yards and
males on pasture spent more time in locomotion than males in
yards. Females on pasture spent the least time in locomotion.
Males on pastures might be expected to show more locomotion than
their mares as they often range over the pasture rounding up stray
mares and checking stud piles, and scanning the fence for 'in-
truders'. With ad libitum forage available and high nutritional demands placed on them during late pregnancy and lactation, females on pasture spend little time in motion that is not part of the
act of foraging. However, food may not be present ad libitum in
yards. Either because they are not occupied with feeding or because they are stressed by confinement, horses in yards spend more
time in motion, but the stallions have less ground to cover in performing their herd-vigilance activities.

   In addition to being in harems, stallions were housed either
solitarily or as members of bachelor groups. One-way analysis of
variance was used to compare the effects of social grouping and
enclosure type on stallion time budgets (Table 11.2). Males in
bachelor groups spent more time playing than solitary or harem
males. Play-fighting is also common in feral horse bachelor groups
and is believed to be important in developing skills necessary to
compete with rivals and obtain females (Hoffmann 1985, Keiper
1985). Solitary males and bachelor group males spent more time
than harem males in locomotion as they would have to do in the
wild to locate females. This locomotion was apparently not due to
aggressive encounters as bachelor males had lower rates of aggression than harem males, and solitary males had no one with whom
to interact. Horses are gregarious by nature so it is not surprising
that solitary males were far more vocal than the other males, pre-

Table 11.2

Male time budgets.

N	All Males 31	By Social Status			By Enclosure Type	
		solitary 5	bachelor 8	harem 18	yard 24	pasture 7
States (% time)						
Feed	48.2±2.2	48.6±2.8	43.5±4.6	50.2±3.1	47.5±2.3	50.6±6.1
Coprophagy	0.2±0.1	0.5±0.3	0.5±0.4	0.1±0.0	0.3±0.2	0.0±0.0
Drink	1.2±0.2	0.9±0.2	1.5±0.4	1.2±0.3	1.4±0.2	0.5±0.3*
Self-Groom	1.1±0.2	0.3±0.1	1.0±0.2	1.3±0.2	0.9±0.1	1.6±0.5
Mutual Groom	0.8±0.2	—	0.8±0.4	1.0±0.3	0.6±0.2	1.6±0.7*
Play	1.7±0.5	0.0±0.0	4.5±1.3	0.9±0.4**	2.1±0.6	0.3±0.2
Standing	22.9±1.8	21.2±2.2	22.4±1.9	23.6±2.9	24.0±1.8	20.4±5.2
Stand Resting	7.7±1.3	7.4±3.9	9.2±2.9	7.2±1.6	7.0±1.4	10.2±3.6
Locomotion	14.1±1.4	20.1±1.9	16.7±3.7	11.2±1.3*	14.5±1.6	12.5±2.8
Recumbency	1.0±0.4	0.2±0.2	0.0±0.0	1.6±0.7	0.5±0.3	2.7±1.4*
Defecation	0.4±0.1	0.3±0.1	0.2±0.0	0.5±0.2	0.4±0.1	0.3±0.1
Urination	0.4±0.1	0.1±0.0	0.2±0.1	0.5±0.2	0.4±0.2	0.2±0.1
Mate	0.1±0.0	—	—	0.2±0.1	0.1±0.1	0.1±0.1
Masturbation	0.2±0.0	0.1±0.1	0.2±0.1	0.1±0.1	0.2±0.1	0.1±0.1
Events (per hour)						
Aggressions	2.0±0.3	—	1.6±0.4	2.8±0.5	1.9±0.4	2.6±0.6
Vocalizations	2.3±0.3	4.1±1.2	1.8±0.2	2.1±0.4*	2.5±0.4	1.9±0.5
Flehmen	0.2±0.1	0.1±0.1	0.2±0.1	0.3±0.1	0.2±0.1	0.3±0.2

Values listed are means ± standard error of the mean.

*ANOVA, significant difference at p<0.05

**ANOVA, significant difference at p<0.01

sumably in an attempt to locate conspecifics. Harem males tended to have a higher rate of aggression than bachelors, probably as they are relatively unrelated to their mares (Boyd 1988a) and trying to exert some control over their harem. As was the case in the previous analysis of harems, males in yards spent more time drinking, and less time mutual grooming and recumbent than males in pastures. The small amount of time they spent mutual grooming can, in part, be explained by the fact that four of the five solitary males were in yards. This can not be the entire explanation, however, because in the previous analysis, harem members of both sexes also spent less time mutual grooming in yards than on pasture. If one assumes that mutual grooming is performed when the horses are relaxed, and not having to devote attention elsewhere, the small amount of mutual grooming in yards tends to support the hypothesis that these are more stressful surroundings than pastures.

A previous study of the effects of female reproductive status on time budgets found that mares who were neither pregnant nor lactating spent less time feeding and more time standing and standing resting than pregnant or lactating mares (Boyd 1988b). Three mares were observed in several reproductive contexts: while pregnant but not lactating they spent 69% of their time feeding, while not pregnant but lactating they spent 73% of their time feeding, and while pregnant and lactating they spent 75% of their time feeding. These percentages correlate well with the increased nutritional demands on mares imposed by late pregnancy and early lactation.

Foal Time Budgets

Fourteen male foals and thirteen female foals under one year of age were observed. Male foals spent less time feeding than female foals (Table 11.3), which is surprising since colts are often larger and might be expected to need more food. Colts spent far more time playing than fillies. Apparently even at this age, like their older bachelor brothers, colts are honing competitive skills through play. Colts also had a tendency to flehmen more often than fillies, which is consistent with the difference in flehmen rates between adult males and females.

Foals in yards spent more time nursing than those on pasture. This was apparently not due to differences in age; the average age of foals in yards was 7.8±1.2 months and the average age of pas-

Table 11.3

Time budgets of foals by gender and enclosure type.

	All Foals	By Gender		By Enclosure Type	
		colts	fillies	yard	pasture
N	27	14	13	8	19
States (% time)					
Feed	50.6±2.6	43.9±0.5	57.0±1.2*	46.1±1.6	54.8±0.6
Coprophagy	0.1±0.1	0.2±0.0	0.0±0.0	0.1±0.0	0.0±0.0
Drink	0.5±0.1	0.4±0.0	0.5±0.1	0.3±0.1	0.6±0.0
Nurse	2.1±0.4	2.8±0.1	1.6±0.2	3.0±0.2	1.4±0.1*
Self-Groom	3.6±0.6	3.3±0.1	2.6±0.3	1.8±0.4	4.1±0.2
Mutual Groom	1.2±0.3	1.2±0.1	0.9±0.1	0.5±0.2	1.5±0.1
Play	1.3±0.4	2.1±0.1	0.5±0.2*	2.0±0.2	0.7±0.1
Standing	15.5±1.6	18.4±0.4	15.0±0.8	20.9±1.1	12.5±0.4*
Stand Resting	4.0±1.0	4.6±0.3	2.9±0.6	2.9±0.8	4.5±0.3
Locomotion	10.2±0.5	11.4±0.1	9.8±0.3	11.7±0.4	9.5±0.1
Recumbency	10.5±1.7	11.4±0.5	8.3±1.0	9.8±1.3	9.9±0.5
Defecation	0.2±0.0	0.1±0.0	0.2±0.0	0.1±0.0	0.2±0.0
Urination	0.2±0.0	0.2±0.0	0.2±0.0	0.1±0.0	0.2±0.0
Events (per hour)					
Aggressions	1.1±0.2	1.1±0.1	1.2±0.1	1.2±0.2	1.1±0.1
Vocalizations	0.9±0.2	0.8±0.1	0.9±0.1	0.8±0.2	0.9±0.1
Flehmen	0.2±0.1	0.3±0.0	0.0±0.0	0.1±0.0	0.2±0.0

Values listed are means ± standard error of the mean.
*ANOVA, significant difference at $p < 0.05$

tured foals was 5.9 ± 0.9 months. Foals in yards spent more time standing than pastured foals. With relatively dry forage compared to pasture and less of it available, perhaps the foals in yards spent more time standing around and nursed for fluid intake and comfort. Such nursing might also represent comfort-seeking after agonistic interactions which Hogan et al. (1988) found to be common in Przewalski's horses kept in yards.

PARTURITION

The most detailed description of the birth of a Przewalski's foal appears in Boyd (1988c). The colt (Belek, #1275 San Diego 40) was born to a primiparous mare (Bessah, #961 San Diego 33) in a 5.3 hectare pasture. Parturient domestic and feral horses are commonly reported to leave their herds before foaling. This mare attempted to leave about twenty minutes before giving birth, but was followed by another herd member and returned to the vicinity of the other herd members. The mare began to lose the amniotic fluid at 1700. Five minutes later the amniotic sac was visible, and the mare lay down after eight additional minutes had elapsed (Figure 11.11). Within four minutes after the mare became recumbent, the foal's forequarters were expelled, and a minute later his struggling broke the amniotic sac. The mother (Belaya, #458 San Diego 2) of the parturient mare approached and began licking the foal. Eleven minutes after the forequarters were expelled, the parturient mare stood, which freed the foal's hindquarters and broke the umbilical cord. The mare immediately joined her mother in nuzzling and licking the foal. Six minutes after standing the afterbirth was expelled. The mare sniffed the afterbirth briefly but ignored it thereafter. The foal began trying to stand twenty minutes after it was born and after ten minutes of attempts finally was successful. By forty-five minutes of age he was walking and approaching other herd members. At the end of the first hour, he passed the meconium and began trying to nurse. Most domestic

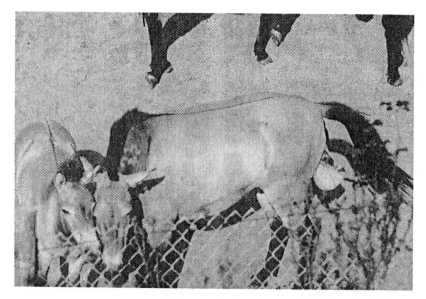

Figure 11.11. The mare Bessah (#961) delivers the forelegs of her colt (#1275), visible within the amniotic sac. The mare lay down to complete the delivery.

horse foals nurse successfully about an hour after they are born (Rossdale 1967, Jeffcott 1972, Tyler 1972, Waring 1982). In spite of his attempts, this foal was not successful because his primiparous mother kept turning to keep him under her nose. The foal lay down to rest an hour and a half after he was born. Darkness precluded further observations, but by morning the foal was nursing successfully. Although the birth and neonatal behavior were typical of what has been described for other equids, with the exception of nursing, the timing of the events was accelerated. Contributing factors might have included the mother's youth and excellent physical condition, the aid given by her mother in cleaning and protecting the foal, and a lack of artificial selection for attributes such as large size which affect the time of first standing in domestic horses (Campitelli et al. 1982/83). The birth was unusual in that the grandmother of the foal was present and assisted in caring for the foal. She and the foal's mother spent similar amounts of time licking the foal during the first hour and both protected it (Boyd 1988a). After the first hour the grandmother ceased most of her assistance.

ONTOGENY OF BEHAVIOR

On the first day of life Przewalski's foals have been observed to stand, walk and trot, rest in standing and recumbent positions, nurse, nibble forage, groom themselves, defecate, paw, snap, neigh and nicker (Boyd 1988c). By the end of their first week they are grazing and eating hay and grain, although the percent of time spent nursing exceeds that spent foraging until they are several weeks old. Coprophagia is common by the end of the first week. Equid foals are thought to obtain gut flora and nutrients through consumption of adult feces (Crowell-Davis and Houpt 1985). The amount of time spent feeding by Przewalski's horse foals increases steadily until at five months of age they are spending at least as much time feeding as are the adults. The biggest decline in nursing occurs between months one and two, when the percent time spent in this behavior drops from 8.5% to 2.4%. This transition coincides with the time when foals are beginning to drink water.

Przewalski's horse foals spend 39% of their time resting during their first month. The amount of time spent resting declines rapidly after the first few months. Recumbency is the most common position of rest in young foals. After two months of age, standing resting is the most common position of rest as it is in adults, however foals continue to exhibit more recumbent rest than adults throughout their first year of life. Similar patterns of resting are exhibited by young domestic horses (Boy and Duncan 1979). Paradoxical sleep usually occurs in the recumbent position and is thought to play a role in memory sorting and consolidation (Dallaire 1986), which would be important to foals as much of what they encounter daily would be novel to them.

Running, solitary play, and kicking defensively appear in the first week of the Przewalski's foal's life. Toward the end of the first month foals begin mutual grooming, initially with their dam, and in subsequent months with other herd members. Mutual play is common by the end of the first month and foals may wander out of sight of their dams and have herd members other than the dam as their nearest neighbor. Foals are involved in little aggression during their first month while they are staying close to their mothers. As they become more independent their involvement in aggression increases, although rates typically are lower than those between adults. Toward the end of their first year colts begin showing male-typical behaviors such as marking and masturbation.

The mother is the foal's nearest neighbor 97% of the time on Day 1 and 95% of the time she is within one meter of the foal. During its first month of life the foal's mother is its nearest neighbor 88% of the time and 83% of the time they are within five meters of each other. From the second month onward the dam is the foal's nearest neighbor only 55% of the time, but 75% of the time they are still within five meters of one another. The association of dam and foal usually continues into adulthood if the offspring are allowed to remain in their natal herd. In contrast, the sire is the nearest neighbor of the foal only about 10% of the time, and during the first week of her foal's life, dams usually prevent the stallion from approaching the foal closely, probably as stallions are occasionally infanticidal, especially toward very young unrelated foals (Boyd 1986, Ryder and Massena 1988). Only 20% of the foal's time was spent within five meters of the stallion during the first month of life and no more than 55% of their time thereafter (Boyd 1988c).

BEHAVIOR PROBLEMS

A knowledge of the typical Przewalski's horse ethogram and time budget facilitates the detection of aberrant behavior or behavior problems. Behavior problems commonly result from a failure to provide for the basic biological needs of equids. Most behavior problems of Przewalski's horses stem from two sources: lack of *ad-libitum* forage to occupy their time, and failure to approximate normal processes of herd formation.

Lack of Ad Libitum Forage

Wild equids spend approximately 70% of their time grazing and roam several kilometers daily while foraging (Salter and Hudson 1979, Kaseda 1983). In captivity, quick consumption of concentrated rations leaves animals with unnatural amounts of time to fill. Lack of oral stimulation may lead to cribbing, woodchewing and coprophagia in Przewalski's horses, just as in their domestic relatives. Ingestion of sand in grassless pastures has also been reported, leading to colic and death (see chapter 9).

Cribbing. Cribbing, which is also referred to as aerophagia or windsucking, is characterized by ingestion of air. Cribbing animals grasp an object with their incisors and pull back while gulping air. Inanimate objects such as stall partitions or hayracks may be used, or the horse may crib on the back or neck of a companion. Cribbing may result in colic and excessive incisor wear (Baker and Kear-Colwell 1974, Frauenfelder 1981, Boyd 1986). Once this behavior becomes established in Przewalski's horses, it is difficult to extinguish (Bouman-Heinsdijk 1982b, Boyd 1986). Even if the cribbing animal is moved from a grassless enclosure to a pasture, the problem is likely to persist. Therefore the best solution is prevention, by providing a higher proportion of roughage in the diet so that a more natural length of time will be spent feeding.

Two horses in this study were observed to crib. One was Colleen, #549 Brookfield 3 (see Figure 11.12a and b). None of the other horses, including four foals pastured with her, began to crib, although this behavior is commonly believed to be learned from other horses. Vecchiotti and Galanti (1986) believe the tendency to crib is inherited in Thoroughbreds, and this may also be true in Przewalski's horses, because the only other observed to crib was Colleen's son Rococco (#753 Topeka 1). He performed the behavior only when he was stabled separate from mares. As previously mentioned, none of the four unrelated foals pastured with Colleen developed the vice of cribbing.

Non-nutritive suckling. Early weaning, like lack of grazing opportunity, can lead to abnormal behavior. Two Przewalski's horse fil-

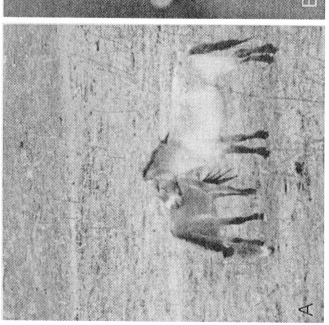

Figure 11.12. a. The mare Colleen (#549) cribs on the back of another herd member. b. The incisors of the cribbing mare in (a) showing excessive incisor wear at the time of her death at age ten. (From Boyd 1986, reprinted with permission of W.B. Saunders Company).

lies, Tina (#1358 London 85) and Betsy (#1365 London 86) and a zebra (*Equus burchelli*), were born by inter-species embryo transfer to Welsh pony mares (see chapter 10 for description). They were weaned at four months of age and housed together. At six months they were transferred to the Zoological Society of London's Regent's Park Zoo. They were housed in a 4.3 x 6.8 meter indoor enclosure. On alternate days all three equids were turned out in a 17 x 5.5 meter paddock for seven to nine hours. They were fed hay *ad libitum* while indoors, given grain twice a day, and carrots two to three times a week.

The only abnormal behavior observed was non-nutritive suckling. Betsy suckled on the ears of her half-sister, Tina. The suckling did not appear to damage the suckled ear nor did the suckled horse aggress against the sucking animal. Tina did, however, terminate suckling bouts by shaking her head or by walking away. Fifty of 136 (36.8%) suckling bouts were terminated by the suckled horse. Overall, 4.7% of the filly's time was spent suckling, but the frequency of the suckling depended on the presence or absence of food. When pellets or carrots were present, 7.9% (about 5 min/hour) of the time was spent suckling, but only 1.4% (less than a minute per hour) when pellets or carrots were not present. Suckling behavior alternated with eating grain in bouts of 10–15 seconds. Eating time was reduced in the suckling horse. She spent 9.1% of her time (5.5 min/hr) eating pellets or carrots when these were available. The suckled horse, Tina, spent 15.2% (9 min/hr) eating, as did the zebra filly. It is likely that the non-nutritive suckling began when the foal was weaned at four months and persisted both because the other filly permitted it and because the suckling filly derived some satisfaction from the activity as other horses do from cribbing.

The suckling horse was the more aggressive of the two. She threatened 9.6 times/hr whereas the suckled horse threatened 2 times/hr. Aggressive episodes occurred when the suckled horse terminated the suckling bouts. The increased aggression was not directed toward the suckled horse but rather was re-directed towards the zebra. The aggression toward the zebra resulted in a change of management; the two species were separated. There was no long-lasting effect on either embryo-transferred Przewalski's horse; both have successfuly reared foals (Houpt and Smith 1993).

Woodchewing. Woodchewing by Przewalski's horses may do extensive damage to wooden fences, doors, and buildings (Boyd 1991). Willard et al. (1977) reported that domestic horses consuming a concentrated feed spent significantly more time chewing wood than horses fed hay.

Coprophagia. Coprophagia is a behavior typical of young equids. It is not generally seen in wild adults, but is a common behavior problem in zoos. It usually occurs among Przewalski's horses housed in small grassless enclosures who do not have hay *ad libitum.* Willard et al. (1977) found that domestic horses fed concentrates exhibited significantly more coprophagia than horses fed hay. Most zoos equids are wormed routinely so this behavior does not add to parasite loads of Przewalski's horses, however it often distresses zoo visitors who observe it. Placing horses on pasture or providing ad libitum hay or browse in grassless enclosures will reduce coprophagia. For example, provision of live oak (*Quercus*) branches eliminated coprophagy by the London Zoo Przewalski's fillies.

Failure to Duplicate Normal Herd Formation Processes

Horses are gregarious by nature; in the wild solitary individuals are seldom seen (Boyd 1980). Solitary animals in captivity are the most likely to develop behavioral aberrations, enhanced by the fact that they are more likely than harems to be kept in small grassless enclosures where lack of foraging opportunities is a problem. In the wild, horses can choose their associates but in captivity humans dictate herd size and composition. Failure to consider the typical social organization of the species can result in problems such as pacing, excessive rates of aggression, impotence and infanticide.

Pacing. Pacing is a stereotyped behavior in which the pacing horse usually walks or trots, often along a barrier such as a wall or fence, with turns occurring at specific locations, following the same pathway repeatedly (Figure 11.13a and b). Pacing may be life-threatening if the horse persists in the behavior during extremely hot weather (Boyd 1986). It may represent a thwarted escape response indicative of harassment by other herd members. It detracts from attempts to create a naturalistic exhibit because zoo visitors are distressed by observing pacing animals, and the behavior can cause extensive soil erosion because the same paths are used repeatedly. Solitary individuals in small enclosures are the horses most likely to show this behavior. Solitary males spend 7% of their time pacing, whereas harem stallions spend 1% of their time pacing (Boyd 1991). An extreme example is the stallion Haldo (#517

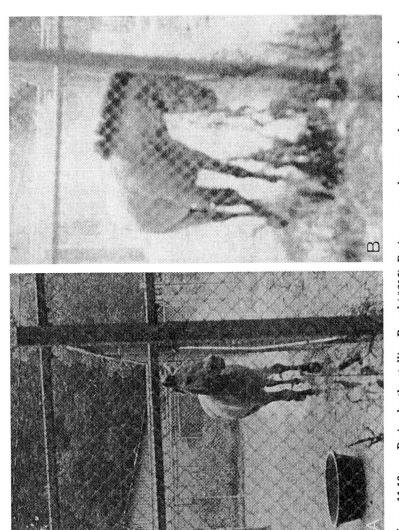

Figure 11.13. a. Pacing by the stallion Roccol (#616). Pacing commonly occurs along a barrier such as a fence. b. The animal typically turns into the barrier at specific locations to repeat the route. (From Boyd 1986, reprinted with permission of W.B. Saunders Company.)

Marwell 3) who spent 82% of his outdoor time pacing when solitary. Most pacing can be alleviated by providing solitary individuals with companions. Pacing can be virtually eliminated by placing groups of horses on pasture. Instead of channeling their energy into pacing, herds in pastures expend their energy foraging and interacting with companions.

Excessive aggression. Hogan et al. (1988) found Przewalski's horses to be more aggressive toward one another when moved into a small enclosure from a pasture, but Boyd (1988b) found no effect of enclosure on aggression rate for either stallions or mares (also see Table 11.1 above). This suggests that it is the actual change from a spacious environment to another more confining one that leads to aggression.

Some Przewalski's stallions are aggressive toward particular mares. Some animals may simply be incompatible and would never have remained together in the wild. When captivity forces them to remain in close proximity, serious aggression results. Separation by transfer of one or more horses to different herds may be the only solution.

Przewalski's stallions frequently become aggressive toward their own offspring when the offspring reach puberty. Since fillies are reproductively mature at an earlier age than colts, they are usually the first victims. In the wild this aggression would drive offspring out of their natal band, and may be a mechanism of inbreeding avoidance. Aggression toward Przewalski's fillies seems to begin when they reach the age of eighteen to twenty-two months (Hutson 1975, Boyd 1986). One stallion became aggressive toward his son when the son was twenty-two months old, although the stallion himself had been tolerated by his own sire until he left the natal band as a three-year-old (Kolter and Zimmermann 1988). The stallion Semari (#392 Catskill 40) tolerated the presence of his son Sembon (#818 Catskill 68) in a small harem until they were separated when the son was five years old. Based on this information, offspring could be removed when eighteen to twenty-two months old, or else closely monitored and removed when aggression towards them begins to escalate.

Grouping young bachelor Przewalski's males together does not usually result in serious aggression, but care must be taken if older experienced breeding stallions are retired into the herd. Reindl and Tilson (1985b) and Boyd (1986) recommend introducing juveniles to one another before older males are added in the hope that they will form a coalition against aggression by older males.

Introducing more than one animal at a time to established groups makes it less likely that one indiviual will bear the brunt of aggression (Tilson et al. 1988). The area containing the bachelor herd should be large enough to allow attacked individuals room to flee and take cover. The presence of mares in nearby enclosures may increase the likelihood of serious aggression (Tilson et al. 1988). Newly formed bachelor herds should be watched closely and facilities should be available for separating individuals if the need arises. Feral horse bachelor herds are fairly fluid in composition; membership changes frequently (Miller 1979). Zoos need to keep in mind that several combinations of male Przewalski's horses may have to be tried before a herd of compatible horses is formed.

Several Przewalski's mares have shown aggression toward the stallion when he attempted to breed other females in the harem. Such behavior seems to be fairly effective in thwarting breeding and, in two cases, the interfering mare had to be removed from the harem temporarily until the other mares conceived (Mackler and Dolan 1980, Boyd 1986, Kolter and Zimmermann 1988). This behavior may be adaptive to the interfering mare by permitting her to monopolize the stallion and prevent competitors from conceiving.

Impotence. Positive experience with mares is a prerequisite if Przewalski's stallions are to be successful breeders. Placing Przewalski's stallions with mares who are older or very dominant can lead to problems (Boyd 1986, 1991, Kolter and Zimmermann 1988). One stallion was placed with mares who were dominant and very aggressive toward him. They bit and kicked him whenever he tried to mount. The stallion became impotent and the mares were shipped elsewhere to be bred. When the mares returned, the stallion became dominant and aggressive toward the mares. He attained an erection and mounted the mares with impunity but failed to intromit (Boyd 1986). This stallion was moved to another zoo and put on pasture with a new harem. He continued to mount without intromission until his death several years later. Another stallion placed in a harem containing older females did become a successful breeder, but bred only those mares in the harem who were his age or younger and to whom he was dominant (Boyd 1991). It is not uncommon for adult Przewalski's mares to reject immature stallions (Bouman-Heinsdijk 1982a, Kolter 1985, Klimov 1988).

This problem also stems from a failure to duplicate herd formation processes which occur in the wild. Juvenile equids typically join bachelor herds upon leaving their natal bands and do not begin to obtain females until they are four or five years old (Keiper

1985, Boyd 1986, Klimov 1988). Older more dominant feral horse bachelors generally oust subordinates in competition for females (Feist and McCullough 1976, Rubenstein 1982, Keiper 1985). The first mares obtained are usually one- and two-year-old fillies dispersing from their natal band. Thus stallions are usually older and more dominant than their first mares. In zoos, juvenile male Przewalski's horses should be left in their natal bands for at least a year so that they can observe mating behavior. They should be placed in bachelor herds when removed from the natal band, and not given harems until they are at least four or five years of age. The first mares placed with the stallion should be younger than he and the harem size should be kept small until the stallion gains age and experience.

Feral horse stallions seldom have harems of more than five or six females (Miller 1981). Przewalski's stallions with harems of thirteen to eighteen females have become overly aggressive toward their mares or apathetic about breeding (Knowles 1980, Keverling Buisman and van Weeren 1982, Keiper 1988). In light of this behavior, harem sizes should not be allowed to grow too large.

Infanticide. Przewalski's stallions occasionally kill foals born into their harem that have been sired by other stallions (Keverling Buisman and van Weeren 1982, Boyd 1986, Ryder and Massena 1988). Male foals are more commonly victims than female foals, perhaps because colts grow up to be competitors while fillies represent future mates (Duncan 1982). Wild stallions might benefit from this behavior because mares which are freed from the physiological stress of lactation are probably more likely to conceive a foal by the new stallion and carry it to term in the following year (Boyd 1986, 1991). Infanticide is problematical in that it does not occur predictably and measures to prevent its occurrence may be disruptive to normal social organization if pregnant mares and those with very young foals are removed from the herd when a new stallion is added. The harems of feral horse stallions are relatively stable and a harem stallion's tenure may be four years or more (Miller 1979). The need to rotate stallions frequently to promote gene flow in inbred zoo populations has probably increased the incidence of this behavior in captivity as compared to the wild.

CONCLUSIONS

Development of an ethogram and data collection protocol are intensive but essential processes for the study of behavior.

Time budgets provide useful information about the activity patterns of horses. Przewalski's horses on pasture in summer spent most of their night-time foraging and sleeping, and their days standing and interacting. Horses in yards spent less time resting and mutual grooming, and more time drinking during the day then horses on pasture. A study of foal time budgets and spatial relationships shows the first month of a foal's life to be a period of dependence on the dam. This is also the time when most behaviors first appear. By the second month, the foal starts to become more independent and socializes with other herd members.

A knowledge of typical activity patterns facilitates the detection of behavior problems. Boredom and lack of forage ad libitum contribute to such problems as cribbing, woodchewing, and coprophagia. Pacing, excessive aggression, impotence, and infanticide can result from failure to consider the social organization of the species. To prevent or alleviate these problems, zoos should, whenever possible, provide plenty of forage and companions, and attempt to mimic the natural processes of juvenile weaning, dispersal, bachelor herd formation and mate acquisition.

ACKNOWLEDGMENTS

The authors would like to thank the following institutions for permitting and facilitating the observation of their Przewalski's horses: Anvers, the Catskill Game Farm, Denver Zoo, London Zoo, Los Angeles Zoo, Memphis Zoo, Minnesota Zoo, Munich Zoo, National Zoo's Conservation and Research Center, Nature Park Lelystad, New York Zoological Park, San Diego Zoo and San Diego Wild Animal Park, Topeka Zoo and Conservation/Propagation Center, Toronto Zoo, and Whipsnade.

Additionally we would like to thank the following for their assistance in data collection: Marjan Bierthus, Denise Carbonaro, Beatrice Ehrsam, Caroline Griffitts, Caroline Hahn, Ron Keiper, Lina de Montigny, Jayme Motler, Daniell Thompson, Carol Popolow, Judy Rosenthal, Ruth Smith and Kim Sweeney.

We are especially grateful to C.E. Houpt for developing the computer programs used to record and compile the time budget data.

12

Social Behavior

Katherine A. Houpt and Lee Boyd

INTRODUCTION

Much information exists about the social behavior of domestic and feral horses (*Equus caballus*) (reviewed by Waring 1983). The behavior of Przewalski's horses has been little-studied. Unfortunately, we will never know what natural Przewalski's horse social behavior was like because little behavioral information was recorded by those who observed the horses in the wild before their extinction. The current population of Przewalski's horses has been in captivity for two to twelve generations (Volf 1990). Thus, we cannot be sure whether any behavioral similarities between Przewalski's and domestic horses exist because of their close evolutionary relationship, or whether similarities exist because of captivity which both species have experienced. Nevertheless, the study of Przewalski's horse behavior is important if this species is to be reintroduced into the wild. If captive Przewalski's horse behavior is similar to captive domestic horse behavior, then one would predict that they might behave like feral horses when released. Horse behavior has been studied on both the western plains and Atlantic and Pacific islands (Pelligrini 1971, Welsh 1975, Feist and McCullough 1976, Salter and Hudson, 1982, Boyd 1980, Miller 1981, Miller and Denniston 1979, Kaseda 1981, Rubenstein 1981, Keiper 1985, Berger 1986) and this knowledge can be used as a basis for managing Przewalski's horses after their reintroduction.

COMMUNICATION

Before the social organization of Przewalski's horses can be understood the means by which they communicate should be considered. Przewalski's horses, like most mammals, communicate via auditory, visual and olfactory means. The vocal, postural, and odor signals used by Przewalski's horses will be described and discussed in relation to that which is known about sensory mechanisms and acuity in *Equus caballus*, the domestic horse.

Perception

Communication depends on the animal's perception. Production of high frequency sounds, for example, will not be an effective means of communication if the recipient cannot hear high frequencies. Perception in Przewalski's horses has not been studied and there is only limited information available on perception in *E. caballus*. All the information on vision and hearing was obtained from domestic horses. We do know that horses have binocular vision in only 60% of their visual field, in comparison to 120° for cats and an even higher percentage in those species such as humans that have eyes located more frontally (Swenson 1984). Lack of binocular vision is balanced in horses by a wide visual field. Horses can see nearly 245° with only their own bodies obscuring the view. When they are grazing with their heads down, horses can see in almost all directions (>300°).

What can horses see? Visual acuity has not been measured although the number of retinal ganglion cells indicates that their acuity is inferior to that of pigs and humans (Hebel 1976). There has been only one study of color vision in horses. Grzimek (1952) trained horses to choose a colored card rather than one of an equal brightness of gray. The horses were able to discriminate green, but not red, from gray. Similar early studies using colored cards in cattle and goats now have been confirmed by more recent studies using more sophisticated methods. Apparently, most animals have color vision, but it is based on two rather than the three pigments on which human color vision is based.

Equine hearing appears to be similar to that of humans (Heffner and Heffner 1983). They can hear slightly higher frequencies, but they are not able to localize the source of a sound well (Heffner and Heffner 1984). Presumably in order to perceive and locate sounds an alert Przewalski's horse has its head up and ears erect, usually pointed in the direction of interest. Even old horses whose ears may normally hang to the side will contract the anterior auricular muscles and thus prick their ears. This can make identification difficult if an old horse has been recognized only by ear position.

Perception of odor by horses has not been investigated except in the context of sexual behavior. Stallions can discriminate mares from stallions on the basis of feces, but they cannot discriminate estrous from non-estrous urine or feces (Stahlbaum and Houpt 1989).

Vocalization

The vocalizations used in communication by the Przewalski's horse are the neigh, nicker, fear snort, and squeal.

Neighs. The neigh is a high amplitude call of long duration that fluctuates in frequency and is given on expiration (see Figure 12.1). The neigh is the separation call usually heard either when a horse is removed from a group or when a horse is heard or seen in the distance. Because separation and movement of horses is a rare event in zoos, neighing is also rare. When neighs are heard under other circumstances, zoo personnel should investigate to ensure that a horse or other equid hasn't left its enclosure. Domestic horse

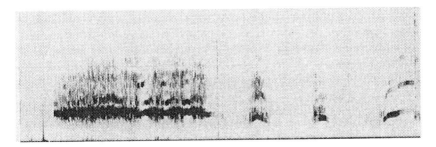

Figure 12.1.   Sound spectrogram of a neigh by the stallion Janus (#718). The frequency in kilohertz is on the ordinate (each horizontal line represents 0.5 Khz) and the time is on the abcissa.

mares appear to be able to recognize their foals' voices, whereas foals respond indiscriminately to mare neighs (Wolski et al. 1980). There are circumstances in the free-ranging situation when vocal communication is very important for reunion of a mare and foal. Foals can become separated from their dams because foals lie and sleep much longer than adult horses (Boy and Duncan 1979, Duncan 1980). Although domestic and feral mares usually will not leave their recumbent foals (Crowell-Davis 1986), they may be frightened away or driven away by a stallion. When the foal awakens, it will neigh and be answered by its dam, or less frequently, by another horse. It can then attempt to locate the source of the adult neighs.

On the basis of data from ten zoos housing forty-seven mares and fourteen stallions, Przewalski's stallions neigh (0.13 ± 0.05 neighs/hr) significantly more often than mares (0.02 ± 0.005 neighs/hr). Stallions neigh once per seven hours and mares once every fifty hours (Mann Whitney U; $P<0.05$). Stallions may neigh to attract mares or to announce their presence to other stallions. Presumably, solitary young horses that have recently left their natal herd neigh when they see a bachelor herd or harem group and will be answered. Three of the fourteen Przewalski's stallions were kept separate from other horses. Two were within hearing distance of others; their rate of neighing was no higher than that of harem stallions 0.007/hr by one stallion and 0.09/hr, by the other). The third stallion, a former harem stallion with no other stallions in the zoo and no visual contact with other horses, neighed nearly once per hour. The role of neighs in stallion encounters is also unknown but may indicate which horses approach and fight and which avoid.

Snorts. There are three types of snort: The frustration snort, the fear snort, and the nostril cleaning snort. The frustration snort is longer in duration and is given when the horse is prevented from doing something it wants to do or is forced to do something it does not want to do. The fear snort is given when the horse is startled. It probably serves to alert the other members of the band. Horses may also snort simply to clear their nostrils of insects or feed. Figure 12.2 is a sonogram of the latter such snort.

Squeals. The squeal is given by horses in antagonistic encounters. Either the initiator or the recipient of aggression may squeal.

Nicker. The nicker is a low amplitude call that fluctuates in frequency and is given in a care-seeking (et-epimeletic) or care-offer-

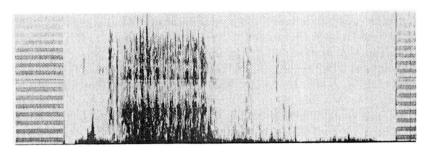

Figure 12.2.   Sound spectrogram of a snort by the mare Tasha (#948) while grazing. The frequency in kilohertz is on the ordinate (each horizontal line represents
0.5 Khz) and the time is on the abcissa.

ing (epimeletic) situation. Stallions nicker when courting mares.
Mares nicker to their foals apparently to encourage them to approach and nurse. Foals, especially newborn foals, nicker to their
dams. Both nicker when reunited after a separation. Adult horses
nicker to their caretakers in anticipation of food. This probably is a
retention of juvenile behavior in the adult.

Postural Communications

Agonistic. The ears are pinned or flattened against the skull when
the horse is threatening another horse or, more rarely, when
threatened. The more severe the threat, the wider the mouth of the
aggressor will be opened and the more the teeth will be exposed.
The muzzle is usually extended toward the recipient of the threat.
The threat can be fulfilled by an actual bite. In most studies of
Przewalski's horses, the ratio of threats to bites is very high
(Hogan et al. 1988, Keiper 1988).

    Agonistic intentions can also be communicated by the hind-
quarters. The tail may be lashed and a hindleg raised. The horse
may kick out with one or both hindlegs. As in the case of threats to
bite, threats to kick occur more often than actual kicks, so their
warning value must be clear to the receiver.

    One of the controversies concerning equine dominance hier-
archies is the function of kicking. Wells and von Goldschmidt-

Rothschild (1979) hypothesized that kicking was mostly directed up the hierarchy. In the tests used to determine dominance in domestic horses, in which two horses competed for a bucket of food fastened to a fence, the dominant animal frequently kicked, especially if the subordinate kept trying to reach the food (Houpt et al. 1978). This indicated that kicking was directed down, not up the hierarchy. The paired feeding situation is artificial in that there is a fence in front of the horses so that any approaches to the food are from the side or rear of the horse. The closest weapon is the hind hooves. For this reason, a more natural situation was investigated. The results of spontaneously occurring aggression between Przewalski's horses during focal sampling of all adults in ten herds were recorded. The hierarchy was constructed on the basis of threats alone and then the percentages of biting (or threats to bite) and kicking (or threats to kick) in which the subordinate aggressed towards a dominant animal were calculated. The herd size and composition varied considerably, but in only two of the ten herds were a greater percentage of kicks directed up the hierarchy than down. A greater percentage of kicks were directed up the hierarchy than were bites in six of the ten cases (see Table 12.1). Kicking may indeed be used predominantly, but not exclusively for defense. To resolve the dispute about the function of kicking, careful studies should be performed in which it is determined whether the initiator of kicking approaches the recipient then turns and kicks or kicks when approached from the rear.

Table 12.1

The percentage of aggressions directed up the dominance hierarchy in Przewalski's horses.

Zoo	N	Percent bites and threats to bite	Percent kicks and threats to kick
Bronx	6	28	41
Catskill A	9	39.6	52.6
Catskill B	4	36.4	35.7
Toronto	4	13.3	7.8
London	2	31.3	0
Anvers	5	25	60.7
Denver	3	22	41.7
Minnesota A	3	27.3	0
Minnesota B	4	33	4
Lelystad	4	27.0	25.0

Snapping, toothclapping, champing. The facial expression of the subadult horse, the Unterlegenheitsgebärde (Zeeb 1959), is one of the most interesting of equid facial expressions. It occurs almost exclusively in subadult horses, but persists in donkeys and zebras as "yawing" exhibited by estrous females. Snapping is characterized by retraction of the lips, opening and closing of the mouth and sometimes by flexure of the carpal and tarsal joints and extended head and neck (Crowell-Davis et al. 1985). It occurs in circumstances in which the foal is probably frightened such as when adult horses are fighting. It is interesting that in some cases the foal appears to place itself deliberately in a fear-producing situation. A colt, for example, will approach a stallion voluntarily and then snap at it. More snapping is directed toward the stallion than toward mares by both colts and fillies. The most common situation to stimulate snapping is aggression either toward the foal or between other horses. Breeding activity also causes foals to snap; the foal may be frightened when the stallion mounts (see Figure 12.3), but remains nearby and snaps. This situation and the occurrence of the expression in estrous donkeys and zebras and the occasional domestic horse mare (Woods and Houpt 1986) have led to the hy-

Figure 12.3. The stallion Vulkan (#606) copulating with a mare at the Bronx Zoo. In the background, a juvenile is exhibiting the snapping facial expression. Photograph by Judy Rosenthal.

pothesis that snapping occurs in approach-avoidance situations. The foal is afraid of the mounting stallion, and might avoid it, but is trying to approach his mother whom the stallion is mounting. Whether or not snapping reduces the probability of aggression by the receiver is difficult to determine. Some bouts of snapping (48%) are directed away from the adult horse and an even larger percentage (75%) are directed away from the adult when the latter is aggressing against the foal and so could not be perceived easily (Boyd 1988a). Crowell-Davis et al. (1985) have postulated that snapping is displaced nursing. Snapping behavior can be used to determine whether a colt is socially mature; if he snaps he is not. Furthermore, he probably will not successfully breed those mares to whom he snapped because he was, or is, subordinate to them.

SOCIAL ORGANIZATION

Apparently wild Przewalski's horses had a harem polygynous social organization (Kaszab 1968, Mohr 1971, MacClintock 1982), although no formal behavioral studies were made. In captivity the social system of Przewalski's horses is determined, not by natural selection, but by those people who manage them in zoos. Most commonly the animals are kept in harem groups with one stallion and several to many mares and their juvenile offspring. In some smaller zoos male-female pairs of horses are maintained.

Harems

There are two reasons for believing that the social systems imposed on Przewalski's horses are natural ones: 1) reports of Przewalski's horses in the wild before they became extinct (Mohr 1971); 2) extrapolation from the behavior of feral *Equus caballus*. In the classification of social groups presented by Emlen and Oring (1977), horses fall into the harem polygynous category. This is a category shared with relatively few other species. Many ungulates form separate male and female groups and males acquire harems or form pair bonds only during the breeding season. The social organization of feral horses in the western United States and on the barrier islands off the eastern coast have been extensively studied (Berger 1986, Keiper and Houpt 1984). In all cases the horses have been found in bands numbering from one to twenty-one mares, foals and juveniles and one stallion. There have been reports of two or more stallions in some larger bands (Miller 1981), but often in these cases one stallion is dominant and does most of the breeding while the subordinate stallions try to repel any marauding stallions. In general, horses are not territorial. It is only in unique situations where water provides two or more boundaries that territoriality has been noted in horses (Rubenstein 1981). Horses, plains zebra (*Equus burchelli*) and mountain zebras (*Equus zebra*) are harem-forming whereas donkeys (*Equus asinus*), onagers (*Equus hemionus*) and Grevy's zebra (*Equus grevyi*) are territorial (Klingel 1974).

Bachelor Groups

The sex ratio of Przewalski's horse is approximately 1:1, but the presumed natural social organization consists of harems each containing one male and several females. This social structure seems to result in optimal reproduction in Przewalski's horses. The problem becomes what to do with surplus males. Reindl and Tilson (1985b) and Boyd (1986) have advocated solving this problem by forming bachelor groups. Feral horse stallions live in bachelor groups from the time they leave their natal herd at age two until they are approximately five years old and have acquired mares of their own. The advantage to the zoo of forming a bachelor herd is that labor and some space is saved if several animals live in one enclosure. Furthermore, young males are playful and will be a more interesting exhibit than the less lively adults. Play in young males is usually interactive play. Play fighting consists of neck wrestling, sparring with the forelegs and nipping, as well as chasing. Mounting may also occur. These activities probably improve the colt's social skills so that he will interact appropriately when placed with mares. He will know how hard he can bite without eliciting true aggression from the victim and he will have perfected combat skills and the motor patterns of mounting.

Recently bachelor groups have been established at a number of zoos. These are usually composed of young stallions, but occasionally adult stallions, some of which are former harem stallions, have been kept in the same enclosure (Tilson et al. 1988).

Not all zoos have several young males at the same time. In that case another equid, such as a pony, can be used as a social companion. This system has been used at the Topeka Zoo and stallions raised that way, such as Marx (#1085 Topeka 7), have become successful harem stallions and sired foals.

DOMINANCE HIERARCHIES

As is true for other equids, members of a Przewalski's horse herd have a dominance hierarchy which is an important part of their social organization. This hierarchy becomes apparent to humans when some horses are observed displacing others, with or without aggression, while feeding or drinking. If a herd is newly formed, dominance interactions may involve frequent aggression. If herd members have been together for a long time and the ranks are well-established, overt aggression may be infrequent and the signs of rank as subtle as who moves aside when a particular horse passes by.

Dominance hierarchies are formed in both harem and bachelor groups of feral horses (Grzimek 1949, Pelligrini 1971, Feist and McCullough 1976, Berger 1977, von Goldschmidt-Rothschild and Tschanz 1978, Wells and von Goldschmidt-Rothschild 1979, Houpt and Keiper 1982). Various benefits accrue to members with high rank. The dominant individual is able to monopolize food, water, and shelter, enabling it to best sustain the body condition needed to maintain its status and reproduce. Additionally, high-ranking individuals have priority access to mates (Boyd 1991).

Feral domestic horse bachelors do not have an opportunity to breed until they are at least four or five years old (see chapter 11), and it is not until they are six to eight years of age that they can successfully obtain mares through combat (Keiper 1985, Berger 1986). High-ranking feral horse bachelors are usually the first to acquire mares (Feist and McCullough 1976, Keiper 1985). If the bachelor group as a unit obtains some mares, the highest ranking bachelor may be able to drive off the other bachelors to become the sole male within a harem. Wild stallions are typically the highest ranking members of their harem. This comes about because, as previously mentioned, dominant individuals are usually the first to acquire mares, and their first mares are likely to be one- or two-year-old inexperienced fillies dispersing from their natal band. In captivity, where humans control herd formation, the Przewalski's stallion may not be the top-ranking individual. These stallions often fail to breed mares that are dominant to them and may fail to breed entirely. If factors affecting dominance are inherited, then it is to the mare's benefit to mate with a dominant stallion that will contribute such traits to her offspring, so that they in turn will be successful in competition for food and mates. In fact, captive Przewalski's mares have been known to aggressively reject breeding attempts by subordinate stallions (see chapter 11). Because dominance appears to affect reproductive success, zoos need to mimic the age differential created in the wild by the gender-specific difference in age at first reproduction, and start stallions with younger mares at least until the stallion gains age and experience.

Benefits to high ranking females within a harem include the ability to monopolize the stallion (Boyd 1991). High status means that their offspring are protected from aggression by other herd members, as long as the offspring remain in their mothers' vicinity.

Age and aggressiveness are factors thought to influence the rank that an individual Przewalski's horse achieves (Lewtas 1973, Feh 1988, Keiper 1988, Klimov 1988, Kolter and Zimmermann 1988, Tilson et al. 1988). In addition to age and aggressiveness, size, length of herd membership, and maternal rank have been suggested to affect hierarchy position in domestic and feral horse herds (Montgomery 1957, Tyler 1972, Houpt et al. 1978, Houpt and Wolski 1980, Pollock 1980, Arnold and Grassia 1982, Keiper and Sambraus 1986, Rutberg and Greenberg 1990). To examine whether there were correlations between these factors and rank in Przewalski's horses, sixteen harems and two bachelor groups were observed. Dominance ranks were determined by use of the Schein and Fohrman (1955) method, in which animals are ranked so that each individual receives threats from the smallest number of individuals below it. Dominance ranks reported in the literature for five harems and two bachelor groups of Przewalski's horses (Feh 1988, Keiper 1988, Kolter and Zimmermann 1988, Tilson et al. 1988) were also included in the analyses. Spearman's rho was used to calculate correlations between the horses' dominance rank and their age, size, aggressiveness, length of herd tenure, and maternal rank. There was a significant positive correlation between rank and a horse's age in nine of the herds large enough to permit statistical testing (Table 12.2). There was a significant positive correlation between rank and size in five of the herds where obvious size differences existed between adult members. There was a significant positive correlation between rank and aggressiveness in eight herds and between rank and length of tenure in three herds. Maternal rank, where known, was significantly correlated with offspring rank in only one herd although the correlation was positive in all but four herds. When overall correlations were calculated, both harems and bachelor groups showed a strong positive correlation between rank and aggressiveness, size, and length of herd ten-

Table 12.2

Spearman correlation coefficients between dominance rank and factors affecting rank.

Herd	N	Age	Size	Aggressions Per Hour	Herd Tenure	Maternal Rank
Harems						
Anvers	6	0.14	—	0.77	—	—
Bronx	12	0.66*	—	0.89**	—	0.47
Catskill 1	4	0.80*	—	0.00	—	—
Catskill 2	9	0.12	—	0.63*	—	0.15
Denver	3	0.50	—	1.00	−0.50	0.87
Front Royal	8	0.99*	0.74*	0.66*	0.37	0.29
Cologne	6	0.94**	—	—	0.94**	—
Lelystad	6	0.06	—	0.75	—	−0.62
London	2	—	—	−1.00	—	—
Los Angeles	2	1.00	—	1.00	1.00	—
Memphis	3	0.50	—	0.50	—	0.40
Minnesota 1	5	0.65	—	0.56	—	—
Minnesota 2	4	0.78	—	0.20	—	−0.05
Munich	6	0.93**	—	1.00**	—	—
San Diego	3	0.87	0.00	1.00	−0.87	0.87
SDWAP 1	8	0.86**	0.54	0.58	0.22	0.04
SDWAP 2	4	0.32	1.00*	0.80*	—	0.89*
Topeka	7	0.62	0.88**	0.79*	0.94**	0.41
Toronto	4	—	—	0.63	—	0.66
overall r=		0.06	0.71**	0.83**	0.61**	0.24
		n=102	n=30	n=96	n=37	n=67
Bachelor Groups						
Minnesota	8	0.88**	—	0.86**	0.84**	−0.33
de Ooij	4	0.89*	—	—	—	—
SDWAP	4	0.78	0.80*	0.95*	0.78	0.79
Topeka	4	0.93*	0.80*	0.40	0.78	−0.55
overall r=		0.29	0.77*	0.93**	0.81**	0.02
		n=20	n=8	n=16	n=16	n=15

—means data was unavailable on this factor for this herd.
*significant at $p<0.05$,
**significant at $p<0.01$
Significance could not be determined for herds with fewer than four members.

ure. Age and maternal rank were also positively correlated to rank, but not significantly so. Thus, large aggressive horses who have been in the herd for a long time have the highest ranks. Older animals whose mothers had high rank also tend to have high rank.

Once they are established, dominance hierarchies are remarkably stable over time. Only one change in rank occurred in the Topeka herd over a four year period, and after eight years only one change had occurred since Mackler and Dolan (1980) studied the exhibit herd at the San Diego Wild Animal Park (Boyd 1991). Change in rank occurs most frequently when there is a change in herd composition. When new herds are formed or new members added, some fighting should be expected as positions in the hierarchy are contested. It is probably best to let this occur without interference to expedite the formation of the hierarchy so that calm can return, unless the fighting seems so severe that permanent injury is probable. It is possible that some individuals will be incompatible and will have to be separated. In the wild, the subordinate horse would have been able to depart for another herd, and zoos, if necessary, should be prepared to duplicate this process. When new members are added to already established Przewalski's horse herds, it is usually the lowest-ranking horse that is most aggressive toward the new animals; these individuals have the most to gain by relegating newcomers to the lowest ranks (Hutson 1975, Mackler and Dolan 1980, Boyd 1986, 1991). Aggression toward new members can sometimes be diluted by adding two or more new animals simultaneously. Providing refuges may help although care should be taken that the shelter not become a place where a horse could become cornered, or impaled upon projections while trying to flee.

MUTUAL GROOMING

Mutual grooming is another obvious form of social interaction. Typically, mutual grooming is initiated when one individual approaches another and begins sniffing or nuzzling the area to be groomed. Often the individual approached is already engaged in self-grooming. If the animal approached does not respond in kind, the interaction ends immediately. If the partner does respond, both will begin using their teeth to gently bite at the other's coat. Occasionally the teeth are not used and the partners rub one another's coat with their muzzles. The partners stand in reverse parallel position and are usually grooming the same general region on their partner that is being groomed on themselves. The areas being groomed are generally along the dorsal surface of the body: the neck, withers, back, and rump. Another common area receiving attention is the hindleg, particularly from the area lateral to the dock of the tail down to the hock. Bouts range from several seconds in length to three or four minutes, with an average length of about one minute, and longer bouts may contain several pauses of a second or two. It is often difficult to determine which individual terminates the bout, because as soon as one horse ceases to nibble, the other will also quit a nibble or two later. It is very rare for a horse to continue to groom another if that animal is not simultaneously reciprocating.

On average, a Przewalski's horse participates in mutual grooming about once every two hours, but there is much individual and seasonal variation. Some horses mutual groom at least once an hour, while others in the herd at the same time participate once every ten hours. For all horses, the frequency of mutual grooming peaks in the spring when their winter coats are shed.

The mutual grooming of equids enables participants to obtain care of the coat for areas of the body difficult to reach by self-grooming (Mazak 1961, Feist and McCullough 1976). It has also been hypothesized that mutual grooming plays a role in strengthening relationships (Mazak 1961, Feist and McCullough 1976, Arnold and Grassia 1982). A second hypothesis is that mutual grooming serves as an appeasement behavior (Feist and McCullough 1976, Kolter and Zimmermann 1988), which may function to minimize aggression between participants (Hogan et al. 1988, Keiper 1988). Data collected on mutual grooming in Przewalski's horses supports the former hypothesis rather than the latter. A horse's most frequent mutual grooming partners are those who aggress against it least (i.e. its closest kin) suggesting that the behavior is distributed nepotistically where possible, that is to aid relatives (Boyd 1988a). At the Topeka Zoo, the horses with the most kin present have the highest frequency of mutual grooming. Those without kin do very little mutual grooming.

KINSHIP

Mutual grooming is not the only behavior of Przewalski's horses which is affected by kinship. Related Przewalski's horses frequently stand, rest, and feed together. For eighteen of twenty-four mares and bachelor males in one study, their closest relative in the herd was the individual most likely to be their nearest neighbor (Boyd 1988a).

One relative may come to another's aid if attacked. Closely

related Przewalski's horses are usually less aggressive toward one another than to more distantly related individuals; less aggression is directed toward members of the closest kin group than would be expected if aggressions were distributed randomly (Boyd 1988a).

Benefits to mares from nepotistic behavior include protection from insect pests (as their neighbors' tails help keep them free of flies), coat care, and development of alliances which provide protection from aggression. Similar benefits accrue to bachelors, and additionally, alliances between related feral horse or feral donkey bachelor males are known to result in the creation of a male coalition that can more readily defeat harem stallions and take over their mares in the wild (McCort 1980, Berger 1986).

Nepotism implies some sort of recognition of kinship. Such recognition is probably learned by association within the natal band (Boyd 1988a). Mothers and offspring are, of course, associated with one another in the natal band, and a foal may learn to identify full siblings through their continued association with its mother. Foals born to other mares in the band could usually be correctly assumed to be half-siblings, having been sired by the same stallion. Somewhat rarer, but not uncommon associations would be between grandmothers and grandchildren, and aunts and nieces or nephews. Foals may also learn their relationship to grandmothers and aunts through the association of these individuals with the foal's mother. When the mother of a four-month-old foal had to be removed from the Topeka Zoo's breeding herd for about six months due to health problems, the foal remained behind with the rest of the herd and its grandmother assumed the role of protecting the foal. The grandmother and foal preferentially associated with one another rather than with any of the other four herd members. In spite of familial resemblances that are obvious even to humans, there is little evidence that horses can recognize unfamiliar kin by phenotype matching, that is, by comparing their own appearance to that of the unfamiliar horse (Duncan et al. 1984, Berger and Cunningham 1987, Boyd 1988a).

REPRODUCTIVE BEHAVIOR

Female Sexual Behavior

A domestic horse mare in estrus urinates frequently, standing in an exaggerated urination position with hind limbs abducted while holding her tail to the side and everting the clitoris, thus stimulating flehmen and eventually the libido of the stallion (Asa et al. 1979). A mare may back into the stallion or paw at him. These are examples of proceptive behavior.

Mares frequently will not accept young stallions, that is stallions less than five years old. The mares are probably socially dominant over an immature stallion and in general, a horse should be dominant to be able to mount another. The effect of sexual rejection and/or overt aggression by mares toward a young stallion may be profound. Several Przewalski's stallions have either become impotent, such as Roccol (#616 Catskill 63) who would mount, but not intromit, or have driven out the older mares once they themselves were mature and dominant (Bektair, #1065 Topeka 5) (see chapter 11).

The mating face. The mating face or Rossigkeitgesicht (Trumler 1959) is that of the estrous mare. Her ears are turned back, but not flattened. Her lips are relaxed and loose. She will squeal, urinate normal amounts and evert the clitoris; the behavior known as clitoral winking. The signals to the stallion are not subtle and should be apparent even from a distance.

Male Sexual Behavior

Flehmen. One of the most striking behaviors of stallions is flehmen (Figure 12.4). Flehmen, or lip curl, is probably not a communication but rather a method of drawing non-volatile material into the vomeronasal organ. The physiological and anatomical information on flehmen and the vomeronasal organ has all been obtained on domestic horses (*Equus caballus*). The vomeronasal organ is a paired hollow tubular structure that lies on the midline between the oral and nasal cavity. In horses the organ opens only into the nasal cavity just caudal to the alar cartilages. Urine on the nose runs into the nasal cavity when the horse lifts its upper lip. The action of flehmen closes off the nares so that there are large pressure changes in the nasal cavity that aspirate fluid into the vomeronasal organ. There are receptors located in the vomeronasal organ of domestic animals and of most other mammals, with the possible exception of primates.

Histologically the epithelium lining the lumen of the vomeronasal organ is similar to that of the nasal cavity in that it is divided into respiratory and olfactory portions. In contrast to the main olfactory receptor cells, those of the vomeronasal organ are not ciliated, but instead have microvilli on their apical border. There are abundant mucous secreting cells in the vomeronasal or-

Figure 12.4. The stallion Vulkan (#606) shows flehmen while marking with urine. Photograph by Judy Rosenthal.

gan. The presence of a large number of blood vessels in the sub-mucosa indicates that the tissue is erectile (Houpt and Guida 1984).

Central neural connections of the vomeronasal organ have not been studied in the horse but have been studied extensively in laboratory animals. The vomeronasal and main olfactory system are relatively independent of each other. The main olfactory connections are primarily with the thalamus and cortex; those of the vomeronasal organ are primarily to the hypothalamus (Johnston 1985).

In addition to the afferent connections of the vomeronasal organ there are also efferent connections. When the parasympathetic fibers to the vomeronasal organ are stimulated, vasodilation occurs and the erectile tissue of the organ becomes engorged with blood. Because the organ is encased in cartilage, expansion occurs only at the expense of the lumen. Narrowing of the lumen squeezes the contents out into the nose. This process empties the organ of both mucus and any material previously aspirated. One can observe mucus dripping from the nostrils of stallions after they flehmen. When the sympathetic nerves are stimulated, vasoconstriction occurs and the organ contracts as blood outflow from the erectile tissue is greater than inflow. Material can then again be aspirated into the lumen of the organ. Stimulation of the vomeronasal organ receptors leads to release of luteinizing hormone from the anterior pituitary which in turn leads to an increase in testosterone and libido of the stallion that exhibited flehmen. Females also flehmen, but more rarely. Twelve of thirteen Przewalski's stallions and the Przewalski's gelding, Alex (#1171 Marwell 69), exhibited flehmen, whereas only fourteen of forty-seven mares exhibited flehmen. The role of flehmen in females is less well understood (see also Table 11.1).

Marking. There are two marking behaviors, performed mostly by stallions, that seem to be stimulated by olfactory input and presumably result in transmission of olfactory information (to the recipient). The behaviors are marking with feces and marking with urine.

Urine marking is performed in such a consistent manner that it could be termed a fixed action pattern. The stallion sniffs urine on the ground and may elevate his head to flehmen. At the same time he moves forward with the front limbs only so that he is straddling the puddle of urine (see Figure 12.4). The stallion then urinates a small amount (50–100 ml) as flehmen is maintained. After urine marking and exhibiting flehmen the stallion may lower his head in order to sniff the urine again and repeat the whole sequence or move forward and walk away from the spot. It has been hypothesized that his urine may mask the scent of estrous mare urine and/or inform the next horse that sniffs the urine that a stallion was present (Turner et al. 1981, Boyd and Kasman 1986). Addition of a mark does not modify a stallion's flehmen or sniffing responses to estrous mare urine, but that does not mean that the stallion cannot discriminate marked from unmarked urine.

Urine marking appears to occur almost exclusively in dominant harem stallions. Most solitary stallions do not urine mark their own urine, although they will fecal mark on their own feces. Female elimination must be the stimulus for urine marking, but is not necessary for defecation marking. Boyd and Kasman (1986) have noted that urine is always marked with urine and that the majority of mare defecations are marked with urine rather than feces. Urine marking is seasonal, occurring most often in the early summer. It is not clear whether the stallion's behavior is seasonal or estrous mare urine is the necessary stimulus which is present in early summer but disappears as the mares become pregnant.

Seven of ten stallions in harem groups marked with urine. Two of the stallions who did not mark were subordinate; Bektair (#1065 Topeka 5), who was subordinate to the mares of his herd when the data was collected, and Sembon (#818 Catskill 68), who was subordinate to his sire, did not urine mark. Urine marking might be used to assess a stallion's dominance.

Domestic horse colts also show marking behavior and flehmen as neonates, but this behavior declines with age until puberty (Crowell-Davis and Houpt 1985). The gonads of equine fetuses at 200 days gestational age are as large as those of their mothers (Ginther 1979) so the colt may still be masculinized as a result of the high levels of gonadotropins to which he was exposed as a fetus. Another reason for the decline in flehmen rate may be that the foal's mother was showing estrous cycles for the first month postpartum, but later became pregnant.

The second marking behavior is fecal marking (see Figure 12.5). Przewalski's stallions may urinate on mare feces, but they are more apt to defecate on male feces. They rarely defecate on mare urine. Stallions defecate on their own feces or those of others producing an accumulation referred to as a stud pile. Solitary stallions defecate on their own feces; the presence of mares is not necessary to stimulate fecal marking. Fecal marking is a male behavior; only two of forty-seven mares were observed to mark with feces. The stud piles of feral horses can become quite tall as various stallions add to the pile (Feist and McCullough 1976). This is espe-

Figure 12.5.   a. The stallion Basil (#293) sniffs a mare's feces and steps over them, b. marking the feces with urine.

cially apt to occur in an area where several herds congregate, such as near a water hole. In the zoo situation the feces are usually removed; nevertheless a stallion may use the same spot. In feral bachelor herds the horse that defecates on the stud pile last is the dominant one and the one most likely to acquire a mare first (Feist and McCullough 1976). It will be interesting to observe Przewalski's bachelor herds, now that several have been formed, to determine if their defecation order is also related to their rank order in the hierarchy.

Courtship

When courting a mare, the stallion investigates her hindquarters and may flehmen. Penile erection will develop during this time. The stallion may lean against the mare's rump, probably to test her willingness to stand. After nipping and sometimes licking the mare he will mount. Some stallions leap so forcefully that all four feet are off the ground (see Figure 12.3). Not every mount results in intromission. When intromission occurs the stallion usually ejaculates. Afterwards he will lay his head on the mare's shoulder and neck in post-copulatory exhaustion for a moment or two before dismounting.

PARENTAL INVESTMENT

Parental investment is defined as anything parents do for their offspring which increases offspring survival at the expense of the parents' ability to produce additional offspring (Trivers 1972). Such investment includes gamete production, gestation and lactation, and protection of the offspring. In polygynous species, males commonly have a greater variance in reproductive success (RS) than females (Bateman 1948, Trivers 1972), and therefore parents might invest more heavily in sons to improve their male offsprings' chances of competing successfully for mates (Trivers and Willard 1973, Maynard Smith 1978, Clutton-Brock et al. 1982). Horses are polygynous, and feral horse males have a greater variance in apparent reproductive success than females (Berger 1986). Therefore, it seems likely that Przewalski's horses might invest more heavily in sons than daughters, as a legacy of their social organization in the wild, and as a result of management polices designed to duplicate this social structure in captivity.

Lactation is one of the most important and costly ways in

which female mammals invest in their offspring. Przewalski's foals weigh 25–30 kg at birth, but double this weight in their first four weeks of life (Mohr 1971). The importance of milk for proper growth of Przewalski's foals became apparent when the foal Coltar (#1130 Topeka 8) was orphaned at two and a half months of age. Despite supplemental feeding, this foal, which was not particularly small at birth, lagged behind his paternal half-siblings' growth, only catching up to them in height at three years of age. In a study of twenty-four foals during their first year of life, it was found that during their first month lactational investment was very high, with foals nursing for one out of every ten minutes (Boyd 1988a). Mares terminated almost half the bouts at this age, perhaps because the frequent nursing interfered with the dam's other activities such as the foraging needed to support lactation. This behavior might also encourage a foal to begin foraging itself to meet some of its energy needs. The amount of time a Przewalski's foal spends foraging increases greatly by month two and at the same time lactational investment declines, primarily due to a decrease in bout frequency to once or twice an hour with bouts continuing to last approximately forty-five seconds. As the foals nurse less frequently, the percent of bouts terminated by the mare declines until weaning. The mares terminate most of the bouts of young foals by moving, rather than by aggression. In contrast, mares weaning foals again terminate about half the bouts, with the number terminated by aggression rising from 5% to 38%. Przewalski's colts tended to spend more time nursing than fillies, because they had longer bouts. Mare-terminated bouts are twenty to thirty seconds shorter than foal-terminated bouts, but there was no evidence that Przewalski's mares terminated bouts of fillies more often than those of colts. This suggests that differential lactational investment in colts versus fillies results from permissive rather than discriminatory behavior by mares. Colts may be nursing longer because they are slightly larger than fillies and require more food.

Przewalski's mares solicit nursing by their foals by using a conspicuous stance with the hindlegs extended beyond vertical and sometimes by nickering to the foal, but these solicitations are rare. More commonly mares facilitate nursing attempts by the foal, through behaviors such as backing out of a crowd of horses around a hayrack so that the foal can reach the udder. Blocking is used by Przewalski's foals to encourage their mothers to stop moving and stand still for nursing. The foal crosses directly in front of the mare's chest on its way around to the udder. If the mare does not halt, the foal circles around and tries again, often with ears back in a threat gesture.

The timing of weaning is affected by the mare's investment in her next offspring. Przewalski's mares who conceive promptly after their foals are born tend to wean their offspring at one year of age, just before the birth of their next foal. Mares who fail to conceive may continue to nurse their offspring for several years until the mare conceives or the juvenile is removed. Mares at two zoos who were receiving exceptionally large amounts of food (17% more digestible energy than horses at other zoos), did not wean their juveniles before the next foals were born and so nursed two offspring simultaneously (Figure 12.6). One mare at the Bronx Zoo, Robin (#498 Catskill 49), had three daughters present in the herd, an eight-year-old, a three-year-old, and a six-month-old foal. Robin nursed the eight-year-old and the foal, as well as the granddaughter born to her three-year-old daughter. The three-year-old nursed her own daughter and her mother's foal. These mares did not nurse

Figure 12.6. The mare Tasha (#948) nursed both her one-month-old filly (#1240) and her yearling filly (#1125). Note that the yearling has approached from the rear, perhaps to avoid attracting her mother's attention. More commonly, suckling foals one month or older stand close to the mother's body in reverse parallel position.

foals belonging to any of the three other kin-lines present in the group (Boyd 1988a).

In addition to their gestational and lactational investment, Przewalski's mares are also very protective of their foals during the first few days of the foal's life, even attacking a normally dominant herd member such as the stallion if it approaches, as has also been reported for domestic horses (Tyler 1972). Foals are particularly vulnerable at this age. Keiper (1985) reports instances in which other members of feral pony herds have kicked newborn foals or inadvertently stepped on them. The mother's protective behavior may also be a guard against infanticidal stallions, or potential predators in the wild. After the first several days, the Przewalski's mares are less protective, but they sometimes come to their offspring's aid. If mothers and daughters remain together, the mother has additional opportunities to invest in her daughter. She may come to her daughter's aid in conflicts with other mares, helping her to improve her dominance rank. She may also aid her daughter at parturition. At the San Diego Wild Animal Park, the birth of the Przewalski's foal Belek (#1275 San Diego 40) was witnessed (see chapter 11). It was unusual in that the mother of the parturient mare began cleaning and protecting the newborn foal before it was completely out of its mother's body (Boyd 1988a).

Przewalski's mares are also their offspring's most frequent grooming partner, from foalhood into adulthood. They also invest in their offspring by preferentially sharing grain with them (Boyd 1991). In the wild, Przewalski's sires probably played an important role in protecting their offspring against predators, and retrieving foals when they strayed from the herd, as has been reported for feral horses (Feist and McCullough 1975, Boyd 1980, Berger and Rudman 1985, Berger 1986). In captivity, sires rarely have occasion to provide this form of parental investment. Sires do appear to aid their offspring by sharing grain with them. Younger offspring are more likely to be permitted to share than older offspring and adult mares (Mackler and Dolan 1980, Boyd 1991). Stallions also tolerate foals grazing in their vicinity (Dobroruka 1961). Przewalski's sires may also take on some of the role of the missing dam for orphaned offspring. The orphaned foal Coltar (#1130 Topeka 8) was twice as likely to be within one meter of his father than were his paternal half-siblings whose mothers were present (Boyd 1988a). The sire was extremely tolerant of Coltar, even permitting the foal to suckle on his sheath during the month after Coltar was orphaned. He allowed Coltar to eat hay and grain alongside him while chasing all other herd members away.

Two Przewalski's colts played frequently with their fathers. Basil (#293 Catskill 17), the father of one of the colts, had been reported by Lewtas (1973) and Hutson (1975) to be very tolerant of play directed at him by some of his other colts. Playing by feral horse stallions with sons may be important in helping sons develop fighting skills necessary to obtain harems in the wild (Berger 1986).

DISPERSAL

Feral horse fillies on Shackleford Island are driven out of their natal herds by the adult mares at two to three years of age. Rubenstein (1982) hypothesized that they were driven out because they competed with their mothers for limited forage. Fillies are ready to breed at two years of age. As stallions rarely breed their own daughters (Berger and Cunningham 1987), the fillies would be wasting breeding opportunities by remaining in their natal band. Driving them out of the band helps to avoid consanguineous matings. Some Przewalski's stallions have become aggressive toward their pubertal daughters, presumably in an attempt to drive them out of the harem. Basil (#293 Catskill 17) chased and bit his twenty-two month-old daughter Hayley (#546 Marwell 8) until she had raw patches on her rump (Hutson 1975). Rolmar (#568 Catskill 61) became aggressive toward his twenty-two month-old daughter Bokalia (#1064 Topeka 4), and as a result she began pacing the fence, presumably in a thwarted escape response, until she was removed and sent to another zoo (Boyd 1988a).

Rubenstein (1982) observed that feral domestic horse colts on Shackleford Island left natal bands on their own accord at about four years of age, rather than being driven out. Colts do not begin to breed before the age of four years (Rubenstein 1982, Kaseda et al. 1984, Berger 1986). If they remain with their natal band until this age they are not missing breeding opportunities or taking mating opportunities away from their father. Instead, by tolerating their sons, parents permit them to postpone having to fend for themselves. The longer a son remains, the greater the likelihood that additional siblings, some of whom will be brothers are born. When sons leave the natal band they join a bachelor herd and Rubenstein (1982) found that brothers dispersing together ranked high in feral horse bachelor herds with rank being a good predictor of which bachelor would be the first to acquire mares. Przewalski's stallions do seem to be more tolerant of sons than daughters, and one colt, Sembon (#818 Catskill 68), was left in his natal herd without incident until he was five years old. At that age he was removed for treatment of laminitis and then could not be returned because he and his father fought.

Based on this information, captive juvenile Przewalski's horses could be left in their natal band until they are at least eighteen months old. The juveniles probably gain social skills through continued association with adults, which would be missed if they were removed too early. In particular, as yearlings they gain the opportunity to observe and interact with neonates, and to observe reproductive behavior during another breeding season.

When juvenile fillies are removed, they can be sent directly to other zoos, and become part of a harem as probably happened in the wild. Juvenile males should be placed in bachelor herds until they are four or five years old. If no other Przewalski's horse bachelors are available, the Topeka Zoo has successfully used pony geldings as bachelor companions. This is much more desirable than housing a young male solitarily or giving him a harem too early, because either of these scenarios commonly results in behavior problems (see chapter 11).

CONCLUSIONS

A knowledge of the social organization of Przewalski's horses is critical to successful captive management and reintroduction efforts. Przewalski's horses were apparently harem polygynous in the wild and duplicating this social organization seems to have contributed to their successful propagation in captivity. Whenever possible, surplus males should be kept in bachelor herds as would have occurred in the wild.

Przewalski's horses communicate by vocal, postural, and olfactory means, and an understanding of these behaviors greatly facilitates the study of the species.

Every herd of Przewalski's horses has a dominance hierarchy. A knowledge of the factors affecting an individual's rank, and of the consequences resulting from that rank, aids in making management decisions. Kinship also influences much of Przewalski's horse behavior and should be taken into consideration as well. Managing Przewalski's horses so as to encourage development of normal reproductive behavior, parental investment patterns, and dispersal mechanisms is essential to ensure the successful propagation of this endangered species.

13

Reintroduction

Inge Bouman, Jan Bouman, and Lee Boyd

CURRENT REINTRODUCTION EFFORTS

China

In 1985 Przewalski's horses were first returned to their historic range: the Dzungarian desert in the Xinjiang-Uygur Autonomous Region of China (Wanyou Zhou and Jun Zhang, personal communication 1992; Ryder 1993). The first shipment of eleven horses from the UK and East Germany spent a year at the Urumqi Zoo (also in the Xinjiang region) before being relocated to the Przewalski Wild Horse Breeding Center in Jimsar County, Xinjiang (Jun et al. 1990). In 1988 an additional five horses were imported to the Xinjiang (or Jimsar) Wild Horse Breeding Center from Tierpark Hellabrunn in West Germany. The first foal was born in 1988 and more than thirty foals have been born in this population since then. The conception rate has typically been around fifty-five percent (Jun et al. 1990). In 1989 two groups of Przewalski's horses (25 animals) were released from four hectare enclosures into a two hundred hectare fenced pasture in the Junggar Basin northeast of Urumqi for several months of the year (Jun et al. 1990, Wanyou Zhou and Jun Zhang, personal communication 1992).

Mongolia

Takhi-Tal. In 1990, the Mongolian government, the Christian Oswald Foundation, and the International Hunter's Association for the Preservation of Wildlife signed a cooperative agreement to reintroduce Przewalski's horses to Takhi-Tal (meaning "valley of the wild horses") and establish a breeding center there (Oswald 1992). Takhi-Tal is located west of Ulan Bator just inside the Mongolian border with Xinjiang, China. Fences were built at Takhi-Tal in 1991, using larch poles brought by train from the taiga two thousand kilometers away. Three small enclosures of one ha each and a large enclosure of one hundred sixty ha were constructed. One of the smaller enclosures contains wooden stalls which are situated behind a 3 meter hill that blocks the wind. The second small enclosure is used to store fodder, and the third is used for quarantine (Oswald 1992). The horses are pastured year-round in the large enclosure. Although up to forty horses could be supported without supplemental feeding, hay and grain are provided during the winter months to spare the grass (Oswald 1992). Water is sluiced to the enclosures from a reservoir.

Two stallions and three mares from Askania Nova were flown to Ulan Bator, and then to Takhi-Tal, where they were greeted enthusiastically by the local population on June 6, 1992 and released into their enclosure. In September 1992 the first foal was born.

Hustain Nuru. At an FAO-sponsored meeting in Moscow in May 1985, the Institute of Evolutionary Animal Morphology and Ecology (IEAME), headed by Academician Sokolov, was asked to look for suitable reintroduction sites in the former Soviet Union and Mongolia and to carry out feasibility studies. Some fifteen areas were investigated, including the Mongolian part of the Dzungarian Gobi (Sokolov et al. 1990). Hustain Nuru, a grassy steppe area with an undamaged ecosystem, important for conservation because of its biological diversity, was chosen as the most suitable reintroduction site. The reintroduction of the Przewalski's horse into Hustain Nuru was proposed by the Mongolian biologists Amarsanaa and Amgalan in 1989 and accepted in a meeting with the chairman of the Central Aimak (province), the owner of the area, the Mongolian Academy of Sciences, the Board of the Mongolian Association for Conservation of Nature and Environment (MACNE), and the Mongolian Horse Society. The administrations of the three surrounding somons (settlements) not only agreed to cooperate, but offered help in building the reserve center. In 1990 the Foundation Reserves for the Przewalski Horse (FRPH) was invited to Mongolia. A contract with the above-mentioned Mongolian organizations was signed aiming at the reintroduction of Przewal-

ski's horses from semi-reserves into Hustain Nuru (IUCN/WWF
project 3077, Bouman and Bouman 1990). Academician Sokolov
and the FRPH extended their contract of cooperation in 1990 to
include the Scientific Institute for Cattle Breeding in the Steppes,
at Askania Nova in the Ukraine. The Mongolian government had
a strong interest in the restoration of its native wildlife and officially endorsed the reintroduction program in 1991. In 1992 the
borders of the state reserve Hustain Nuru, measuring fifty thousand ha, were officially laid down by the Mongolian State Committee for Environment Control. Hunting and access of livestock to
the reserve had been forbidden earlier. The FRPH and MACNE
prepared the reintroduction program for the Przewalski's horses,
and a special program for management of the steppe biotope at
Hustain Nuru to ensure the conservation of its biodiversity.

Hustain Nuru is a mountainous steppe area in the lower spurs
of the southern part of the Chentai mountains some 115 km from
Ulan Bator. It lies isolated between three somons, each situated
some 15–30 km from the borders of the reserve, and it has sporad-
ically been used for livestock grazing. No people permanently lived
in the area. On the mountain tops and north slopes (highest altitude of 1841 meters), birch woods grow which provide food and protection from the extreme winters for the Przewalski's horses and
other wildlife. The mountain valleys and slopes (elevation of 1340
meters above sea level) have a typical steppe vegetation containing
vast stands of fescue, brome grass, koeleria, and feathergrasses.
Several natural springs, which do not dry up in summer, are present. The mountains and valleys offer a variety of food and water
sources, which permit year-round grazing and satisfies the needs of
Przewalski's horses within the reserve boundaries, helping to prevent wide dispersal. Competition with other wildlife and livestock
for food or water should pose no problems in Hustain Nuru. Experience with domestic horses in comparable areas of Mongolia gives
reliable indications that some five hundred Przewalski's horses can
live in the wild state in the reserve. Proper studies of feeding ecology, habitat use, spatial distribution, movement patterns and social organization of the released Przewalski's horses, starting in
1993, will refine this estimate.

Hustain Nuru has a diverse fauna with typical steppe animals
like the bobak marmots, susliks, steppe lemmings, and a variety of
other rodents. Several wild ungulates, like the red deer and some
wild sheep migrate to and from surrounding nature reserves
around Ulan Bator to Hustain Nuru. The main predators are

Figure 13.1. a and b. Horses in the semi-reserve in Hustain Nuru, Mongolia.

wolves (local population estimated at twenty) which may prey on Przewalski's horses, the lynx, the Pallas's cat and the steppe polecat. Bird life is abundant with quite a few birds listed as endangered in the Red Data Book such as the steppe eagle.

It is obvious that the support of the local people for such a project is essential. The local authorities and local herdsmen have offered help in many ways: land for the reserve, agricultural land for extra food supply for the horses, and grazing pastures outside the reserve for livestock of the reserve staff. They helped with the building of the administration center and the fences of the acclimatization areas. Electricity was provided by MACNE, and a bridge built and some parts of the road leveled to make transport of the horses possible. Although the reserve is large and has some natural boundaries like the Tuul River to the south, not all valleys and mountain passes can be closed. It must be expected that some Przewalski's horses will succeed in crossing the borders, so surveillance is needed to prevent disperal in the direction of the somons. Each released group of Przewalski's horses will have its own ranger who will follow them. With the help of the local people and the wardens living along the border of the reserve, the Przewalski's horses will be herded back into the reserve if they disperse too widely.

Several criteria are used to select individual Przewalski's horses for reintroduction. One is genetic composition. All of the original founders should be represented in the horses selected for return to the wild. Askania Nova and the FRPH maintain more than a fifth of the world population, comprising the descendants of all thirteen founders. The genetic composition of the combined population of horses provides a sufficiently broad base to minimize any foreseeable risks posed by inbreeding. Projected inbreeding coefficients can be kept below 0.16 with a maximum of 0.20 for some combinations of horses.

A second important criteria for selection is an individual's ability to adapt to natural conditions. The horses will be selected from animals which have been bred in semi-reserves for some generations in Askania Nova (Ukraine), in The Netherlands, and Germany. They have learned to exist with a minimum of human intervention by searching for their own food and withstanding harsh weather conditions. Research carried out in the semi-reserves has shown that the horses develop a normal social organization and behavioral repertoire (Feh 1988, Klimov 1988, Keiper 1990, Sauerland 1991, Keiper and Receveur 1992, Leboucher 1992), and reproduce successfully (Bouman and Bouman 1990). Leboucher (1992) observed the Przewalski's bachelor group in The Netherlands to provide basic information for a proper choice of the stallions for release in Mongolia. The four-year-old stallion Khaan was chosen because he demonstrated arousal, fecal marking, herding behavior, and exhibited leadership in situations with novel stimuli. Experience in the semi-reserves has shown that Przewalski's mares of two to three years adapt easily to new environments and integrate easily into new social groups, so mares of this age group will be chosen for reintroduction.

On June 5, 1992 a group of eight Przewalski's horses from Askania Nova and eight from the FRHP arrived at the airfield of Ulan Bator. They were met by hundreds of Mongolians who were very excited about the return of the wild horse or "takh". Many old herdsmen still remember the wild horses and they are featured frequently in songs, poetry and stories. Soon after their arrival, the sixteen individually-crated Przewalski's horses were transported by trucks to Hustain Nuru. A group of five young females from Askania Nova were released separately from a similar group of females from the FRPH. Unfortunately one Askania Nova mare died due to a fall in the crate before release. To each group of mares was added an unfamiliar and unrelated four-year-old stallion. A third group, the bachelor group, contained stallions from Askania Nova and the FRPH of varying age, but younger than the harem stallions to prevent strong competition with the harem stallions directly after release. The repeated release of groups with ages as described above will guarantee the building up of an appropriate age structure in the released population in the coming ten years. To establish the proper sex ratio, an equal number of mares and stallions will be released through the year 2000.

Repeated releases are necessary to build up a self-sustaining population. The Przewalski's horses will be selected from different bloodlines from a variety of breeding groups in the semi-reserves. After the first release, four more releases of sixteen animals are planned from 1994–2000. It is envisaged that after ten years, a population of some two hundred Przewalski's horses (eighty introduced horses plus their offspring) will live in Hustain Nuru, and new genetic contributions for the breeding groups in the semi-reserves will be sought from cooperating zoos.

Endangered species need proper preparation and acclimatization prior to reintroduction. "Hard releases", in which animals are neither prepared nor monitored cannot be justified, especially given their limited numbers (no Przewalski's horses in the wild and just over one thousand in captivity). It is important to give the horses time to acclimatize, to become familiar with the new location, new food and new physical conditions, and familiar with one another as a group. Group cohesion is necessary to be able to cope with the many unfamiliarities in the new environment and to withstand predation by wolves.

At the center of the Hustain Nuru reserve three enclosures, each some 45–65 ha large, were built out of sight of each other for keeping the three groups of Przewalski's horses during the first year after their arrival. The natural vegetation of the enclosures consists of a variety of grasses, herbs and some small bushes, providing sufficient food in summer. Extra food will probably have to be supplied in winter and good quality hay is available. A small stream runs through all enclosures. Wire-netting fences 75 cm high and mounted on high-tension steel wire were constructed (Blaak 1992) The wire-netting extends underground to make a good earth connection and discourage wolves from getting through the fence. Above the wire-netting five high-tension steel wires extend the fence to a height of 1.6 meters and are connected to a Gallagher MB 200 energizer to electrify the fence. Adjacent to each enclosure, a holding pen of 1 ha was built, where the crates were opened on arrival. The fences of these pens were wire-netting to a height of 1.5 meters with two electrified high-tension wires above and two on brackets inside the netting to teach the horses to respect the electric fence (Blaak 1992). The horses stayed one week in the holding pen to recover from their 40–60 hour journey by airplane and truck to the site. After three to four days the horses already stayed together as a group and had learned to avoid the shock of the electric fence. A week after their arrival all groups were released from the pens into the enclosures. All groups were closely watched by their own Mongolian wildlife ranger living nearby. A Dutch biologist familiar with the Przewalski's horses stayed at Hustain Nuru to train the rangers, the Mongolian biologist, and the reserve manager in monitoring, making systematic observations, and writing reports.

The Przewalski's horses will be considered ready for release into the steppe of Hustain Nuru if they are fully acclimatized and if they have become integrated groups to discourage scattering of individual horses after release into the reserve. Mongolia has a much more rigorous climate than the south of the Ukraine or The Netherlands. The average January temperature is $-25°C$ with an absolute minimum of $-40°C$. Large differences in temperature occur between day and night. Snow cover lasts about one hundred days with a depth of snow varying from 20–40 cm with deeper snow occurring in crevices. The degree of physiological acclimatization will not be easy to assess, but vitality, activity level, seasonal condition, seasonal coat change, and the erectness of the mane will give indications of the well-being of the horses.

The development of group integration is probably easier to observe. Synchronization of activity patterns, changes in the amount and kind of aggression within the group, and the emergence of a settled dominance hierarchy will provide indications of group integration. Group cohesion will probably be strongest when foals are born. Therefore, it is planned to wait until after some foals have been born in 1993 before releasing a group.

All twelve staff members (reserve manager, biologist, administrative personnel, technicians, wildlife rangers and wardens for surveillance) are Mongolians employed by MACNE and living permanently at Hustain Nuru. Seven of them were recruited from the surrounding local herdsmen and several have visited The Netherlands to get acquainted with the Przewalski's horses before arrival. Financial support from the Dutch government for five years will be provided for technical field equipment (jeeps, telemetry, etc.). It will also provide support for foreign experts to train the Mongolian personnel in preparing ecological maps, in monitoring wildlife (modern observation techniques, data handling and analyses) and monitoring the grazing impact of the main herbivores on vegetation of the steppe biotope. The training will further concentrate on assisting the staff with development of a long-term management plan and creation of the necessary infra-structure to protect the reserve and its wildlife in the future. The detailed monitoring of the Przewalski's horses after release will be an important part of the total program. Most of the daily observations will be provided by the rangers following the groups of Przewalski's horses, and the wardens who are responsible for surveillance in and outside the reserve. The rangers will monitor the location of the horses and other herbivores, size and composition of their groups, activities and interactions between groups, sexual activity, wandering off of individual horses, and the presence of predators. The collected data will explain the distribution and habitat selection of the horses. The unstructured observations of the rangers will be supplemented with more systematic observations of feeding behavior by the biologists. The monthly condition scoring of the horses will be an important measure for estimating the adaptation process. Examination of feces for parasites will occur regularly. Any remains of dead animals will be located and new births recorded to get an insight into the nature of population fluctuations. Annual reports will be written and published.

The wild horse was once an integral part of the steppe ecosystem to which it had become adapted. Reintroduction of the Przewalski's horse to Hustain Nuru will restore this ecological association and preserve an endangered steppe ecosystem for future generations. The return of the wild horse can be seen as a vehicle for a conservation education program for the Mongolians. They will not only become proud of their "takh" but also will become sensitized to the value of, and the threats to, the steppe of their region. Therefore, an information center will be established by MACNE with financial aid from the Dutch government. In this information center in-service training for teachers on environmental issues will be possible. Local herdsmen living near the border of the reserve can be trained as reserve scouts. The goodwill of the local people and the involvement of MACNE gives much hope that these plans will be realized in the coming years.

14

Conclusion

Lee Boyd and Katherine A. Houpt

LESSONS LEARNED

The history of Przewalski's horse is replete with ironies. Przewalski's horse is certainly the closest living relative of domestic and feral horses. It is ironic that domestic horses made possible the human exploration and expansion that in turn almost led to the extinction of their wild relatives. Domestic horses even played a direct role in the chase and capture of Przewalski's horses, and acted as nursemares for captured foals. Although domestics competed with the last wild Przewalski's horses for food and water, it was in part due to the obviously close evolutionary relationship of the discovered species with a familiar one, that Przewalski's horses were interesting enough for people to be motivated to save them. One reason that captive propagation of Przewalski's horses has been so successful is accumulated experience of industry and science in managing domestic and feral horses.

A similar ironic relationship exists between Przewalski's horses and humans. We nearly sent this species to extinction several times. Our interactions with Przewalski's horses contributed to their extinction in the wild. Bringing some into captivity saved the species as a whole from extinction, but then the captive population was nearly lost in World War II. Thanks to the efforts of many individuals we currently have a world population of over one thousand Przewalski's horses in captivity and are trying to re-establish wild populations.

Today we deplore the death of so many wild Przewalski's horses at the turn of the century during attempts to catch and transport foals, but we must consider that this was the technology available at the time. Had those captures not taken place, the species almost certainly would be extinct. No one seems to have predicted the decline of the wild populations in time to prevent their demise. It is difficult to argue with those who today believe that preserving habitat is the best means of saving endangered species. But the example of Przewalski's horse conservation shows us that extinction events may be difficult to predict and how important it is to have a captive population to draw upon should reintroductions become necessary. Maintaining such healthy captive populations has become a major role of modern zoos, receiving at least equal priority with their traditional mission of public education.

That Przewalski's horses were saved from extinction can be attributed to a number of people who have devoted a great part of their life toward this goal. Each has had their own area of interest and in promoting that area have had a profound impact on the conservation of Przewalski's horses. Erna Mohr chronicled the history of the species and began the studbook which was to become the model for others to follow. This task was continued by Jiri Volf giving us what are probably more complete records on this species than any other, including most domestic breeds. Heinz Heck is responsible for initiating the discussion of type and establishing the prolific herd of horses at the Catskill Game Farm from which most North American horses trace their ancestry. Heinrich Dathe published the proceedings of the international symposia on Przewalski's horses making possible the dissemination of that information. Through his interest in the genetics of the species, Oliver Ryder encouraged the exchange of horses, most notably between North America and the Soviet Union. Jan and Inge Bouman have worked tirelessly to see that Przewalski's horses are returned to the wild. Fortunately, the species is charismatic enough that these devotees were able to attract proponents to aid them in their mission. The individual efforts of these people and many others have synergistically brought us to where we are today, working towards returning the species to the wild.

The history of Przewalski's horses in captivity has certainly taught us 'not to put all our eggs in one basket.' The captive population was nearly lost in World War II, and as pointed out by Houpt (chapter 9), infectious diseases also have the ability to wipe out a herd. Zoo populations should be kept small and scattered worldwide. Not only does this prevent wide-scale population crashes due to disease, war or natural disaster, but it enables the greatest number of people to see and learn about this endangered species and come to appreciate them, and ensures that harems do not become so artificially large that identification of the horses becomes difficult and behavior problems arise.

The problems resulting from the old management practices of unilateral breeding and selling horses in related pairs are well-documented. The current strategy of considering the horses worldwide as one population is sound in theory, with horses continuing to be exchanged between zoos to minimize inbreeding. The largest problem with this scheme currently seems to be in the implementation; in the logistics of working out exchanges, which are costly and slow to proceed. Facilitation of these exchanges should be a goal that is attended to in the immediate future.

Several themes have come up again and again in this volume. Because it was recognized early on that this was a rare and interesting species, detailed records were initiated and maintained to document the captive population. These have proven to be invaluable in studying and managing the species. What an asset this is can be realized in comparison with current problems experienced by managers of species once considered more common, such as orangutans and tigers, where a lack of record-keeping in the past is leading to problems with subspecies identification within captive populations.

We have learned that roughage needs to be provided to maintain gastrointestinal populations of cellulytic microorganisms and prevent the development of behavioral vices such as cribbing and coprophagia. Vitamin E supplementation at high levels has been shown to be necessary in some local populations of horses. Rather than a genetic neurological disease, there is a genetically determined large requirement for vitamin E, a deficiency of which can lead to neurological signs.

The behavior of a species is often one of the last areas of their biology to be studied and one of the last aspects to be considered in making management decisions. The numerous behavior studies of captive Przewalski's horses within the last decade are now affecting management policies. We have extrapolated from the social organization of the species and from studies of captive behavior that surplus males should be maintained in bachelor groups, that young males should not be placed with older mares initially, and harems should be kept small and dispersal mechanisms and harem acquisition strategies from the wild should be mimicked in captivity to ensure optimal reproduction and prevent the development of behavior problems.

POINTS OF CONTROVERSY

The naming of the species: *Equus ferus*, or *Equus przewalskii* by tradition? Actually our tradition is somewhat flawed. Przewalski was not actually the first discoverer of the horses, but merely the first to bring them to the attention of the western world.

What is the relationship of *Equus przewalskii* to *Equus caballus*? They have different chromosome numbers, although the difference is easily explained. They readily hybridize. The behavior of the two species seems to be identical as far as can be determined. Relationships between horses, asses, zebras, and hemiones in general are unclear.

How much has captivity changed Przewalski's horses? Undoubtedly there have been some changes in temperament, as those who could not adjust to captivity died without reproducing.

How pure were the original founders? Do white marks indicate the admixture of domestic blood into the wild populations prior to capture of the founders? Or are these marks a natural trait of wild equids, providing a variant that humans might have positively selected for during domestication, as a means of identification or for aesthetic purposes, increasing the frequency of occurrence and thereby setting up our present-day association of this trait with domestic blood?

What should be done about the Prague versus the Munich lines? As a stallion has the potential to sire more offspring in a lifetime than does a mare, the plan of using Munich line stallions to breed Prague line mares (chapter 2) seemed a reasonable way to mix the two lines while reducing the contribution of the domestic mare. Unfortunately her genetic contribution is tied to that of two other founders whose contributions would also be reduced (chapter 6). As this problem seems insoluble, the domestic alleles do not seem to be disrupting the genome (chapter 6), and we cannot be sure that the wild-caught founders were pure themselves, it seems time to put the Prague versus Munich distinction behind us and manage the two bloodlines as one population.

Should we be selecting for type? The European breeders are selecting against individuals known to carry the fox-colored or chestnut gene (chapter 2) and yet fox-colored individuals evidently existed in the wild population prior to extinction (chapter 5).

AREAS FOR FUTURE RESEARCH

Although we have repeatedly stated that the species' record is remarkable and unique, and provides a wealth of data, data on additional topics could be compiled. In particular, the studbook records do not show herd composition, which makes it impossible to determine average ages at first reproduction, or individual lifetime reproductive success because there is no information on breeding opportunities versus breeding successes. Necropsies are not always performed, and if they are, the findings are not always sent to the studbook keeper, nor does the cause of death appear in the studbook. Almost no data on foal growth exists. Estimates of normal foal height and weight at various ages would be useful in husbandry of orphaned foals or those who fail to thrive. This would also provide a baseline so that ages of wild foals could be estimated in the future and their growth assessed without having to capture them. Finding ways to encourage the report of such information and standardizing the reporting should be a top priority.

Etorphine, the drug of choice for immobilization, is no longer available in North America. Unless that situation is reversed, new drugs must be developed and investigated for this purpose.

Mitochondrial DNA studies are relatively new and hold promise for studying the relationship of Przewalski's horses to other equids.

The reproductive physiology of male Przewalski's horses is relatively unstudied, but of obvious importance to the propagation of the species.

We have the technology to do embryo-transfers. But should we be performing such transfers in a population that already has over 1000 individuals, and from which we hope to obtain individuals competent to be returned to the wild? One consideration is that cryopreservation of sperm and embryos, especially from under-represented individuals, would be desirable as a hedge against loss of genetic diversity in case of natural or un-natural disasters.

Neonatal deaths are now the largest class of mortality. Ways to reduce the likelihood of such deaths should be examined.

Many aspects of Przewalski's horse behavior need further study. It would be interesting to determine if horses on exhibit in small yards make up at night for their lack of diurnal rest. Whether the horses direct kicks up or down the dominance hierarchy is still controversial. The function of snapping behavior is still not well understood. An examination of how well harem stallion behavior correlates with the estrogen metabolites in his mares' urine would be interesting. Bachelor herds could be studied to see if dominance rank correlates with the order in which the stallions defecate on stud piles.

RECOMMENDATIONS FOR REINTRODUCTION

All of the original founders should be represented in horses selected for return to the wild. Groups to be released should be composed so as to minimize the inbreeding coefficients of the offspring. As Przewalski's horses are harem polygynous, leading to a surplus of males, it is logical that expendable bachelors be released first to see how they fare in a given area. Proper ages and group composition need to be determined. Horses should spend some time in semi-reserves at potential reintroduction sites to become acclimated to the region before being released. One strategy calls for the animals originally brought to the semi-reserves to be kept there, and only their offspring, who have always fended for themselves, will be released. However, personal observations (Boyd) of horses that have recently gone feral in the deserts of Wyoming, some branded and still wearing halters, suggest that horses can leave captivity already behaviorally competent to find forage, water, shelter, and interact with other horses to form harem and bachelor groups. A Shetland pony gelding was a member of one bachelor group in the Red Desert and ran wild for several years, surviving the third worst winter in Wyoming's history. As these domestic horses have been in captivity for many more generations than Przewalski's horses and still retain the ability to fend for themselves, it is reasonable to assume that Przewalski's horses are capable of the same. However there is an important difference which Przewalski's horses will have to overcome. When domestic horses turn feral in areas such as the Red Desert, they become incorporated into bands whose members were born in the wild and know where to find water, forage, etc. The first reintroduced Przewalski's horses will not have that advantage. Feral horses who are unfamiliar with an area are sometimes at risk; the Committee on Wild Horse and Burro Research (1991) reported deaths when 133 feral horses were driven from their home range to a neighboring area, marked and released at that site. Upon release in the unfamiliar area, 48 of the horses were evidently unable to find water or the gaps in a fence that would have allowed them to return to their home range, and they walked the fence until they died of dehydration.

The Przewalski's horses must be prevented from contacting domestic horses or the species will be diluted by hybridization and cease to exist as such, except in captivity.

Predators are another problem that must be addressed. It is not clear how well horses retain the ability to respond appropriately to predators, since few large predators remain in areas of North America where the feral horse populations have been studied. Predators are less likely to bother the horses if there is an adequate base of available prey that is easier to catch. The current and projected population sizes of potential predators and their prey need to be evaluated prior to the release of the horses. Even if predation on horses becomes a problem, mass predator extermination is not an appropriate response in today's world. Elimination of specific individuals causing the problem, and population management of other species on which these predators may prey should minimize attacks on Przewalski's horses.

Care must be taken so that fences erected to enclose the horses do not exclude other wildlife from critical resources such as water holes, or interfere with traditional migration routes.

Radio telemetry would be a useful technique for re-locating released Przewalski's horses. Radio collars have been used successfully on horses in the past (Keiper 1985). However, recent use of radio collars has resulted in some problems (Committee on Wild Horse and Burro Research 1991). Collars became either too loose, slipped over the horses' ears, and were lost or too tight. Loose collars caused sores on the horses' ears from banging against them as the horse grazed or drank. Tight collars abraded the horses' necks, especially under the radio transmitter, causing sores that became infected. In other cases the horse grew and the collar became imbedded in the neck. No horses were known to have died or been permanently injured as a result of poorly fitting collars, but affected animals had to be caught, the collars removed, and the wounds treated. Some wounds did result in scars. These problems were attributed to weight gain or loss subsequent to collaring caused by fluctuations in forage abundance. Many horses were two to five years old when collared and may have outgrown their collars as they matured. This would particularly be a problem with Przewalski's stallions whose neck girth increases considerably with maturity. Collars provided a focus of attack during fights between stallions and so were torn off more readily than expected (Siniff et al. 1990). Solutions to these problems should be explored if reintroduced Przewalski's horses are to be tracked using radio telemetry. An expandable segment might be built into the collar to permit size changes, although the collar might then need to be designed with a breakaway feature, should the horse somehow put a foot through it or snag the collar on something while scratching or grazing. Only fully mature horses should be candidates for collaring. Mares would be better candidates than stallions as they generally have less change in neck size; their fights are more infrequent and usually do not involve biting at each other's neck. Tracking by satellite would allow one to determine how far the horses move.

Local personnel in Mongolia and China should be involved and trained to implement long-term monitoring and management of the populations. Creating reserves to save the Przewalski's horse will provide refuge for other native species. These areas will become prime sites for ecological research and may eventually create opportunities for tourism that will benefit the local economy.

References

Alford, B.T., R.L. Burkhart, and W.P. Johnson. 1974. Etorphine and diprenorphine as immobilizing and reversing agents in captive and free-ranging mammals. Journal of the American Veterinary Medical Association 164:702–705.

Allen, J.L. 1992. Immobilization of Mongolian wild horses (*Equus przewalskii przewalskii*) with carfentanil and antagonism with naltrexone. Journal of Zoo and Wildlife Medicine 23:422–425.

Altmann, J. 1974. Observational study of behavior: sampling methods. Behavior 49:227–267.

Amos, N. 1987. The status and conservation of the British population of Przewalski's horse. M.S. Thesis, University College, London.

Animal Welfare Act of 1970. 1970. Public Law No. 91–579.

Anonymous. 1884. Przevalsky's wild horse. Nature 30:391–392.

Anthony, D., D.Y. Telegin, and D. Brown. 1991. The origin of horseback riding. Scientific American 265(6):94–100.

Antonius, O. 1912. Was ist der "Tarpan?" Naturwissenschaftliche Wochenschrift, N.F. 11, 33:513–517.

Arnold, G.W., and A. Grassia. 1982. Ethogram of agonistic behaviour for Thoroughbred horses. Applied Animal Ethology 8:5–25.

Arnold, S.J. in press. Monitoring quantitative variation and evolution in captive populations. *in* Ballou, J.D., M. Gilpin, and T.J. Foose (eds.). Population Management for Survival. University of Chicago Press, Chicago.

Asa, C.S., D.A. Goldfoot, and O.J. Ginther. 1979. Sociosexual behavior and the ovulatory cycle of ponies (*Equus caballus*) observed in harem groups. Hormones and Behavior 13:49–65.

273

Ashton, D.G. 1984. A survey of diseases of the Przewalski horse. Equus (Berlin) 2(2):179–188.

Ashton, D.G., and D.M. Jones. 1979. Some diseases of the Przewalski horse. Pages 149–156 *in* de Boer, L.E.M., J. Bouman and I. Bouman (eds.). Genetics and Hereditary Diseases of the Przewalski Horse. Foundation for the Preservation and Protection of the Przewalski Horse, Rotterdam, The Netherlands.

Avise, J.C. 1989. A role for molecular genetics in the recognition and conservation of endangered species. Trends in Ecology and Evolution 4:279– 281.

Avise, J.C., J. Arnold, R.M. Ball, E. Bermingham, T. Lamb, J.E. Neigel, C.A. Reeb, and N.C. Saunders. 1987. Intraspecific phylogeography: the mitochondrial DNA bridge between population genetics and systematics. Annual Review of Ecology and Systematics 18:489–522.

Azzaroli, A. 1966. Pleistocene and living horses of the old world. Palaeontographia Italica 61:1–15.

———. 1985. An Early History of Horsemanship. Brill/Backuys, Leiden. 201 pp.

Back, D.G., B.W. Pickett, J.L. Voss, and G.E. Seidel, Jr.. 1974. Observations on the sexual behavior of nonlactating mares. Journal of the American Veterinary Medical Association 165:717–720.

Bader, H., S. Gremmes, H. Sieme, M. Paar, H.O. Hoppen, and K.P. Brandt. 1991. Subfertility in the male Przewalski horse. Journal of Reproduction and Fertility, Supplement 44:676–677.

Bagtache, B., D. Hadjouis, and V. Eisenmann. 1984. Présence d'un Equus caballin (*E. algericus* n.sp.) et d'une autre espèce nouvelle d'Equus (*E. melkiensis* n.sp.) dans l'Atérien des Allobroges, Algérie. Compte Rendu de l'Academie des Sciences, Paris II 298:609–612.

Bahn, P.G. 1980. Crib-biting: Tethered horses in the Paleolithic? World Archeology 12(2):212–217.

Baker, G.J., and J. Kear-Colwell. 1974. Aerophagia (windsucking) and aversion therapy in the horse. Proceedings of the American Association of Equine Practitioners 20:127–130.

Ballou, J. 1983. Calculating inbreeding coefficients from pedigrees. Pages 509–520 *in* Schonewald-Cox, C.M., S.M. Chambers, B. MacBryde, and W.L. Thomas (eds.). Genetics and Conservation. The Benjamin/Cummings Publishing Company, Menlo Park, California.

Ballou, J.D., and T.J. Foose. in press. Demographic and genetic management of captive populations. *in* Lumpkin, S., and D.G. Kleiman (eds.). Wild Mammals in Captivity.

Bannikov, A.G. 1958. Distribution géographique et biologie du cheval sauvage et du chameau de Mongolie (*Equus przewalskii* et *Camelus bactrianus*). Mammalia 22(1):152–160.

Bannikov, A.G., and N.W. Lobanov. 1980. Przewalski horse (in Russian). Priroda 3:100–105.

Barclay, H.B. 1980. The Role of The Horse in Man's Culture. J.A. Allen, London. 398 pp.

Bateman, A.J. 1948. Intra-sexual selection in *Drosophila*. Heredity 2:349–368.

Beck, B.B., and C.M. Wemmer, 1983. The Biology and Management of an Extinct Species, Pere David's Deer. Noyes Publications, Park Ridge, NJ. 193 pp.

Benirschke, K., N. Malouf, R.J. Low, and H. Heck. 1965. Chromosome complement: differences between *Equus caballus* and *Equus przewalskii*, Poliakoff. Science 148:382–383.

Bennett, D.K. 1980. Stripes do not a zebra make, Part I: A cladistic analysis of Equus. Systematic Zoology 29(3):272–287.

Berger, J. 1977. Organizational systems and dominance in feral horses in the Grand Canyon. Behavioral Ecology and Sociobiology 2:131–146.

———. 1983. Induced abortion and social factors in wild horses. Nature 303:59–61.

———. 1986. Wild Horses of the Great Basin. The University of Chicago Press, Chicago, 326 pp.

Berger, J., and C. Cunningham. 1987. Influence of familiarity on frequency of inbreeding in wild horses. Evolution 41:229–231.

Berger, J., and R. Rudman. 1985. Predation and interactions between coyotes and feral horse foals. Journal of Mammalogy 66(2):401–402.

Bibikova, V.I. 1967. Studies in ancient domestic horses in eastern Europe (in Russian). Bjull. Moskowsk. Obshchestva Ispytatelei Prirody, Otd. Biol. 3.

Bingaman, L., and J.D. Ballou. 1986. DEMOGPHY: Lotus 1–2–3 Spreadsheet Demographic Model. National Zoological Park, Washington, D.C.

Blaak, H. 1992. Putting up electric fences in Mongolia. Przewalski Horse 29:5–9.

Blanchard, J. 1964. Informations recherchees d'après les équidés européens figurés. Pages 3–34 *in* Garcia, L.P., and E.R. Perello (eds.). Prehistoric Art of the Western Mediterranean and the Sahara. Wenner Gren Foundation for Anthropological Research, Inc., New York.

Boddaert, P. 1785. Elenchus Animalium, 1. C.R. Hake, Rotterdam. 174 pp.

Bökönyi, S. 1974. The Przevalsky Horse. Souvenir Press, London. 140 pp.

Bouman, I., and J.G. Bouman. 1989. Gefangenschaftszucht des Przewalski-Pferdes: Uberleben der Przewalski-ähnlichen Abkömmlinge oder die Rettung des Pferdes? Pages 269–305 *in* Schneider, E., H. Oelke, and H. Grob (eds.). Die Illusion der Arche Noah. Gefahren für die Arterhaltung durch Gefangenschaftzucht. Echo Verlag, Göttingen.

Bouman, I., and J. Bouman. 1990. Report on the semi-reserves project IUCN/WWF no. 3077. Proceedings of the 5th International Symposium on the Preservation of the Przewalski Horse. Zoologischer Garten Leipzig:184–190.

Bouman, J. 1977. The future of Przewalski horses in captivity. International Yearbook 17:62–68.

———. 1980. Eine Analyse der Stammbuch-Daten und einige Konklusionen hinsichtlich der zukünftigen Züchtung der Przewalskipferde in Gefangenschaft. Equus (Berlin) 2(1): 21–42.

———. 1982. The history of breeding the Przewalski horse in captivity. Pages 17–64 *in* Bouman, J., I. Bouman, and A. Groeneveld (eds.). Breeding Przewalski Horses in Captivity for Release into the Wild. Foundation for the Preservation and Protection of the Przewalski Horse, Rotterdam, The Netherlands.

Bouman, J.G., and H. Bos. 1979. Two symptoms of inbreeding depression in Przewalski horses living in captivity. Pages 111–117 *in* de Boer, L.E.M., J. Bouman, and I. Bouman (eds.). Genetics and Hereditary Diseases of the Przewalski Horse. Foundation for the Preservation and Protection of the Przewalski Horse, Rotterdam, The Netherlands.

Bouman, J.G., and I. Bouman-Heinsdijk. 1979. The introduction of the Przewalski horse in the wild. Pages 165–168 *in* de Boer, L.E.M., J. Bouman, and I. Bouman (eds.). Genetics and Hereditary Diseases of the Przewalski Horse. Foundation for the Preservation and Protection of the Przewalski Horse, Rotterdam, The Netherlands.

Bouman, J., I. Bouman, and A. Groeneveld. 1982. Breeding Przewalski Horses in Captivity for Release into the Wild. Foundation for the Preservation and Protection of the Przewalski Horse, Rotterdam, The Netherlands. 240 pp.

Bouman-Heinsdijk, I. 1982a. Is re-introduction of Przewalski horses into the wild an realistic idea? Pages 177–220 *in* Bouman, J., I. Bouman, and A. Groeneveld (eds.). Breeding Przewalski Horses in Captivity for Release into the Wild. Foundation for the Preservation and Protection of the Przewalski Horse, Rotterdam, The Netherlands.

————. 1982b. Semi-reserves for the Przewalski horse as an intermediary step between captivity and reintroduction into the wild and an international stallion exchange strategy to reduce inbreeding in captivity. Pages 221–229 *in* Bouman, J., I. Bouman, and A. Groeneveld (eds.). Breeding Przewalski Horses in Captivity for Release into the Wild. Foundation for the Preservation and Protection of the Przewalski Horse, Rotterdam, The Netherlands.

Bowling, A.T., and O.A. Ryder. 1987. Genetic studies of blood markers in Przewalski's horses. The Journal of Heredity 78:75–80.

————. 1988. Switched identity of two Przewalski's horse mares detected by blood typing. Zoo Biology 7:81–84.

Boy, V., and P. Duncan. 1979. Time-budgets of Camargue horses. I. Developmental changes in the time-budgets of foals. Behaviour 71:187–202.

Boyd, L.E. 1980. The natality, foal survivorship, and mare-foal behavior of feral horses in Wyoming's Red Desert. M.S. Thesis, University of Wyoming, Laramie, Wyoming. 137 pp.

Boyd, L. 1986. Behavior problems of equids in zoos. Pages 653–664 *in* Crowell-Davis, S.L., and K.A. Houpt (eds.). Behavior. The Veterinary Clinics of North America: Equine Practice 2(3). W.B. Saunders Company, Philadelphia.

————. 1988a. The behavior of Przewalski's horses. Ph.D. Thesis, Cornell University, Ithaca, NY. 290 pp.

————. 1988b. Time budgets of adult Przewalski horses: effects of sex, reproductive status, and enclosure. Applied Animal Behaviour Science 21:19–39.

————. 1988c. Ontogeny of behavior in Przewalski horses. Applied Animal Behaviour Science 21:41–69.

————. 1991. The behavior of Przewalski's horses and its importance to their management. Applied Animal Behaviour Science 29:301–318.

Boyd, L., and L. Kasman. 1986. The marking behavior of male Przewalski's horses. Pages 623–626 *in* Duvall, D., D. Müller-Schwarze, and R.M. Silverstein (eds.). Chemical Signals in Vertebrates 4. Plenum Press, New York.

Boyd, L.E., D.A. Carbonaro, and K.A. Houpt. 1988. The 24-hour time budget of Przewalski horses. Applied Animal Behaviour Science 21:5–17.

Brentjes, B. 1967. Einige Darstellungen des Przewalskipferdes aus Vorderasien und Kaukasien. Equus (Berlin) 1(1):285–291.

Brentjes, V.B. 1972. Das pferd im Alten Orient. Säugetierkundlich Mitteilungen 20:325–353.

Bridges, W. 1974. Gathering of Animals: An Unconventional History of the New York Zoological Society. Harper and Row, New York. 518 pp.

Brincken, J. 1826. Memoire descriptif sur la forêt Impériale de Bialovieza en Lithanie. Warsaw.

Brown, W.M., M. George, Jr., and A.C. Wilson. 1979. Rapid evolution of animal mitochondrial DNA. Proceedings of the National Academy of Sciences, USA 76:1967–1971.

Bubenik, A.B. 1961. Vierundzwanzigstunden-Rhythmus des Przewalski-Pferdes (*Equus przewalskii* Pol. 1881) während der Laktation und beginnender Brunst. Equus (Berlin) 1:122–140.

Buisman, A.K., and R. van Weeren. 1982. Breeding and management of Przewalski horses in captivity. Pages 77–160 *in* Bouman, J., I. Bouman, and A. Groeneveld (eds.). Breeding Przewalski Horses in Captivity for Release into the Wild. Foundation for the Preservation and Protection of the Przewalski Horse, Rotterdam, The Netherlands.

Campitelli, S., C. Carenzi, and M. Verga. 1982/83. Factors which influence parturition in the mare and development of the foal. Applied Animal Ethology 9:7–14.

Caughley, G. 1977. Analysis of Vertebrate Populations. John Wiley & Sons, New York. 234 pp.

CBSG. 1991. Final report on transponder system testing and product choice as a global standard for zoological specimens. CBSG News 2(1):3–4.

Clay, C.M., E.L. Squires, R.P. Amann, and B.W. Pickett. 1987. Influences of season and artificial photoperiod on stallions: testicular size, seminal characteristics and sexual behavior. Journal of Animal Science 64:517–525.

Clutton-Brock, J. 1981. Domesticated Animals from Early Times. University of Texas Press, Austin. 208 pp.

Clutton-Brock, T.H., F.E. Guinness, and S.D. Albon. 1982. Red Deer: behavior and ecology of two sexes. The University of Chicago Press, Chicago. 378 pp.

Cohen, M. 1983. Tetanus. Pages 27–29 *in* Robinson, N.E. (ed.). Current Therapy in Equine Medicine. W.B. Saunders Company, Philadelphia.

Cole, H.H., and H. Goss. 1943. The source of equine gonadotrophin. Pages

107–119 *in* Essays in Biology in Honor of Herbert M. Evans. University of California Press, Berkeley.

Comben, N., R.J. Clark, and D.J.B. Sutherland. 1984. Clinical observations on the response of equine hoof defects to dietary supplementation with biotin. Veterinary Record 115:642–645.

Committee on Wild Horse and Burro Research, National Research Council. 1991. Wild horse populations: field studies in genetics and fertility. National Academy Press, Washington, D.C. 42 pp.

Conway, W.G. 1980. An overview of captive propagation. Pages 199–208 *in* Soule, M.E., and B.A. Wilcox (eds.). Conservation Biology: An Evolutionary-Ecological Perspective. Sinauer, Sunderland, MA.

Corbet, G.B., and J. Clutton-Brock. 1984. Appendix: Taxonomy and nomenclature. Pages 434–438 *in* Mason, I.L. (ed.). Evolution of Domesticated Animals. Longman, London.

Craig, A.M., L.L. Blythe, E.D. Lassen, K.E. Rowe, R. Barrington, and M. Slizeski. 1989. Variations of serum vitamin E, cholesterol, and total serum lipid concentrations in horses during a 72-hour period. American Journal of Veterinary Research 50:1527–1531.

Crowell-Davis, S.L. 1983. The behavior of Welsh pony foals and mares. Ph.D. Thesis, Cornell University, Ithaca, NY. 284 pp.

———. 1986. Spatial relations between mares and foals of the Welsh pony (*Equus caballus*). Animal Behaviour 34:1007–1015.

Crowell-Davis, S.L., and K.A. Houpt. 1985. The ontogeny of flehmen in horses. Animal Behaviour 33:739–745.

Crowell-Davis, S.L., K.A. Houpt, and J.S. Burnham. 1985. Snapping by foals of *Equus caballus*. Zeitschrift für Tierpsychologie 69:42–54.

Czekala, N.M., L.H. Kasman, J. Allen, J. Oosterhuis, and B.L. Lasley. 1990. Urinary steroid evaluations to monitor ovarian function in exotic ungulates: VI. Pregnancy detection in exotic Equidae. Zoo Biology 9:43–48.

Dallaire, A. 1986. Rest behavior. Pages 591–607 *in* Crowell-Davis, S.L., and K.A. Houpt (eds.). Behavior. The Veterinary Clinics of North America: Equine Practice 2(3). W.B. Saunders Company, Philadelphia.

Dathe, H. 1984. Conclusions and Recommendations. 4th International Symposium on the Preservation of the Przewalski Horse. Equus (Berlin) 2(2):246–247.

Dathe, H., and A. Wünschmann. 1980. Einführung. Equus (Berlin) 2(1):5–7.

de Boer, L.E.M., J. Bouman, and I. Bouman. 1979. Genetics and Hereditary Diseases of the Przewalski Horse. Foundation for the Preservation and Protection of the Przewalski Horse, Rotterdam, The Netherlands. 176 pp.

de Sélincourt, A. 1954. (Translation of) Herodotus, The Histories. Penguin
Books, London.

Dietz, O., and E. Wiesner. 1984. Diseases of the Horse. A Handbook for
Science and Practice, Part 2/II. S. Karger, Basel. 478 pp.

Dobroruka, L.J. 1961. Eine Verhaltensstudie des Przewalski-Urwild-
pferdes (*Equus przewalskii* Poliakov 1881) in dem Zoologischen Garten Prag. Equus (Berlin) 1:89–104.

Dodman, N.H., L. Shuster, M.H. Court, and J. Patel. 1988. Use of a narcotic antagonist (nalmefene) to suppress self-mutilative behavior in
a stallion. Journal of the American Veterinary Medical Association
192:1585–1586.

Dolan, J.M. 1982. Przewalski's horse, *Equus przewalskii*, Poliakov, 1881,
in the United States prior to 1940 and its influence on the present
breeding. Zoologische Garten 52:49–65.

Dovchin, N. 1961. The Przewalski horse in Mongolia. Equus (Berlin) 1:22–
27 (translated from Russian by E. Geldermans).

Dover, G., S. Brown, E. Coen, J. Dallas, T. Strachan, and M. Trick. 1982.
The dynamics of genome evolution and species differentiation.
Pages 343–372 *in* Dover, G.A., and R.B. Flavell (eds.). Genome Evo-
lution. Academic Press, New York.

Dubrovskaya, R.M., I.M. Starodumov, and V.V. Klimov. 1982a. Hereditary
polymorphism in proteins, ferments and blood groups of Przewalski's horses in Askania Nova reserve (in Russian). Proceedings of
the 3rd Congress of the All-Union Theriological Society 34:Mam-
mals I.

Dubrovskaya, R.M., I.M. Starodumov, and V.V. Klimov. 1982b. Hereditary
polymorphism in proteins, ferments and blood groups of Przewalski's horses in the USSR (in Russian). Proceedings of the 4th Congress of the All-Union Society of Geneticists and Selectionists 4:192.

Duncan, P. 1980. Time-budgets of Camargue horses. II. Time-budgets of
adult horses and weaned sub-adults. Behaviour 72:26–49.

———. 1982. Foal killing by stallions. Applied Animal Ethology 8:567–
570.

Duncan, P., C. Feh, J.C. Gleize, P. Malkas, and A.M. Scott. 1984. Reduction of inbreeding in a natural herd of horses. Animal Behaviour
32:520–527.

Durrant, B.S. 1990. Semen characteristics of the Przewalski's stallion (*Equus przewalskii*). Theriogenology 33:221.

Durrant, B.S., and M.L. Hoge. 1988. Ultrasonography in a Przewalski's horse mare, *Equus przewalskii*. Theriogenology 29:240.

Durrant, B.S., J.E. Oosterhuis, and M.L. Hoge. 1986. The application of artificial reproduction techniques to the propagation of selected endangered species. Theriogenology 25:25–32.

Eisenmann, V. 1982. Le cheval et ses proches parents: évolution et phylogénie. CEREOPA 1982, 8ème journee d'etude:9–26.

Emlen S.T., and L.W. Oring. 1977. Ecology, sexual selection, and the evolution of mating systems. Science 197:215–223.

Evans, K.L., L.H. Kasman, J.P. Hughes, M. Couto, and B.L. Lasley. 1984. Pregnancy diagnosis in the domestic horse through direct urinary estrone conjugate analysis. Theriogenology 22:615–620.

Feh, C. 1988. Social behaviour and relationships of Przewalski horses in Dutch semi-reserves. Applied Animal Behaviour Science 21:71–87.

Feist, J.D., and D.R. McCullough. 1975. Reproduction in feral horses. Journal of Reproduction and Fertility, Supplement 23:13–18.

———. 1976. Behavior patterns and communication in feral horses. Zeitschrift für Tierpsychologie 41:337–371.

Fisher, R.A. 1930. The Genetical Theory of Natural Selection. Clarendon Press, Oxford, England. 272 pp.

Fisher, R.A., W. Putt, A.M. Scott, C.M. Hawkey, P.D. Butcher, D.G. Ashton, and P. Bircher. 1979. Gene markers in 40 Przewalski horses. International Zoo Yearbook 19:228–235.

Foose, T.J. 1983. The relevance of captive populations to the conservation of biotic diversity. Pages 374–401 *in* Schonewald-Cox, C.M., S.M. Chambers, B. MacBryde, and W.L. Thomas (eds.). Genetics and Conservation. The Benjamin/Cummings Publishing Company, Menlo Park, California.

Forfa, T. 1987. Working on a wobbles cure. Equus 120(10):65–67.

Forsten, A. 1988. The small caballoid horse of the upper Pleistocene and Holocene. Journal of Animal Breeding and Genetics 105:161–176.

Fowler, M.E. 1986. Zoo & Wild Animal Medicine. W.B. Saunders Company, Philadelphia. 1127 pp.

Frauenfelder, H. 1981. Treatment of crib-biting: a surgical approach in the standing horse. Equine Veterinary Journal 13:62–63.

Frechkop, S. 1965. La spécificité du cheval de Prjewalsky. Bulletin de l'Institut royale des Sciences naturelles de Belgie 41, no. 29, 17 pp.

Garner, H.E. 1980. Update on equine laminitis. Pages 25–32 *in* Moyer, W. (ed.). Veterinary Clinics of North America: Large Animal Practice 2(1). W.B. Saunders Company, Philadelphia.

Garutt, V.E.W., I.I. Sokolov, and T.N. Salesskaja. 1965. Erforschung und Zucht des Przewalski-Pferdes (*Equus przewalskii* Poljakoff) in der Sowjetunion. Zeitschrift für Tierzüchtung und Züchtungsbiologie 82(4):377–426.

George, M., Jr., and O.A. Ryder. 1986. Mitochondrial DNA evolution in the genus Equus. Molecular Biology and Evolution 3:535–546.

Geyer, C.J., and E.A. Thompson. 1988. Gene survival in the Asian wild horse (*Equus przewalskii*):I. Dependence of gene survival in the Calgary breeding group pedigree. Zoo Biology 7:313–327.

Geyer, C.J., E.A. Thompson, and O.A. Ryder. 1989. Gene survival in the Asian wild horse (*Equus przewalskii*):II. Gene survival in the whole population, in subgroups, and through history. Zoo Biology 8:313–329.

Gibbons, E.F., Jr., and B.S. Durrant. 1987. Behavior and development in offspring from interspecies embryo transfer: theoretical issues. Applied Animal Behaviour Science 18:105–118.

Ginther, O.J. 1974. Occurrence of anestrus, estrus, diestrus and ovulation over a 12-month period in mares. American Journal of Veterinary Research 35:1173–1179.

———. 1979. Reproductive Biology of the Mare. Basic and Applied Aspects. McNaughton and Gunn, Inc., Ann Arbor, MI. 413 pp.

Gmelin, S.G. 1774. Reise durch Russland. St. Petersburg.

Goldschmidt-Rothschild, von B., and B. Tschanz. 1978. Soziale Organisation und Verhalten einer Jungtierherde beim Carmargue-Pferd. Zeitschrift für Tierpsychologie 46:372–400.

Gorgas, M. 1966. Betrachtung zur Hirnschädelkapazität zentralasiatischer Wildsäugetiere und ihrer Hausformen. Zoologischer Anzeiger 176:227–235.

Groves, C.P. 1974. Horses, Asses and Zebras in the Wild. Ralph Curtis Books, Hollywood, Florida. 192 pp.

———. 1986. The taxonomy, distribution and adaptations of recent equids. Pages 11–65 *in* Meadow, R.H. , and H.P. Uerpmann (eds.). Equids in the Ancient World. Dr. Ludwig Reichert Verlag, Wiesbaden. 421 pp.

Groves, C.P., and D.P. Willoughby. 1981. Studies on the taxonomy and phylogeny of the genus *Equus*. I: Subgeneric classification of the recent species. Mammalia 45:321–354.

Gruenerwald, W. 1982. A Computer Analysis of Studbook Data for the Przewalski Horse (*Equus przewalskii*). Canyon Colorado Equid Sanctuary, Wagon Mound, New Mexico. 432 pp.

Gruenerwald, W. 1985. A Computer Analysis of Studbook Data for the Przewalski Horse (*Equus przewalskii*). Supplement I 1982–1983. Canyon Colorado Equid Sanctuary, Wagon Mound, New Mexico. 140 pp.

Grum-Grzhimailo, G.E. 1892. The wild horse (*Equus przewalskii*). From the diary of a travel to China in 1889–1890 (translated by Aleinikov, P.). Niva 17.

Grzimek, B. 1949. Rangordnungsversuche mit Pferden. Zeitschrift für Tierpsychologie 6:455–464.

Grzimek, V.B. 1952. Versuche über das Farbsehen von Pflanzenessern. I. Das farbige Sehen (und die Sehschärfe) von Pferden. Zeitschrift für Tierpsychologie 9:23–39.

Hagenbeck, C. 1926. Auf Tierfang-Pfaden in der Mongolei. Carl Hagenbeck's illustrierte Tier und Menschenwelt. Jahrgang I, Heft 3:49–54.

Haigh, J.C. 1990. Opioids in zoological medicine. Journal of Zoo and Wildlife Medicine 21:391–431.

Harper, F. 1940. The nomenclature and type localities of certain old world mammals. Journal of Mammalogy 21:191–203.

Harrell, F.E. 1985. The LOGIST Procedure. Pages 181–202 in SUGI Supplemental Library, Version 5.0. SAS Inst., Inc., Cary, North Carolina.

Hawkes, J., M. Hedges, P. Daniluk, H.F. Hintz, and H.F. Schryver. 1985. Feed preferences of ponies. Equine Veterinary Journal 17:20–22.

Hearn, J.P., and P.M. Summers. 1986. Experimental manipulation of embryo implantation in the marmoset monkey and exotic equids. Theriogenology 25:3–11.

Hebel, R. 1976. Distribution of retinal ganglion cells in five mammalian species (pig, sheep, ox, horse, dog). Anatomy and Embryology 150:45–51.

Heck, H. 1967. Die Merkmale des Przewalskipferdes. Equus (Berlin) 1:295–301.

Hedrick, P.W., P.F. Brussard, F.W. Allendorf, J.A. Beardmore, and S. Orzack. 1986. Protein variation, fitness and captive propagation. Zoo Biology 5:91–99.

Heffner, H.E., and R.S. Heffner. 1984. Sound localization in large mammals: Localization of complex sounds by horses. Behavioral Neuroscience 98:541–555.

Heffner, R.S., and H.E. Heffner. 1983. Hearing in large mammals: Horses (*Equus caballus*) and cattle (*Bos taurus*). Behavioral Neuroscience 97:299–309.

Heiss, L. 1970. Askania Nova, Animal Paradise in Russia. The Bodley Head, London. 175 pp.

Hemmer, H. 1983. Domestikation: Verarmung der Merkwelt. Vieweg, Braunschweig & Wiesbaden. 160 pp.

Hennecke, D.R., G.D. Potter, and J.L. Kreider. 1981. A condition score relationship to body fat content of mares during gestation and lactation. Pages 105–110 *in* Proceedings of the 7th Equine Nutrition Physiology Symposium.

Henry, M., A.E.F. Figueiredo, M.S. Palhares, and M. Coryn. 1987. Clinical and endocrine aspects of the oestrous cycle in donkeys (*Equus asinus*). Journal of Reproduction and Fertility, Supplement 35:297–303.

Heptner, V.G. 1955. Notes on the Tarpans (in Russian). Zoologicheski Journal 34:1404–1423.

———. 1961. Distribution, geographical variability and biology of wild horses on the territory of the USSR. Equus (Berlin) 1:28–41.

Heptner, V.G., A.A. N. simovitch, and A.G. Bannikov. 1961. Mammals of the Soviet Union. Volume I. Artiodactyla and Perissodactyla (in Russian). Vysshaya Shkola Publishers, Moscow. (German version, Die Saügetiere der Sowjetunion, pub. Stuttgart, 1966: English version, Mammals of the Soviet Union, The National Science Foundation, Washington, D.C. 1988).

Herre, V.W. 1961. Grundsätzliches zur Systematik des Pferdes. Zeitschrift für Tierzüchtung und Züchtungsbiologie 75(1):57–78.

Herre, W. 1967. Gedanken zur Erhaltung des Wildpferdes, *Equus przewalski* Poljakow 1881. Equus (Berlin) 1(1):304–325.

Hillman, R.B., and R.G. Loy. 1975. Oestrogen excretion in mares in relation to various reproductive states. Journal of Reproduction and Fertility, Supplement 23:223–230.

Hilzheimer, M. 1909. Was ist *Equus equiferus* Pallas? Naturwissenschaftliche Wochenschrift 8:810–812.

Hintz, H.F. 1983. Horse Nutrition. A Practical Guide. Arco Publishing, Inc., New York. 228 pp.

Hintz, H.F., C.J. Sedgewick, and H.F. Schryver. 1976. Some observations on digestion of a pelleted diet by ruminants and non-ruminants. International Zoo Yearbook 16:54–57.

Hoffmann, R. 1985. On the development of social behaviour in immature males of a feral horse population (*Equus przewalskii* f. caballus). Zeitschrift für Saugetierkunde 50:302–314.

Hogan, E.S., K.A. Houpt, and K. Sweeney. 1988. The effect of enclosure size on social interactions and daily activity patterns of the captive Asiatic wild horse (*Equus przewalskii*). Applied Animal Behaviour Science 21:147–168.

Houpt, K.A. 1983. Self-directed aggression: A stallion behavior problem. Equine Practice 5(2):6–8.

Houpt, K.A., and L. Guida. 1984. Flehmen. Equine Practice 6(3):32–35.

Houpt, K.A., and R. Keiper. 1982. The position of the stallion in the equine dominance hierarchy of feral and domestic ponies. Journal of Animal Science 54:945–950.

Houpt, K.A., and R. Smith. 1993. Animal Behavior Case of the Month. Journal of the American Veterinary Medical Association 203:377–378.

Houpt, K.A., and T.R. Wolski. 1980. Stability of equine hierarchies and the prevention of dominance related aggressions. Equine Veterinary Journal 12:18–24.

Houpt, K.A., K. Law, and V. Martinisi. 1978. Dominance hierarchies in domestic horses. Applied Animal Ethology 4:273–283.

Hughes, J.P., G.H. Stabenfeldt, and J.W. Evans. 1975. The oestrous cycle of the mare. Journal of Reproduction and Fertility, Supplement 23: 161–166.

Hutson, A.D. 1975. Aspects of the social behaviour of Przewalski's horse. Department of Biological Science, Portsmouth Polytechnic, Portsmouth, U.K. 57 pp.

Jalanka, H.H., and B.O. Roeken. 1990. The use of medetomidine, medetomidine-ketamine combinations, and atipamezole in nondomestic mammals: A review. Journal of Zoo and Wildlife Medicine 21:259–282.

Janis, C. 1976. The evolutionary strategy of the Equidae and the origins of rumen and cecal digestion. Evolution 30:757–774.

Janssen, D.L., and J.E. Oosterhuis. 1984. Guaifenesin for muscle relaxation in immobilized hoofstock. Page 59 *in* Proceedings of the American Association of Zoo Veterinarians.

Jeffcott, L.B. 1972. Observations on parturition in crossbred pony mares. Equine Veterinary Journal 4:209–213.

Johnston, J. 1987. Tetanus. Pages 370–373 *in* Robinson, N.E. (ed.). Current Therapy in Equine Medicine, 2nd ed. W.B. Saunders Company, Philadelphia.

Johnston, R.E. 1985. Olfactory and vomeronasal mechanisms of communication. Pages 322–346 *in* Pfaff, D.W. (ed.). Taste, Olfaction, and the Central Nervous System. Rockefeller University Press, New York, N.Y.

Jun, Z., Y. Hui, and M.C. De. 1990. Przewalski's horse breeding report (1987–1990). Chinese Wildlife 90(6): (in Chinese).

Kapitzke, G. 1973. Wildlebende Pferde. Paul Parey, Berlin and Hamburg. 168 pp.

Kaseda, Y. 1981. The structure of the groups of Misaki Horses in Toi Cape. Japanese Journal of Zootechnical Science 52:227–235.

———. 1983. Seasonal changes in time spent grazing and resting of Misaki horses. Japanese Journal of Zootechnical Science 54:464–469.

Kaseda, Y., K. Nozawa, and K. Mogi. 1984. Separation and independence of offsprings from the harem groups in Misaki horses. Japanese Journal of Zootechnical Science 55(11):852–857.

Kaszab, Z. 1968. Entgegnung auf die Bemerkungen von Jiri Volf bezüglich: "New Sighting of Przewalski horses?" Zeitschrift für Saugetierkunde 33:62–63.

Keiper, R.R. 1985. The Assateague Ponies. Tidewater Publishers, Centreville, Maryland. 101 pp.

———. 1988. Social interactions of the Przewalski horse (*Equus przewalskii* Poliakov, 1881) herd at the Munich Zoo. Applied Animal Behaviour Science 21:89–97.

———. 1990. Social interactions of free-ranging Przewalski horses in semi-reserves. Proceedings of the 5th International Symposium on the Preservation of the Przewalski Horse. Zoologischer Garten Leipzig:176–183.

Keiper, R., and K. Houpt. 1984. Reproduction in feral horses: an eight-year study. American Journal of Veterinary Research 45:991–995.

Keiper, R.R., and M.A. Keenan. 1980. Nocturnal activity patterns of feral ponies. Journal of Mammalogy 61:116–118.

Keiper, R.R., and H. Receveur. 1992. Social interactions of free-ranging Przewalski horses in semi-reserves in The Netherlands. Applied Animal Behaviour Science 33: 303–318.

Keiper, R.R., and H.H. Sambraus. 1986. The stability of equine dominance hierarchies and the effects of kinship, proximity and foaling status on hierarchy rank. Applied Animal Behaviour Science 16:121–130.

Keverling Buisman, A., and R. van Weeren. 1982. Breeding and management of Przewalski horses in captivity. Pages 77–160 *in* Bouman, J., I. Bouman, and A. Groeneveld (eds.). Breeding Przewalski Horses in Captivity for Release in the Wild. Foundation for the Preservation and Protection of the Przewalski Horse, Rotterdam, The Netherlands.

Kirkpatrick, J.F., L.H. Kasman, B.L. Lasley, and J.W. Turner, Jr. 1988. Pregnancy determination in uncaptured feral horses. Journal of Wildlife Management 52:305–308.

Kirkpatrick, J.F., B.L. Lasley, and S.E. Shideler. 1990a. Urinary steroid evaluations to monitor ovarian function in exotic ungulates: VII. Urinary progesterone metabolites in the Equidae assessed by immunoassay. Zoo Biology 9:341–348.

Kirkpatrick, J.F. S.E. Shideler, and J.W. Turner, Jr. 1990b. Pregnancy determination in uncaptured feral horses based on steroid metabolites in urine-soaked snow and free steroids in feces. Canadian Journal of Zoology 68:2576–2579.

Klimov, V.V. 1988. Spatial-ethological organization of the herd of Przewalski horses (*Equus przewalskii*) in Askania-Nova. Applied Animal Behaviour Science 21:99–115.

Klingel, H. 1974. A comparison of the social behaviour of the Equidae. Pages 124–132 *in* Geist, V., and F. Walther (eds.). The Behaviour of Ungulates and its Relationship to Management. IUCN Publ. No. 24, Morges, Switzerland.

Knowles, J.H. 1980. History of the Marwell Zoological Park's herd of Przewalski horses. Equus (Berlin) 2:73–78.

Kock, R.A., P.C. Pearce, and P. Taylor. 1988. The use of detomidine and butorphanol in zoo equids. Pages 188–191 *in* Proceedings of the American Association of Zoo Veterinarians.

Kolter, L. 1985. Soziale Beziehungen zwischen den Przewalskipferden (*Equus p. przewalskii*) im Kölner Zoo. Zeitschrift des Kölner Zoo 4(28):193–201.

Kolter, L., and W. Zimmermann. 1988. Social behaviour of Przewalski horses (*Equus p. przewalskii*) in the Cologne Zoo and its consequences for management and housing. Applied Animal Behaviour Science 21:117–145.

Kuttner, C., and H. Wiesner. 1987. Changes in blood values of Przewalski horses (*Equus przewalski przewalski*) and zebras (*Equus zebra hartmannae*) during chemical immobilization. Journal of Zoo Animal Medicine 18:144–147.

Lacy, R.C. 1987. Loss of genetic diversity from managed populations: in-

288 *References*

teracting effects of drift, mutation, immigration, selection and population subdivision. Conservation Biology 1:143–158.

──. 1988. Documentation to GENES software. Chicago Zoologial Park, Brookfield, IL.

──. 1989. Analysis of founder representation in pedigrees: founder equivalents and founder genome equivalents. Zoo Biology 8:111–123.

Lasley, B., D. Ammon, P. Daels, J. Hughes, C. Munro, and G. Stabenfeldt. 1990. Estrogen conjugate concentrations in plasma and urine reflect estrogen secretion in the nonpregnant and pregnant mare: a review. Equine Veterinary Science 10(6):444–448.

Leboucher, A. 1992. Behavioural study of the Przewalski stallions living in the semi-reserve of the Goudplaat, The Netherlands. Towards reintroduction: which stallion is behaviourally fitted for survival in Mongolia? Unpublished report. 163 pp.

Lee, E.T. 1980. Statistical Methods for Survival Data Analysis. Lifetime Learning Publications, Belmont, California. 557 pp.

Lehner, P.N. 1979. Handbook of Ethological Methods. Garland STPM Press, New York. 403 pp.

Leroi-Gourhan, A. 1971. Préhistoire de l'art occidental. Éditions D'art Lucien Mazenod, Paris. 482 pp.

Lewtas, P.N. 1973. Aspects of social behaviour of Mongolian wild horses. Department of Biological Sciences, Portsmouth Polytechnic, Portsmouth, U.K. 42 pp. (unpubl).

Liu, I.K.M. 1983. Equine herpesvirus. Pages 4–5 *in* Robinson, N.E. (ed.). Current Therapy in Equine Medicine. W.B. Saunders Company, Philadelphia.

Liu, S.K., E.P. Dolensek, C.R. Adams, and J.P. Tappe. 1983. Myelopathy and vitamin E deficiency in six Mongolian wild horses. Journal of the American Veterinary Medical Association 183:1266–1268.

Lovell, J.D., G.H. Stabenfeldt, J.P. Hughes, and J.W. Evans. 1975. Endocrine patterns of the mare at term. Journal of Reproduction and Fertility, Supplement 23:449–456.

Lundholm, B. 1947. Abstammung und Domestikation des Hauspferdes. Zoologisk Bidrag Uppsala, 27, 288 pp.

Lydekker, R. 1912. The Horse and its Relatives. The Macmillan Company, New York and George Allen & Co., Ltd., London. 286 pp.

MacClintock, D. 1982. Where have all the horses gone? Animal Kingdom 85(5):26–31.

MacCluer, J.W., J.L. VandeBerg, B. Read, and O.A. Ryder. 1986. Pedigree analysis by computer simulation. Zoo Biology 5:147–160.

Mackler, S.F., and J.M. Dolan, Jr. 1980. Social structure and herd behavior of *Equus przewalskii* Poliakov, 1881 at the San Diego Wild Animal Park. Equus (Berlin) 2(1):55–69.

Mansmann, R.A., E.S. McAllister, and P.W. Pratt. 1982. Equine Medicine and Surgery, Third Edition. American Veterinary Publications, Santa Barbara, CA. 1417 pp.

Martin-Rosset, W., and J.P. Dulphy. 1987. Digestibility interactions between forages and concentrates in horses: Influence of feeding level —comparison with sheep. Livestock Production Science 17:263–276.

Matschie, P. 1903. Giebt es in Mittelasien mehrere Arten von echten Wildpferden? Naturwissschaftliche Wochenschrift 18:581–583.

Matthews, J.G., and J.D.A. Delhanty. 1979. Chromosome studies in Przewalskis horses, (*Equus przewalskii*). Pages 71–83 *in* de Boer, L.E.M., J. Bouman, and I. Bouman, (eds.). Genetics and Hereditary Diseases of the Przewalski Horse. Foundation for the Preservation and Protection of the Przewalski Horse. Rotterdam, The Netherlands.

Mayhew, I.G., C.M. Brown, H.D. Stowe, A.L. Trapp, F.J. Derksen, and S.F. Clement. 1987. Equine degenerative myeloencephalopathy: A vitamin E deficiency that may be familial. Journal of Veterinary Internal Medicine 1:45–50.

Maynard Smith, J. 1978. The Evolution of Sex. Cambridge University Press, Cambridge. 222 pp.

Mazák, V. 1961. Die Hautpflege bei dem Przewalski-Urwildpferd (*Equus przewalskii przewalskii* Poliakov). Equus (Berlin) 1:105–121.

———. 1962. Haarwechsel und Haarwuchs bei Przewalski-Pferd und Onager im Prager Zoologischen Garten wahrend der Jahre 1958–1960. Vestnik Ceskoslovenski Spolecnosti Zoologicke 26:271–286.

———. 1966. "Bars" - hřebec koně Prževalského, *Equus przewaksii* Poliakov, 1881, v zoologické zahradě v Praze. Lynx, new series, 7:23–28.

Mazák, V., and L.J. Dobroruka. 1967. Rekonstruktion des Przewalskipferdes, eine Grundlage fur die negative Selektion in der Prager Urwildpferde-Zucht. Equus (Berlin) 1:329–349.

McAllister, E.S. 1982. Viral respiratory infections. Pages 732–734 *in* Mansmann, R.A., E.S. McAllister, and P.W. Pratt (eds.). Equine Medicine and Surgery, Third Edition. American Veterinary Publications, Santa Barbara, CA.

McCort, W.D. 1980. The behavior and social organization of feral asses

(*Equus asinus*) on Ossabaw Island, Georgia. Ph.D. Thesis, The Pennsylvania State University, University Park, Pennsylvania. 219 pp.

McDonald, L.E. 1980. Veterinary Endocrinology and Reproduction, Third Edition. Lea & Febiger, Philadelphia, Pennsylvania. 560 pp.

Miller, R. 1979. Band organization and stability in Red Desert feral horses. Pages 113–128 *in* Denniston, R.H. (ed.). Proceedings of the Symposium on the Ecology and Behavior of Wild and Feral Equids. University of Wyoming, Laramie, Wyoming.

————. 1981. Male aggression, dominance, and breeding behavior in Red Desert feral horses. Zeitschrift für Tierpsychologie 57:340–351.

Miller, R., and R.H. Denniston, II. 1979. Interband dominance in feral horses. Zeitschrift für Tierpsychologie 51:41–47.

Miller, R.E., W.J. Boever, R.E. Junge, L.P. Thornburg, and M.F. Rasibeck. 1990. Acute monensin toxicosis in Stone sheep (*Ovis dalli stonei*), blesbok (*Damaliscus dorcus phillipsi*) and a Bactrian camel (*Camelus bactrianus*). Journal of the American Veterinary Medical Association 196:131–134.

Mohr, E. 1959. Das Urwildpferd. A. Ziemsen Verlag, Wittenberg Lutherstadt. 144 pp.

Mohr, E. 1971. The Asiatic Wild Horse. J.A. Allen & Co. Ltd., London. 124 pp.

Mohr, E., and J. Volf. 1984. Das Urwildpferd, *Equus przewalskii*. A. Ziemsen Verlag, Wittenberg, Lutherstadt. 128 pp.

Monfort, S.L., N.P. Arthur, and D.E. Wildt. 1991. Monitoring ovarian function and pregnancy by evaluating excretion of urinary oestrogen conjugates in semi-free-ranging Przewalski's horses (*Equus przewalskii*). Journal of Reproduction and Fertility 91:155–164.

Montgomery, G.G. 1957. Some aspects of the sociality of the domestic horse. Transactions of the Kansas Academy of Science 60:419–424.

Morton, N.E., J.F. Crow, and H.J. Muller. 1956. An estimate of the mutational damage in man from data on consanguineous marriages. Proceedings of the National Academy of Sciences 42:855–863.

Moyer, W. 1980. Symposium on Equine Lameness. The Veterinary Clinics of North America, Large Animal Practice 2(1). W.B. Saunders Company, Philadelphia. 204 pp.

Munro, C.D., J.P. Renton, and R. Butcher. 1979. The control of oestrous behaviour in the mare. Journal of Reproduction and Fertility, Supplement 27:217–227.

National Research Council. 1978. Nutrient requirements of horses. NRC-NAS. National Academy Press, Washington, D.C. 100 pp.

———. 1989. Nutrient requirements of horses. NRC-NAS. National Academy Press, Washington, D.C. 100 pp.

Nett, T.M., D.W. Holtan, and V.L. Estergreen. 1975. Oestrogens, LH, PMSG and prolactin in serum of pregnant mares. Journal of Reproduction and Fertility, Supplement 23:457–462.

Noack, T. 1903. Zur Entwicklung von Equus przewalskii. Zoologischer Anzeiger 26:370–373.

Nobis, G. 1955. Beiträge zur Abstammung und Domestikation des Hauspferdes. Zeitschrift für Tierzüchtung und Züchtungsbiologie 64(3): 201–246.

———. 1971. Vom Wildpferd zum Hauspferd. Fundamenta, ser. b, 6. Böhlau Verlag Koln Wien. 96 pp.

Oosterhuis, J.E. 1979. Immobilization of nondomestic equidae at the San Diego Wild Animal Park (1975–1979). Pages 118–119 in Proceedings of the American Association of Zoo Veterinarians.

Oswald, C. 1992. Wiederinbürgerung des Urwildpferdes in China und der Mongolei. Christian Oswald Stiftung, Oberlaufing 5, D-8017 Ebersberg, Germany.

Paklina, N., and M.K. Pozdnyakova. 1989. Why the Przewalski horses of Mongolia died out. Przewalski Horse 24:30–34.

Pallas, P.S. 1811. Zoographia Rosso-Asiatica. St. Petersburg 1.

Palmer, E., and B. Jousset. 1975. Urinary oestrogen and plasma progesterone levels in non-pregnant mares. Journal of Reproduction and Fertility, Supplement 23:213–221.

Pashen, R.L., and W.R. Allen. 1979. The role of the fetal gonads and placenta in steroid production, maintenance of pregnancy and parturition in the mare. Journal of Reproduction and Fertility, Supplement 27:499–509.

Pashen, R.L., E.L. Sheldrick, W.R. Allen, and A.P.F. Flint. 1982. Dehydroepiandrosterone synthesis by the fetal foal and its importance as an oestrogen precursor. Journal of Reproduction and Fertility, Supplement 32:389–397.

Pelligrini, S.W. 1971. Home range, teritoriality and movement patterns of wild horses in the Wassuk Range of western Nevada. M.S. Thesis, University of Nevada, Reno. 39 pp.

Podliachouk, L., and M. Kaminski. 1971. Comparative investigations of Equidae. A study of blood groups and serum proteins in a sample of

Equus przewalskii Poliakoff. Anim. Blood Grps biochem. Genet. 2:239–242.

Poliakov, I.S. 1881. Przewalski's horse (*Equus przewalskii* n. sp.). Isvestia Russki Geographicheski obsch-va, St. Petersburg 17:1–20.

Pollock, J.I. 1980. Behavioural Ecology and Body Condition Changes in New Forest Ponies. RSPCA Scientific Publications, Horsham, U.K. 119 pp.

Prost, J.H. 1965. A definitional system for the classification of primate locomotion. American Anthropologist 67:1198–1214.

Pruski, W. 1959. Dzikie konie wschodniej Europy. Polska Akademia Nauk, Warsaw 85D:1–132.

Przewalski, N. 1884. Reisen in Tibet und am oberen Lauf des Gelben Flusses in den Jahren 1879 bis 1880. Stein Nordheim, Jena. 269 pp.

Putt, W., and R.A. Fisher. 1979. An investigation of some 36 genetically determined enzyme and protein markers in Przewalski and domestic horses. Pages 21–32 *in* de Boer, L.E.M., J. Bouman, and I. Bouman (eds.). Genetics and Hereditary Diseases of the Przewalski Horse. Foundation for the Preservation and Protection of the Przewalski Horse, Rotterdam, The Netherlands.

Radulesco, C., and P. Samson. 1962. Quelques observations sur *Equus scythicus*. Zoologischer Anzeiger 169:347–356.

Raeside, J.I., and R.M. Liptrap. 1975. Patterns of urinary oestrogen excretion in individual pregnant mares. Journal of Reproduction and Fertility, Supplement 23:469–475.

Raeside, J.I., R.M. Liptrap, and F.J. Milne. 1973. Relationship of fetal gonads to urinary estrogen excretion by the pregnant mare. American Journal of Veterinary Research 34:843–845.

Ralls, K., and J. Ballou. 1983. Extinction: lessons from zoos. Pages 164–184 *in* Schonewald-Cox, C.M., S.M. Chambers, B. MacBryde, and W.L. Thomas (eds.). Genetics and Conservation. The Benjamin/ Cummings Publishing Company, Inc., Menlo Park, California.

Ralls, K., J.D. Ballou, and A. Templeton. 1988. Estimates of lethal equivalents and the cost of inbreeding in mammals. Conservation Biology 2:185–193.

Randall, G.C.B. 1984. Perinatal adaptation. 10th International Congress on Animal Reproduction and Artificial Insemination 4:43–50.

Rayfield, D. 1977. Lhasa war sein Traum. F.A. Brockhaus, Wiesbaden. 278 pp.

Reindl, N.J., and R.L. Tilson. 1985a. Bachelor herds and stallion depots (videotape). Minnesota Zoological Garden, Apple Valley, 20 min.

———. 1985b. Bachelor herds and stallion depots: a new approach to an old problem. Pages 530–537 *in* Proceedings of the American Association of Zoological Parks and Aquariums Annual Conference.

Roberts, S.J. 1986. Abortion and other gestational diseases in mares. Pages 705–710 *in* Morrow, D.A. (ed.). Current Therapy in Theriogenology 2. W.B. Saunders Company, Philadelphia.

Robinson, N.E. 1983. Current Therapy in Equine Medicine. W.B. Saunders Company, Philadelphia. 637 pp.

———. 1987. Current Therapy in Equine Medicine, Second Edition. W.B. Saunders Company, Philadelphia. 761 pp.

Rossdale, P.D. 1967. Clinical studies on the newborn thoroughbred foal. I. Perinatal behaviour. British Veterinary Journal 123:470–481.

Rossdale, P.E., and S.W. Ricketts. 1980. Equine Stud Farm Medicine, Second Edition. Lea & Febiger, Philadelphia. 564 pp.

Rubenstein, D.I. 1981. Behavioural ecology of island feral horses. Equine Veterinary Journal 13(1):27–34.

———. 1982. Reproductive value and behavioral strategies: coming of age in monkeys and horses. Pages 469–487 *in* Bateson, P.P.G., and P.H. Klopfer (eds.). Perspectives in Ethology, Vol. 5., Plenum Press, New York.

Rutberg, A.T., and S.A. Greenberg. 1990. Dominance, aggression frequencies and modes of aggressive competition in feral pony mares. Animal Behaviour 40:322–331.

Ryder, O.A. 1988. Przewalski's horse—putting the wild horse back in the wild. Oryx 22:154–157.

———. 1991a. Putting the wild horse back in the wild. Proceedings of the 5th International Symposium on the Preservation of the Przewalski Horse. Zoologischer Garten Leipzig: 328–331.

———. 1991b. Goals of Przewalski's horse breeding. Proceedings of the 5th International Symposium on the Preservation of the Przewalski Horse. Zoologisher Garten Leipzig: 105–106.

Ryder, O.A. 1993. Przewalski's horse: prospects for reintroduction into the wild. Conservation Biology 7(1):13–15.

Ryder, O.A., and S.K. Hansen. 1979. Molecular cytogenetics of the equidae. I. Purification and cytological localization of a (G+C)-rich satellite DNA from *Equus przewalskii*. Chromosoma 72:115–129.

Ryder, O.A., and R. Massena. 1988. A case of male infanticide in *Equus przewalskii*. Applied Animal Behaviour Science 21:187–190.

Ryder, O.A., and E.A. Wedemeyer. 1982. A cooperative breeding program for the Mongolian wild horse, *Equus przewalskii*, in the United States. Biological Conservation 22:259–271.

Ryder, O.A., J. Ballou, J.M. Dolan, T.J. Foose, N.J. Reindl, E.A. Thompson, and C.M. Wemmer. 1989. Asian Wild Horse Species Survival Plan: Masterplan 1989. Zoological Society of San Diego, San Diego, CA. 69 pp.

Ryder, O.A., A.T. Bowling, P.C. Brisbin, P.M. Carroll, I.K. Gadi, S.K. Hansen, and E.A. Wedemeyer. 1984. Genetics of *Equus przewalskii* Poliakov, 1881: analysis of genetic variability in breeding lines, comparison of equid DNAs, and a brief description of a cooperative breeding program in North America. Equus (Berlin) 2(2):207–227.

Ryder, O.A., P.C. Brisbin, A.T. Bowling, and E.A. Wedemeyer. 1981. Monitoring genetic variation in endangered species. Pages 417–424 *in* Scudder, N.G.K., and J.L. Reveal (eds.). Evolution Today. Proceedings of the Second International Congress of Systematic and Evolutionary Biology.

Ryder, O.A., N.C. Epel, and K. Benirschke. 1978. Chromosome banding studies of the equidae. Cytogenetics and Cell Genetics 20:323–350.

Ryder, O.A., R.A. Fisher, W. Putt, and D. Whitehouse. 1982. Genetic differences among subgroups of a captively-bred endangered species: The case of the Mongolian wild horse, *Equus przewalskii*. Pages 91–102 *in* Proceedings of the American Association of Zoological Parks and Aquariums Annual Conference.

Ryder, O.A., A. Trommershausen-Smith, S.K. Hansen, Y. Suzuki, M.C. Sparkes, R.S. Sparkes, J.B. Clegg, J.E. Oosterhuis, L.S. Nelson, P.T. Robinson, J.E. Meier, and K. Benirschke. 1979. Genetic variation in Przewalski's horses, *Equus przewalskii*, of the Munich line in the United States. Pages 41–60 *in* de Boer, L.E.M., J. Bouman, and I. Bouman (eds.). Genetics and Hereditary Diseases of the Przewalski Horse. Foundation for the Preservation and Protection of the Przewalski Horse. Rotterdam, The Netherlands.

Salensky, W. 1902. Wissenschaftliche Resultate der von N.M. Przewalski nach Central-Asien unternommenen Reisen. Kaiserlichen Akademie der Wissenschaften, Zoologischer Theil (St. Petersburg) 1(2):1–74.

———. 1907. Prjevalski's Horse (*Equus prjewalskii*, Pol.). Hurst and Blockett, Ltd., London.

Salter, R.E., and R.J. Hudson. 1979. Feeding ecology of feral horses in western Alberta. Journal of Range Management 32:221–225.

———. 1982. Social organization of feral horses in Western Canada. Applied Animal Ethology 8:207–223.

Samson, P. 1975. Les Equidés fossiles de Roumanie (Pliocène moyen—Pléistocène supérieur). Geologica Romana 14:165–352.

Sauerland, M. 1991. Przewalski Pferde im Semi-Reservat: Ethologische Studien unter besonderer Berücksichtigung der einbindung des Hengstes in die soziale Organisation des Familienverbandes. Diplomarbeit für das Fachebereich Biologie Westfallische Wilhelms-Universität Munster. 122 pp.

Schein, M.W., and M.H. Fohrman. 1955. Social dominance relationships in a herd of dairy cattle. British Journal of Animal Behaviour 3:45–55.

Schmidt, C.R. 1987. The European Breeding Program (EEP). International Zoo News 205 34(6):4–7.

Schwarzenberger, F., E. Mostl, E. Bamberg, and G. von Hegel. 1992. Monitoring of corpus luteum function by measuring progestagens in faeces on non-pregnant mares (Equus caballus) and Przewalski mares (Equus przewalskii). Animal Reproductive Science 29:263–273.

Scott, A.M. 1979. Red-cell groups and serum types in the Przewalski horse (Equus przewalskii). Pages 33–40 in de Boer, L.E.M., J. Bouman, and I. Bouman (eds.). Genetics and Hereditary Diseases of the Przewalski Horse. Foundation for the Preservation and Protection of the Przewalski Horse. Rotterdam, The Netherlands.

Seal, U.S., T. Foose, R.C. Lacy, W. Zimmermann, O. Ryder, and F. Princee. 1990. Przewalski's horse, Equus przewalskii, Global Conservation Plan Draft. Captive Breeding Specialist Group. SSC/IUCN, Apple Valley, MN. 230 pp.

Sher, A.V. 1986. On the history of mammal fauna of Beringida. Quartär-paläontaologie 6:185–193.

Shields, W.M. 1982. Philopatry, Inbreeding and the Evolution of Sex. State University of New York Press, Albany, NY. 245 pp.

Short, C.E., K. Otto, M. Gilbert, and G.A. Maylin. 1989. The responses to detomidine usage as a sole agent or in combination in the horse. Pages 153–166 in Proceedings of the Annual Convention of the American Association of Equine Practitioners, Boston, MA.

Short, R.V. 1975. The evolution of the horse. Journal of Reproduction and Fertility, Supplement 23:1–6.

Short, R.V., A.C. Chandley, R.C. Jones, and W.R. Allen. 1974. Meiosis in interspecific equine hybrids. II. The Przewalski horse/domestic horse hybrid (Equus przewalskii X E. caballus). Cytogenetics and Cell Genetics 13:465–478.

Simerson, C. 1988. Hoof maintenance of captive ungulates. Pages 97–101 *in* Proceedings of the American Association of Zoological Parks and Aquariums Annual Conference.

Singer, M.F. 1982. Highly repeated sequences in mammalian genomes. International Review of Cytology 76:67–112.

Siniff, D.B., J.R. Tester, and E.D. Plotka. 1990. Fertility control in wild horses. Final report to the U.S. Department of the Interior, Bureau of Land Management, November 30. University of Minnesota, Minneapolis, MN, and Marshfield Medical Research Foundation, Marshfield, WI. 79 pp.

Skorkowski, E. 1946. Systematyka konia i zasady jego hodowli (Systematics of the horse and the principles of his breeding). Krakow.

––––––. 1961. Unterarten in den Pferdepopulationen und deren Frühgeschichte. Zeitschrift für Tierzüchtung und Züchtungsbiologie 76: 209–224.

Smith, C.H. 1841. The Natural History of Horses. Jardine's Naturalist's Library, Mammalia, v. 12. W.H. Lizars, Edinburgh. 352 pp.

Sokolov, I.I. 1959. Mammals of the USSR: Perissodactyla and Artiodactyla. Fauna of the USSR, vol. 1. Leningrad.

Sokolov, V., N. Paklina, G. Amarsanaa, M. Pozdnjakova, and E. Rachkovskaja. 1990. Das letzte Przewalskipferdeareal und seine geobotanische Charakteristik. Proceedings of the 5th International Symposium on the Preservation of the Przewalski Horse. Zoologischer Garten Leipzig:213–218.

Soulé, M.E., and B.A. Wilcox. 1980. Conservation Biology: An Evolutionary-Ecological Perspective. Sinauer Associates, Inc., Sunderland, MA. 395 pp.

Spöttel, W. 1926. *Equus przewalski* Polj., 1881 mit besonderer Berrücksichtigung der im Tierzuchtinstitut der Universität Halle gehaltenen Tiere. Kühn-Archiv-Verlagsbuchhandlung. Paul Parey, Berlin. 137 pp.

Stabenfeldt, G.H., and J.P. Hughes. 1977. Reproduction in horses. Pages 401–431 *in* Cole, H.H., and P.T. Cupps (eds.). Reproduction in Domestic Animals. Academic Press, New York.

Stahlbaum, C.C., and K.A. Houpt. 1989. The role of the flehmen response in the behavioral repertoire of the stallion. Physiology and Behavior 45:1207–1214.

Stecher, R.M. 1961. The Przewalski horse: Notes on variations in the lumbo sacral spine. Equus (Berlin) 1:191–196.

Summers, P.M., A.M. Shephard, J.K. Hodges, J. Kydd, M.S. Boyle, and

W.R. Allen. 1987. Successful transfer of the embryos of Przewalski's horses (*Equus przewalskii*) and Grant's zebra (*E. burchelli*) to domestic mares (*E. caballus*). Journal of Reproduction and Fertility, Supplement 80:13–20.

Swenson, M.J. 1984. Duke's Physiology of Domestic Animals, Tenth Edition. Comstock Publishing Associates, Ithaca, NY. 922 pp.

Tan, B. 1981. Wild horses found in northern China. International Zoo News 170, 28(1):16–17.

Taussky, H.H. 1954. A microcolorimetric determination of creatine in urine by the Jaffe reaction. Journal of Biological Chemistry 208: 853–861.

Taylor, P.M., A.P. Browning, and C.P. Harris. 1988. Detomidine-butorphanol sedation in equine clinical practice. The Veterinary Record 123:388–390.

Templeton, A.R., and B. Read. 1984. Factors eliminating inbreeding depression in a captive herd of Speke's gazelle (*Gazella spekei*). Zoo Biology 3:177–199.

Templeton, A.R., H. Hemmer, G. Mace, U.S. Seal, W.M. Shields, and D.S. Woodruff. 1986. Local adaptation, coadaptation, and population boundaries. Zoo Biology 5:115–125.

Tilson, R.L., K.A. Sweeny, G.A. Binczik, and N.J. Reindl. 1988. Buddies and bullies: Social structure of a bachelor group of Przewalski horses. Applied Animal Behaviour Science 21:169–185.

Tong, B.D., and O.A. Ryder. 1983. Restriction mapping of the ribosomal genes of the family Equidae. Journal of Cell Biology 97:382a.

Trivers, R.L. 1972. Parental investment and sexual selection. Pages 136–179 *in* Campbell, B. (ed.). Sexual Selection and the Descent of Man 1871–1971. Aldine Publishing Company, Chicago.

Trivers, R.L., and D.E. Willard. 1973. Natural selection of parental ability to vary the sex ratio of offspring. Science 179:90–92.

Trommershausen-Smith, A., Y. Suzuki, C. Stormont, K. Benirschke, and O.A. Ryder. 1980. Blood type markers in five Przewalski's horses. Equus (Berlin) 2:52–54.

Trumler, V.E. 1959. Das "Rossigkeitgesicht" und ähnliches Ausdrucksverhalten bei Einhufern. Zeitschrift für Tierpsychologie 16:478–488.

———. 1961. Entwurf einer Systematik der rezenten Equiden und ihrer fossilen Verwandten. Saugetierkundliche Mitteilungen 9:109–125.

Turner, J.W., Jr., A. Perkins, and J.F. Kirkpatrick. 1981. Elimination marking behavior in feral horses. Canadian Journal of Zoology 59:1561–1566.

Tyler, S.J. 1972. The behaviour and social organization of the New Forest Ponies. Animal Behaviour Monographs 5(2):85–196.

Ucko, P.J., and A. Rosenfeld. 1967. Palaeolithic Cave Art. World University Library, McGraw-Hill Book Company, New York. 256 pp.

Udén, P., and P.J. Van Soest. 1982. Comparative digestion of timothy (*Phleum pratense*) fibre by ruminants, equines and rabbits. British Journal of Nutrition 47:267–272.

Udén, P., T.R. Rounsaville, G.R. Wiggans, and P.J. Van Soest. 1982. The measurement of liquid and solid digesta retention in ruminants, equines and rabbits given timothy (*Phleum pratense*) hay. British Journal of Nutrition 48:329–339.

USDA. 1973. Animal Welfare Act: part 9 CFR and amendments. United States Department of Agriculture, Animal and Plant Health Inspection Service, Washington, D.C.

Vecchiotti, G.G., and R. Galanti. 1986. Evidence of heredity of cribbing, weaving and stall walking in Thoroughbred horses. Livestock Production Science 14:91–95.

Velle, W. 1963. Metabolism of estrogenic hormones in domestic animals. General and Comparative Endocrinology 3:621–635.

Veselovsky, Z., and J. Volf. 1965. Breeding and care of rare asian equids at Prague Zoo. International Zoo Yearbook 5:28–37.

Vetulani, T. 1936. Die Wiedereinfuhrung des Waldtarpans in den Urwald von Bialowieza (Bialowies). Bulletin international de l'Academie Polonaise des Sciences et Lettres, Classe des Sciences mathematiques et naturelles, ser. B, Sciences naturelles:3–4.

Volf, J. 1960–1990. Pedigree Book of the Przewalski Horse. Zoological Garden Prague, Czechoslovakia, published annually.

———. 1967. New sighting of Przewalski horses? Zeitschrift für Saugetierkunde 32:245–246.

———. 1970. Der Einfluss der Domestikation auf die Formentwicklung des Unterkiefers beim Pferd. Equus (Berlin) 1(2):401–406.

———. 1974. Die Färbung des Przewalski-Wildpferdes (*Equus przewalskii* Poljakov 1881) und ihre Variabilität. Zoologische Garten, Neue Folge 44:64–73.

———. 1975. Breeding of Przewalski Wild Horses. Pages 263–270 *in* Martin, R.D. (ed.). Breeding Endangered Species in Captivity. Academic Press, London.

———. 1979a. Tarpanoidni kun ("konik") a jeho chov v Popielne (Polsko)/ The tarpanoid horse ("konik") and its breeding in Popielno (Poland). Gazella 2:67–73.

———. 1979b. Der Tarpan und das polnische "konik". Zeitschrift des Kölner Zoo 4(21):119–124.

———. 1980. General Pedigree Book of the Przewalski Horse. Zoological Garden Prague, Czechoslovakia.

———. 1989. Die "wilde" oder gezielte Aufzucht von Przewalskipferden (*Equus przewalskii* Polj., 1881)? Zoologische Gärten 59(5/6):402–410.

Volf, J., and O. Chagdarsouren. 1975. Nouvelles données sur le cheval de Przewalski (*Equus przewalskii* Polj. 1881) en captivité et dans la nature. Mammalia 39(1):31–37.

Volf, J., E. Kůs, and L. Prokopová. 1991. General Studbook of the Przewalski Horse. Zoological Garden Prague, Prague, Czechoslovakia.

von Hegel, G., H. Weisner, and T. Hänichen. 1990. Proceedings of the 5th International Symposium on the Preservation of the Przewalski horse. Zoologischer Garten Leipzig:263–268.

Waring, G.H. 1982. Onset of behavior patterns in the newborn foal. Equine Practice 45:28–34.

Waring, G.H. 1983. Horse Behavior: The Behavioral Traits and Adaptations of Domestic and Wild Horses, including Ponies. Noyes Publications, Park Ridge, New Jersey. 292 pp.

Weeks, M. 1977. The Last Wild Horse. Houghton Mifflin, Boston. 144 pp.

Wells, S.M., and B. von Goldschmidt-Rothschild. 1979. Social behaviour and relationships in a herd of Camargue horses. Zeitschrift für Tierpsychologie 49:363–380.

Welsh, D.A. 1975. Population behaviour and population ecology of the horses of Sable Island, Nova Scotia. Ph.D. Thesis, Dalhousie University, Halifax, Nova Scotia. 403 pp.

Wildt, D.E. 1989. Strategies for the practical application of reproductive technologies to endangered species. Zoo Biology Supplement 1:17–20.

Wildt, D.E., A.M. Donoghue, L.A. Johnston, P.M. Schmidt, and J.G. Howard. 1991. Species and genetic effects on the utility of biotechnology for conservation. Zoological Society of London.

Willard, J.G., J.C. Willard, S.A. Wolfram, and J.P. Baker. 1977. Effect of diet on cecal pH and feeding behavior of horses. Journal of Animal Science 45:87–93.

Wilson, J.H. 1987. Eastern equine encephalomyelitis. Pages 345–347 *in* Robinson, N.E. (ed.). Current Therapy in Equine Medicine, Second Edition. W.B. Saunders Company, Philadelphia.

Wintzer, H.J. 1986. Equine Diseases. A Textbook for Students and Practitioners. Springer Verlag, New York. 439 pp.

Wolski, T.R., K.A. Houpt, and R. Aronson. 1980. The role of the senses in mare-foal recognition. Applied Animal Ethology 6:121–138.

Woods, G.L., and K.A. Houpt. 1986. An abnormal facial gesture in an estrous mare. Applied Animal Behaviour Science 16:199–202.

Zeeb, K. 1959. Die "Unterlegenheitsgebärde" des noch nicht ausgewachsenen Pferdes (*Equus caballus*). Zeitschrift für Tierpsychologie 16: 489–496.

Zeuner, F.E. 1963. A History of Domesticated Animals. Harper & Row Publishers, New York. 560 pp.

Zevegmid, D. 1959. Protection of the very rare animals of world's fauna. Priroda Moskva 5:52–53 (in Russian).

Zevegmid, D., and N. Dawaa. 1973. Die seltenen Großsäuger der Mongolischen Volksrepublik und ihr Schutz. Arch. Naturschutz u. Landschaftsforsch Berlin 13(2):87–106.

Zimmermann, W. 1985. 20 Jahre Przewalskipferde (*Equus p. przewalskii*) im Kölner Zoo. Zeitschrift des Kölner Zoo 4:171–187.

Contributors

Nicole P. Arthur received a Bachelor of Science degree in Animal Production from Pennsylvania State University in 1988. During her senior year in college, Ms. Arthur initiated a project to study reproductive endocrinology in Przewalski's mares by evaluating estrogen metabolites in voided urine. Between 1987 and 1989, Ms. Arthur collected daily urine samples, recorded behavioral observations and performed laboratory analyses of urinary estrogen levels from eight Przewalski's mares maintained at the National Zoo's Conservation and Research Center. Since 1988, Ms. Arthur has been employed as a full-time research assistant in the Endocrine Research Laboratory at the National Zoological Park's Conservation and Research Center.

Jonathan Ballou is the Population Manager at the Smithsonian Institution's National Zoological Park. He is currently working on his Ph.D. in Population Biology at the University of Maryland. He has a masters in Statistics from George Washington University. Mr. Ballou specializes in the genetic and demographic management of small populations, both wild and in captivity and has worked with such species as the golden lion tamarin (he is the International Studbook Keeper for this species), black lion tamarin, black-footed ferret, Guam rail, Sumatran tiger and Przewalski's horse.

Jan G. Bouman and Inge Bouman-Heinsdijk founded the Foundation for the Preservation and Protection of the Przewalski Horse in 1977. This foundation publishes a magazine, organizes exhibitions to propagate interest in the Przewalski's horse, publishes articles, stimulates research, and administers an extensive computerized studbook data system on the Przewalski's horse based on information and elaborations of the studbook maintained in Prague (Volf, 1960 et seq.). Together with the World Wildlife Fund-Netherlands they founded the Foundation Reserves for the Przewalski's Horse and its sister foundation in Germany in 1990. Five semi-reserves for the Przewalski horses were established in the Netherlands and in Germany (semi-reserve project no. 3077 IUCN/WWF). The present sixty Przewalski's horses are kept in large territories to give them the chance to get accustomed to freedom and more natural conditions with a minimum of human intervention. The ultimate aim is to release the descendants of the breeding groups into reserves in Central Asia and Mongolia.

Lee Boyd received her B.S. degree in Biology from St. Mary's College of Maryland and her M.S. degree from the University of Wyoming. Her master's thesis concerned the natality, foal survivorship, and mare-foal behavior of feral horses. Her Ph.D. from Cornell University covered the behavior of Przewalski's horses. Over the past ten years she has spent more than one thousand hours observing various Przewalski's horse herds and is currently a consultant to the Equid Taxon Advisory Group. She is interested in animal behavior as it applies to wildlife conservation and management. Her research also emphasizes social behaviors such as parent-offspring relationships, dominance hierarchies, mutual grooming, and mate choice. She has been teaching at Washburn University since 1982.

Colin Groves obtained his B.Sc. and Ph.D. at London University. He has taught at the University of California (Berkeley), in London and Cambridge Universities, and at the Australian National University where he now works. He is author of over one-hundred-twenty papers on mammalian taxonomy and evolution, and has done field work mainly related to conservation work in East Africa, Indonesia, India and Iran. He has a special interest in Perissodactyla, of which he reckons there are sixteen living wild species (seven equids, four tapirs, five rhinos), and is delighted to report that he has seen living examples of every one; the moment when he finally notched up number sixteen (*Rhinoceros sondaicus*) was very nearly his last, owing to an unaccountable fit of animosity on the part of the perissodactyl in question.

Harold F. Hintz is a Professor of Animal Nutrition and Chairman of the Department of Animal Science, Cornell University. He has been a member of the Equine Research Program at Cornell since 1967. He teaches courses in horse production, companion animal nutrition and exotic animal nutrition to undergraduate students and a course in livestock nutrition to veterinary students.

Katherine Houpt obtained her veterinary degree (V.M.D.) and her Ph.D. at the University of Pennsylvania. Her research interests are broad—spanning behavior of all the domestic species, but equine behavior in general and equine welfare in particular predominate. She is a professor of physiology and the first woman full professor at the New York State College of Veterinary Medicine, where she directs the Animal Behavior Clinic and teaches Problems in Dog, Cat and Horse Behavior and Farm Animal Behavior. She is a diplomate of the American College of Veterinary Behaviorists.

Mike LaRue began his work at the Topeka Zoo while at the University of Kansas in 1966. After earning a degree in Zoology, he worked as a full time keeper beginning in 1970. He was then promoted to Zoologist, then General Curator, Assistant Director and finally Director in 1993. Mike has been active in zoo conservation issues for a number of years. He currently serves on the propagation committees for the Orangutan and the Przewalski's horse. He is the regional studbook keeper for the North American captive population of the Mandrill baboon. Mike is also a member of the Baboon and Equid Taxon Advisory Groups. Mike was instrumental in acquiring and establishing the Topeka Zoo's Conservation/Propagation Center located on 160 acres.

Mike has traveled and studied wildlife in Australia, New Zealand, Zambia and Zimbabwe. He backpacks in his spare time.

Steven L. Monfort received a degree in veterinary medicine from the University of California, Davis in 1986 and between 1986 and 1988, he participated in a two year post-doctoral fellowship at the Smithsonian Institution's National Zoological Park in Washington, D.C. Currently, Dr. Monfort is employed as a Research Veterinarian at the National Zoological Park's Conservation and Research Center in Front Royal, Virginia where he specializes in the reproductive physiology of endangered species. Dr. Monfort has ten years of training in reproductive endocrinology with particular expertise in the application of non-invasive urinary hormone monitoring techniques for tracking reproductive status in wildlife species.

Oliver A. Ryder received his doctorate from the University of California, San Diego in 1975. As Geneticist with the Center for Reproduction of Endangered Species at the San Diego Zoo, he manages a highly productive laboratory and has applied his background in molecular genetics to the science of conservation biology. He is the Species Coordinator for the Asian Wild Horse SSP and a member of the steering committee for the Przewalski's horse Global Management Plan Working Group.

Jiri Volf studied biology at the Faculty of Natural Sciences at Charles University in Prague. After getting his degree, he started to work as zoologist at the Prague Zoo. He specializes mostly in comparative anatomy, influence of domestication, biology of reproduction, and the postnatal development and handrearing of mammals. From 1959 to 1990 he was the studbook keeper for Przewalski's horses (after wisents, the second International Studbook of Endangered Species). He is the author of twenty-two books, eighty scientific papers and communications, one hundred and twenty professional articles and the same number of popularized articles.

David E. Wildt received his doctorate in Physiology and Animal Science from Michigan State University in 1975. Since 1983, Dr. Wildt has served as head of the Reproductive Physiology Program at the National Zoological Park, Washington, D.C. Dr. Wildt has extensive research experience in the area of reproductive physiology of wildlife species with particular expertise in endocrinology, embryology and andrology.

Index

305

Printed in the United States
31265LVS00008BA/18